AF801346

The Psychology Behind Design

Jeongmin Lee · Wujin Chu · Chris Baumann

The Psychology Behind Design

A Marketing Perspective

Springer

Jeongmin Lee
Industrial Design Department
Gachon University
Seongnam City, Korea (Republic of)

Wujin Chu
College of Business Administration
Seoul National University
Seoul, Korea (Republic of)

Chris Baumann
Macquarie Business School
Macquarie University
Sydney, NSW, Australia

ISBN 978-981-97-3425-2 ISBN 978-981-97-3426-9 (eBook)
https://doi.org/10.1007/978-981-97-3426-9

© The Editor(s) (if applicable) and The Author(s), under exclusive license to Springer Nature Singapore Pte Ltd. 2024

This work is subject to copyright. All rights are solely and exclusively licensed by the Publisher, whether the whole or part of the material is concerned, specifically the rights of translation, reprinting, reuse of illustrations, recitation, broadcasting, reproduction on microfilms or in any other physical way, and transmission or information storage and retrieval, electronic adaptation, computer software, or by similar or dissimilar methodology now known or hereafter developed.
The use of general descriptive names, registered names, trademarks, service marks, etc. in this publication does not imply, even in the absence of a specific statement, that such names are exempt from the relevant protective laws and regulations and therefore free for general use.
The publisher, the authors and the editors are safe to assume that the advice and information in this book are believed to be true and accurate at the date of publication. Neither the publisher nor the authors or the editors give a warranty, expressed or implied, with respect to the material contained herein or for any errors or omissions that may have been made. The publisher remains neutral with regard to jurisdictional claims in published maps and institutional affiliations.

This Springer imprint is published by the registered company Springer Nature Singapore Pte Ltd.
The registered company address is: 152 Beach Road, #21-01/04 Gateway East, Singapore 189721, Singapore

If disposing of this product, please recycle the paper.

Preface

Embarking on the journey to write this book has been both a challenging and rewarding experience. Our ambition was to demystify the complex interplay between consumer psychology and design, making it accessible, engaging, and, most importantly, applicable to our daily lives. We also intended for this book to be accessible not only to professionals in marketing and design but also to anyone intrigued by the psychological implications of design in their everyday lives. Therefore, this book is not just a collection of theoretical insights. It is a deep dive into the mind tricks, turning everyday design into a peek into our psyche.

The chapters unfold a narrative that journeys through the equilibrium of design and psychology, the subtle nudges that influence our decisions, the social dynamics at play in our perceptions, and the visual dominance that shapes our environment. Beyond these, the book also delves into the psychological constructs of the self, cognitive biases, the allure of minimalism, and the hedonics of design, among other topics.

This book is a manifestation of our belief that understanding the psychology behind design can enrich our daily experiences, offering insights into how and why certain designs resonate with us. That is, we're here not just to convey knowledge; we're inviting readers on a treasure hunt to spot those psychological gems hidden right before their eyes. We mixed in some laughs and real-life design stories to make sure this ride is as fun as it is enlightening. Therefore, this book is intended to be not just read but experienced—an opportunity to see the world anew through the lens of consumer behavior and design psychology. We hope every page-turn lights up a little spark of discovery on the psychological wonders behind our daily encounters with design, from the mundane to the extraordinary.

In writing this book, we also aimed to share our passion for the subject, hoping to show you the powerhouse that design can be, not just as a tool for aesthetics or function but as a fundamental component of our psychological landscape. May this journey freshen up how you look at design and consumer psychology.

In bringing this book into the world, special appreciation is due to our publisher. This collaboration has not only enriched the book but also made the process a gratifying experience. A big thanks for making our dream a reality.

Seongnam City, Korea (Republic of) Jeongmin Lee
Seoul, Korea (Republic of) Wujin Chu
Sydney, Australia Chris Baumann

Contents

Chapter 1
The Symphony of Equilibrium

"You must be kidding! You call that art? Come off it!".

At some modern art exhibition, confronted by artwork made of junk materials, we've all grumbled something like this, haven't we? Maybe we didn't voice it, but the thought bubble was definitely bobbing around our heads. After all, it's an art exhibition. No need to turn a searchlight on our cultural naivete. But still... There was an undeniable itch, a sense that this artist was twisting our arms, forcing us to swallow this unsavory dish.

There was even an artist who, literally and seriously, was kidding about art. In an act of defiance to traditional art, Marcel Duchamp granted artistic dignity to a genuine urinal, a readymade product, not a painstakingly crafted artwork (Fig. 1.1). He autographed it, named it "Fountain," and dusted off his hands. And the audience? Well, their response was probably along the lines of, "You must be kidding! You call that art? Come off it!".

If I attempted something like this, people would say that I started with a sort of rubbish and wrapped it up as complete rubbish.[1] When Duchamp does it, it's "Art" with a capital A. Why? Can a great artist get away with anything?

However, beneath the surface of his seemingly shambolic urinal, Duchamp was slipping a groundbreaking concept into the art scene. His point was that it's the artist's ideas, not physical artwork, which should be admired, that art is brainwork, not handwork. He kindled a new direction in art. That's the difference between my humble attempt and Duchamp's game-changer. As Derek Matravers said, "The difference between Duchamp's urinal and a common-or-garden urinal is that Duchamp linked his urinal to the art world, and that's what makes it a work of art."[2] And yet, that's also what makes it an unreachable work of art. In some sense, it's a league of their own.

---

[1] On October 23, 2022, extracted and revised from https://upjoke.com/sculpture-jokes.

[2] Edmonds and Warburton (2010).

© The Author(s), under exclusive license to Springer Nature Singapore Pte Ltd. 2024
J. Lee et al., *The Psychology Behind Design*,
https://doi.org/10.1007/978-981-97-3426-9_1

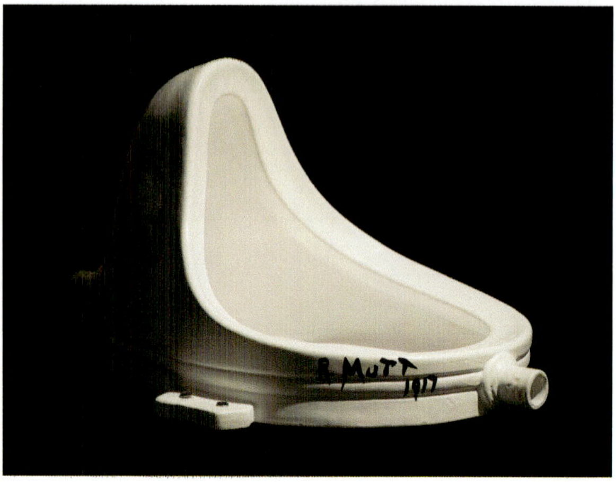

Fig. 1.1 Fountain, Marcel Duchamp, 1917 (Dima Moroz/Shutterstock)

However, something doesn't add up in our attitude, either. For instance, take Einstein's famed formula for special relativity, "$E = mc^2$," which represents the equivalence of mass and energy. An equation as elegant as it is enigmatic. I'm pretty sure most of us wouldn't know what it means, even though it is a cornerstone of modern physics. Asked if I understand it, my honest reply would be, "Relatively…"[3] However, do you feel angry or alienated? We don't need to be embarrassed by our ignorance about concepts that we didn't study.

Then, why do we bristle or feel frustrated when faced with baffling artwork that is above our heads? Are we subconsciously demanding that all artworks be as graspable as a leisurely Sunday comic strip, despite our lack of academic engagement? Perhaps we subconsciously believe art should always be relatable, given its status as the playground for our innate expressive energy. If art goes too fast, leaving us far behind, our subconscious will kick up a fuss, "Nope! It can't and shouldn't."

Similar sentiments intervene in the realm of design. A CEO once quipped about board meetings: only experts weigh in on technical issues, but when it comes to advertising or product design, suddenly, every member voices a statement out loud. Sure, design is also a specialized field, but we can't help but meddle since it's tightly woven into the tapestry of our everyday lives. It's the familiar backyard that we want to adorn ourselves. On that score, design and politics share a common thread—every Tom, Dick, and Harry has a say.

Please don't take it the wrong way, though. We, the "ordinary" folks, also look ahead to a better future and are looking for visionaries willing to venture off the beaten path, forging new trails. Extraordinary artists capable of changing the status quo? They're cherished! Sure, we celebrate them, so long as they don't upheave our non-extraordinary daily life, so long as we are not muddle-headed with their coups every day.

---

[3] On October 23, 2022, extracted and revised from https://upjoke.com/einstein-jokes.

Fig. 1.2 Tilted Arc, Richard Serra, 1981 (Norman Owen Tomalin/Alamy Stock Photo)

"Tilted Arc" by Richard Serra, a lengthy steel slab installed in the Federal Plaza of New York (Fig. 1.2), was an example of this issue. It provoked a most notorious controversy regarding public sculpture, a fierce battle between the outraged public and the defenders of artistic liberty. It was a real clash of two polemic opinions.[4]

According to the public's gripes, this artwork sliced up the plaza space into two and blocked the view. It was made of steel, which became rusty with time. Worse still, it was an obstacle that made plaza crossing very difficult: it turned a simple shortcut into an inconvenient detour around its bulky perimeter.

On the other hand, from the point of artistic defenders, what Serra did was an upheaval to the artistic world of the period—incorporating the site, time, and change into plastic art. As Serra himself put it, "The viewer becomes aware of himself and of his movement through the plaza. Step by step, the perception not only of the sculpture but of the entire environment changes." To achieve this artistic goal means it should be in their way.

A stroke of artistic genius? Yes! However… What about the social role of the plaza that the public has already been enjoying there? In my view, the real kicker was the obstacle course it created for passersby. After all, it shook up the public both psychologically and physically. While I tip my hat to Serra's revolutionary idea, imposing it on the public by throwing a wrench in their daily lives would be a different ball game.

The upshot of it all? Serra's Tilted Arc was removed. The plaza and the public breathed a sigh of relief, and Serra went on with his experiment elsewhere. After all is said and done, Serra's artistic concept, once an upheaval, has become a widely accepted art form now. It's not unusual to encounter public sculptures today that play with site, time, or change. So, at the end of the day, it seems both parties won.

---

[4] Dosch (2018).

As seen in this case, there is always a balancing act between two opposite powers in one way or another. It reminds me of a witty rivalry of tooth-and-tongue: when teeth threaten the tongue, "If I just press a little, you'll get cut," the tongue can reply, "If I misuse a single word, all 32 of you will come out."[5] And just like that, the mouth regains its peace and balance.

Related to this balancing act, let me bring up another case, a tantalizing tidbit. Parisians hated the Eiffel Tower when it first showed up for the 1889 Paris Expo. They complained that this ugly metallic structure was a total blemish amid their city's chic charm and that the sheer size of the monument would dwarf all other historical monuments in the city. Over time, however, the people of Paris became familiar with this once-alien structure, and it found a new lease on life as a hosting place of communication devices. Eventually, it outlasted the controversy and has become an iconic landmark of Paris today.[6] Even though it had initially irked the Parisians' aesthetic sensibilities, at least it didn't bother them physically or trip them up in their daily routine. That's what made Parisians bear this eyesore until familiarity could feed preference. That's what Serra's Tilted Arc lacked.

So, let's not forget that we inhabit a universe that is carefully held in equilibrium between centrifugal and centripetal forces. Tweak that balance even a tad, and we're headed for cosmic chaos. Given this fact, it's only natural that most of us yearn for a harmonious balance between opposing forces. Still and all, some people are radically unconventional, but rest assured, there must be a similar number of people who are utterly conventional. The balance, after all, earns both of its wings again. Thus, when you're about to unleash a groundbreaking idea, bear in mind that there'll be a counterforce punching the clock to guard the balance. The finest strategy to avoid a knee-jerk reaction from the opposing pole is to coax them along the journey, not to bully them into submission by twisting their arms. Keep in mind that the best trick is allowing time for your innovation to simmer down from a coup to a comforting norm.

Owl of Minerva Behind the Scene

In this book, each chapter has three sections. First up, we dive into a narrative prologue (an episode section), like the one you've just read. Picture it as a window into the chapter's central theme, drawing you in with relatable stories and slices of everyday experiences. Next, we venture into the heart of the matter in a main section (sections which follow "Owl of Minerva Behind the Scene"). Here, we explore psychological theories, all intricately linked to the central theme. We also bring them to life with concrete design examples that illustrate these concepts in action. Our final section is the supplementary section (a section titled "More Design Insights Added to the Scene"). It's where we delve into additional design cases that didn't quite fit in the main section but are very intriguing. This section is optional and can be omitted if no further elucidation is required.

---

[5] On June 17, 2023, extracted and revised from http://www.funny-jokes-quotes.com/daily-life-situations.html.

[6] Thompson (2000).

Now, shall we talk about the psychological underpinnings of our first episode? The Owl of Minerva, the symbol of wisdom, will spread its wings[7] to tell the psychological and visual stories ducked behind this scene of "universal equilibrium."

Equilibrium Everywhere

First, let's zero in on our main theme—the *universal law of equilibrium*. As I hinted at the opening episode, the unerring equilibrium between centrifugal and centripetal forces holds the reins over the operation of the cosmos. Human lives are also under the energy of this grand principle, and whether we realize it or not, it's a part of our daily experiences.

Admittedly, I might have asserted this law's societal footprints without scientific proof. However, Hegel, the distinguished philosopher, stepped up with social proof—the *thesis-antithesis-synthesis theory of Hegelian dialectics* (Fig. 1.3). I found this theory illuminating in its explanation of social changes and in its comprehension of social equilibrium.

Want more relatable evidence from life experiences? Let's borrow some old wisdom: "With the good comes the bad," or "Every cloud has a silver lining." How about tongue-in-cheek laws that echo daily life's ironical equilibrium?

Law of variation: Switching traffic lanes? Prepare to watch your old lane zip past you (works every time). Ultimately, all lanes achieve equilibrium in speed.[8]

Law of arena: At any event, the arrival time of the people is always proportional to the distance of their seat from the aisle, and the number of times you should stand up is inversely proportional to the distance of your seat from the aisle. (Is the aisle seat really better?).[9]

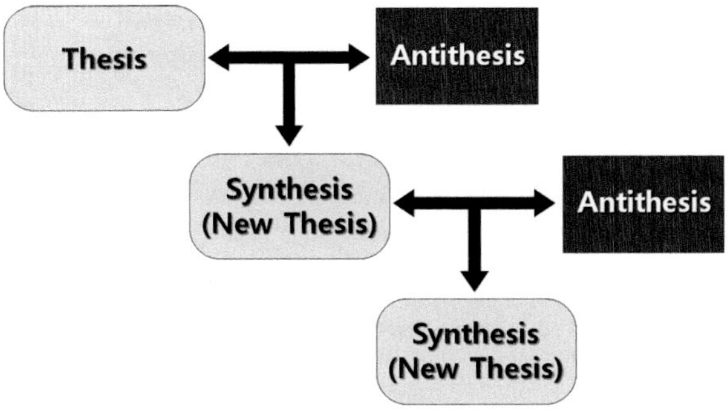

Fig. 1.3 Hegelian dialectic (created by Jeongmin Lee, 2023, Author's Collection)

[7] Warburton (2011).

[8] On October 23, 2022, extracted and revised from https://funnyfunnyjokes.org/2011/09/06/universal-laws/.

[9] See Footnote 8.

Law of silence: People who don't say much consist of two groups—those who are very quiet and those who excessively talk a lot.[10]

MAYA: Where Innovation Meets Familiarity

This unseen energy of equilibrium also comes into play in the world of design. A design principle called MAYA, short for Most-Advanced-Yet-Acceptable, urges designers to find a balance between the warm blanket of familiarity and the spicy kick of novelty for their creations to resonate in the market. It's because innovation for the future matters much for customers, as does familiarity with the present.[11]

Most customers don't want to be bored with the same-o-same-o design, nor do they appreciate designs that are too far out there, like those in Fig. 1.4. Striking a balance between novelty and familiarity, that elusive sweet spot, isn't an easy task. But check out the Yamaha electric violin in Fig. 1.5. It seems to find this sweet spot: the traditional violin's soundbox disappeared, but its shadow still lingers. That sketchy shadow of a soundbox provides a cozy den where we can breathe easy in the whirlwind of innovation.

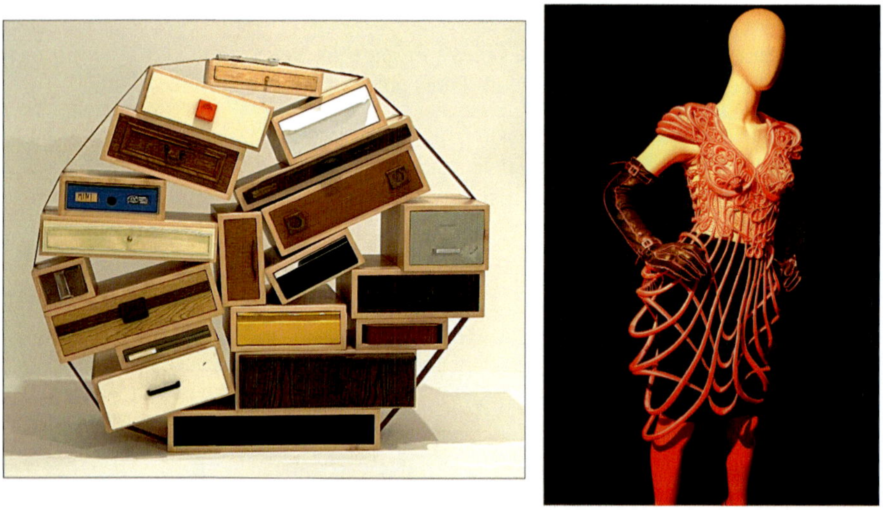

Fig. 1.4 Left—Chest of Drawers, Droog, 1981/Right—The Boudoir, Jean Paul Gaultier, from the Sidewalk to the Catwalk Exhibit, 2011 (Left: David Grossman/Alamy Stock Photo) (Right: Devon Meunier/Meunierd/Shutterstock)

[10] On June 17, 2023, extracted and revised from HUMORTHATWORKS.COM.

[11] Blum (2004).

Fig. 1.5 Yamaha electric violin (Lebedinski Vladislav/ Shutterstock)

Let's take a gander at another MAYA design example. The bookshelf in Fig. 1.6 is not your grandma's bookshelf, that's for sure. Instead of the usual vertical-horizontal lines, this one's lines are all in the diagonal direction, which gives it a new twist. But here's where it nails the MAYA principle: despite its boldness, it still has that unmistakable vibe of a bookshelf. It's a bit of a show-off, but it's also incredibly down-to-earth when it comes to doing its job—holding books.

Why do designers have to consider MAYA carefully? No-brainer! It's because the ultimate goal of any design is to sell. It means the puppeteer orchestrating the designer's performance is none other than customers' preferences. But, let's face it, being educated in the field of creative work, designers are more inclined to be innovative than conventional. Even so, to wear the badge of "genuine professional," designers must rein in their avant-garde instincts and tune in to the customers' likes and dislikes. They should keep in mind that their profession means wearing the shackles of customers' preferences.

Let's wade deeper into the water of the MAYA principle, this time focusing on the psychological underpinnings. The magic of the MAYA principle lies in the partnership of the "mere-exposure effect" and the "isolation effect"—another equilibrium between opposite poles. The *mere-exposure effect* means familiarity breeds affection. The more you encounter something, the better it gets.[12] That was what happened to

[12] Zajonc (2001).

Fig. 1.6 MAYA example: Innovative bookshelf design (Somil Bhandari/ Shutterstock)

Parisiens as regards the Eiffel Tower. It is understandable in terms of evolutionary psychology: familiarity means that it is something that doesn't threaten our survival.

Yet, we humans also tend to remember the outlandish over the ordinary. That is, we remember the supernormal stimulus much better than the normal, familiar stimulus. So, even if the avant-garde designs in Fig. 1.4 made you raise an eyebrow, they've probably etched themselves onto your memory. Similarly, encountering many stimuli simultaneously, we tend to pay more attention to the stimulus clearly distinguished from the other stimuli. For example, in "EVF4WRB," you will likely spot the "4" first, and later, you will say, "4 was definitely there, but I am not sure about other letters." This cognitive phenomenon is known as the *isolation effect*.[13] Evolutionary psychology can explain it, too: human cognition wants to check whether this novel, unfamiliar stimulus can be a possible menace to our survival. It's like our cognitive system has its own security guard.

Steve Jobs' wardrobe choice for presentations is a brilliant example of this effect. Amid the convention of suits for formal presentations, his jeans and black turtleneck stood out, making them as memorable as his presentations. I'm pretty sure that he "carefully" chose this "casual-looking" attire.

As we can see, both the comfort of familiarity (the mere-exposure effect) and the refreshing power of novelty (the isolation effect) make us feel alive. Thus, it's natural for humans to be drawn to things that stoke both feelings, and that's why the MAYA principle works for customers' preferences. Two opposite poles usually attract each other, even in the human psyche. The funny thing is opposites sometimes share some

[13] Hunt (1995).

commonalities, too. Consider the adventurous explorers and the committed couch potatoes. These two extremes are both looking for the remote.[14]

Psychological Equilibrium: More Principles

There are more psychological principles that aim to seek a balance between two extremes. I will usher into a few of them. First, there is the *Yerkes-Dodson law*. It points out that human performance gets a shot in the arm with physiological or mental arousal, but only to a certain degree. When levels of arousal become higher than a critical point, performance decreases.[15] It underscores that humans want some arousal while they want some rest to lower it. We are always on the journey of hunting for that elusive sweet spot of equilibrium.

Big retail brands apply this law when designing their megastores. That is, they strategically position resting spots along the customers' shopping odyssey. Their bet? These pit stops would boost the customers' shopping performances, making them linger a little longer, explore a little further, and, consequently, lighten their wallets a bit more.

Next up is the *choice overload effect*. It says that both too few options and too many options can steer customer satisfaction down the drain.[16] Consumers are stuck between a rock and a hard place—making the best decision and having the freedom of many options. The problem is that the latter could trigger cognitive overload and lead to regrettable decisions. Think about the number of toothpaste brands we should weigh in the supermarket. This overload is precisely why Costco, a successful warehouse retailer, decided to provide fewer options instead of more. A happy byproduct? Costco could deliver better discount pricing as well.[17]

Another example of applying the choice overload effect is IKEA's showroom design strategy, which can ease the cognitive load of selecting items. Amidst the ocean of products in its mega-sized stores, IKEA offers a lot of carefully curated showroom designs. They can coax customers into bulk-buying a whole room setup rather than agonizing over individual pieces. To egg customers on this approach, the total price of the showroom design is displayed, along with prices for individual items. A smart strategy to minimize choice paralysis, isn't it?

Let's delve into the third compelling lead related to the psychological equilibrium, this time in our perception—the *optical illusion of a bent straight line*. Take a look at the left image of Fig. 1.7, where the top line of the square appears to dip slightly in the middle. Grab a ruler and check. It's a straight line! This optical illusion is born from the powerful upward current in the background lines. Rob the image of its backdrop, and all you have is a well-behaved square (Fig. 1.7 right). A complex

[14] On June 18, 2023, extracted and revised from https://upjoke.com/explorer-jokes.

[15] Hanoch and Vitouch (2004).

[16] Iyengar and Lepper (2000).

[17] Mothersbaugh et al. (2020).

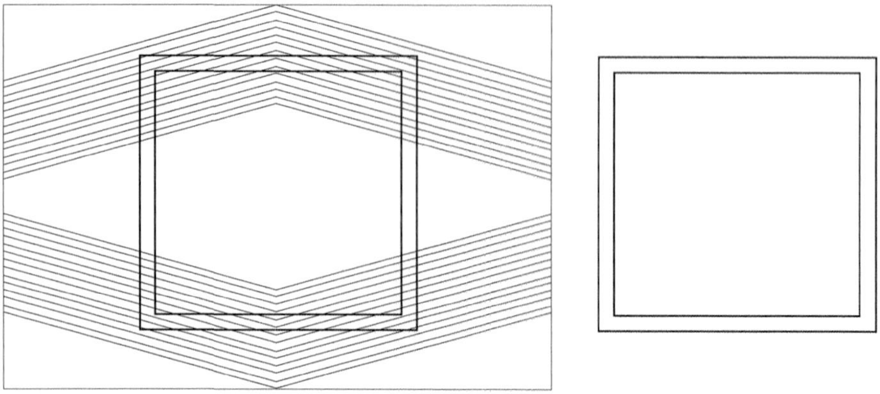

Fig. 1.7 Optical illusion of the straight line (created by Jeongmin Lee, 2023, Author's Collection)

explanation should be involved, but, in layman's terms, our perception doesn't like leaning too heavily in one direction. Therefore, to maintain balance, it makes a downward adjustment. The same thing happens with the lower line of the square. So, here's a little wisdom for the creatives: sometimes, designers should not draw a straight line really straight if it is intended to be seen straight!

As we can see, the principles we've discussed above highlight the need for a "Goldilocks zone" in consumer experiences. Striking this balance is key to creating preferable products and services. Understanding this equilibrium is crucial, not just in design and marketing, but as a universal approach to resonating with our inherent human preferences.

Nudge: Balanced Persuasion

Now, allow me to usher you into *nudge*, another area where equilibrium does its thing. It is a gentle way to steer people in the direction you propose. Nudge will be investigated more deeply in the next chapter, so here, the focus is on its relationship with equilibrium.

According to Richard Thaler (Nobel laureate) and Cass Sunstein, it's possible to shape an environment that respects people's freedom of choice while encouraging them toward better decisions.[18] They called it *libertarian paternalism*. That sounds like an odd mix, a coupling of two polar opposite ideologies. Some critics argue that it's an incompatible pairing, and there can be ethical problems. However, I believe it can be both feasible and beneficial, provided it's done under proper ethical codes. After all, the unions of conflicting psychological phenomena worked behind several principles we've already explored. So, why not with nudging?

[18] Thaler and Sunstein (2008).

The virtue of nudging lies in maintaining people's sense of self-control and free will. That's the "libertarian" part. At the same time, it presents a desirable option with a more accessible or more attractive wrapping, so it takes effort to reject this option. That's the "paternalistic" part.

There are various methods for applying nudges, with the *Default Strategy* being one notable example. It is the option that is automatically opted for if you don't change to the other option, and people usually settle upon the option that doesn't badger them anymore. This leads to the default option being chosen more often, but it doesn't rob anyone of their right to select another option.

Behind this default strategy, you'll find a curious character at work, a cognitive bias known as the *availability heuristic*. It leads you to rely on what's readily available rather than laboriously rummage for more accurate information when making decisions. Who would want to dive into a vast library when there's a catchy headline at hand?

IKEA skillfully incorporates default strategy into the store design—its famous one-way layout. Once you step into an IKEA store, you're on a fixed path with a one-way direction. It is designed to make you bump into everything IKEA offers, from a wide variety of showrooms to a million and one products. Sure, there are a few shortcuts, which means IKEA isn't stripping you of your choice to pass up unwanted sections. However, these shortcuts are not easy to find. It's certainly there, but it's questionably not there. This design strategy works so well that most customers think they voluntarily follow this stamina-consuming one-way journey.

In a nutshell, by gently guiding choices while preserving autonomy, nudges embody a balanced approach, merging respectful guidance with individual decision-making. This approach illustrates how an understanding of psychological equilibrium can transform the way we influence behaviors—less about overt persuasion and more about facilitating smarter choices in a seemingly effortless manner.

More Design Insights Added to the Scene

Before we end our discussion about the universal equilibrium, let's delve into two more masterpieces that are undoubtedly noteworthy.

Earlier, we explored the public uproar over Serra's Tilted Arc. Another famous public sculpture that stirred up a hornet's nest was Picasso's "Untitled" in Chicago, more affectionately known as the "Chicago Picasso" (Fig. 1.8). A throng of curious onlookers, full of anticipation, filled the Daley Plaza for the unveiling ceremony. After all, it was Picasso. However, in no time, they were bewildered by this funny-looking cubist sculpture that dared to have no resounding theme either. Before this work, motifs of public sculptures in Chicago were mainly historical figures. Not to mention furious criticism, it mustered a hot debate over what on earth it portrayed. Picasso remained silent.[19]

[19] Lopez (2017).

Fig. 1.8 Untitled (Chicago Picasso), Pablo Picasso, 1967, Daley Plaza, Chicago, USA (photographed by Jeongmin Lee, 2016, Author's Collection)

Speculations ranged from a baboon, an aardvark, Picasso's pet Afghan Hound, the Anubis (Fig. 1.9), to one of his models. Not surprising, given the human knack for fabricating misinterpretations at their pleasure —like misreading "Copyright" as an instruction to "Copy right" or assuming "money laundering" as "cleaning the purse."[20] Some people cast ridicule, saying that it belonged to a zoo. Anything can be possible if you don't know what you are talking about. This was the case for the critics of the time. To Chicagoans, accustomed to noble depictions in public sculptures, this alien creation with a long, seemingly goofy face was far from the majestic symbol they believed befitting their city's grand plaza.

It was not removed, though, probably by virtue of the name "Picasso." And then again, with time, its strangeness faded into familiarity, which in turn kindled preference. Today, this once-ridiculed object has become Chicago's favorite artwork—a local landmark and a beloved playground teeming with joyous climbers and sliders (Fig. 1.10).

---

[20] "Copyright" as "Copy right": On October 23, 2022, extracted and revised from https://upjoke.com/familiar-jokes.

"Money laundering" as "Cleaning the purse": On October 23, 2022, extracted and revised from Reader's Digest Canada, https://www.readersdigest.ca/culture/70-funniest-jokes-readers-digest/ (Shinae Hartley).

Fig. 1.9 Left—Baboon/Right—The Anubis (detail of the wall in the tomb of Horemheb), the Valley of the Kings, Egypt (Left: Edwin Butter/Shutterstock) (Right: Jakub Kyncl/Shutterstock)

Fig. 1.10 Children playing on the Chicago Picasso (Conchi Martinez/Shutterstock)

Lastly, let's touch on a renowned example that corrected the illusions of the "bent straight line." Previously, I pointed out that sometimes, designers should not draw a straight line really straight if it is intended to be seen straight. The Parthenon in Athens is perhaps the most famous architectural exemplar of the *optical corrections of straight lines*.[21]

[21] Bondarko et al. (2021).

Every architectural line of this magnificent temple looks straight. However, in reality, it has few straight lines. The horizontal lines of the stylobate and entablature (Fig. 1.11, left) are subtly arched upwards, and the temple's base is also slightly domed (Fig. 1.11, right). It corrects the optical illusion that the long horizontal line looks a bit sagged in the middle. So, to make the horizontal lines appear straight, the architect employed an upward curvature, which is almost imperceptible to the casual observer. Figure 1.12 explains it better. The design would appear like (A) if created with truly straight lines. Therefore, it was crafted like (B) to appear like (C).

A similar optical illusion plays out with vertical lines. The long vertical lines of the columns with frieze and pediment seem to bow inward slightly. To counter this, the Parthenon's architect made the columns slightly convex in the middle.

Apart from these crafty manipulations of straight lines, the Parthenon abounds with other optical adjustments. It's awe-inspiring that the architect of this temple, way back in the fifth BC, was well aware of these perceptual illusions and ingeniously adjusted them in this magnificent edifice—a task that would have been herculean in its complexity. A level of perfection is just sublime excellency, worthy of the gods!

Alright, let's wrap up our exploration into the symphony of equilibrium in art, design, and human psychology. Think of it as a gentle seesaw, where we've been

Fig. 1.11 Parthenon, Ictinus and Callicrates, 5th BC, Athens, Greece (Dmitry Vinogradov/Lucky-photographer/Shutterstock) (text added by Jeongmin Lee)

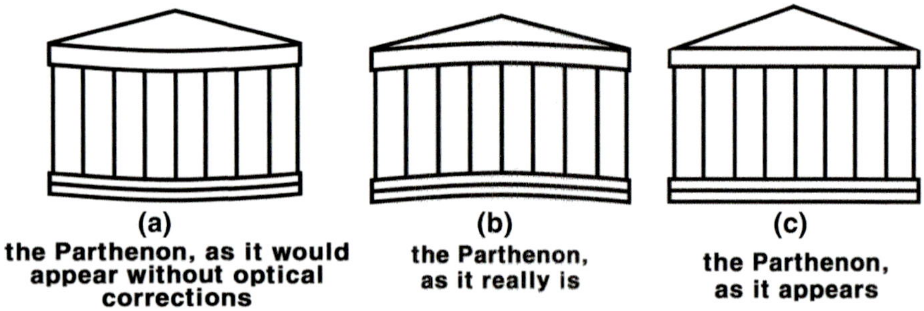

Fig. 1.12 Optical corrections of straight lines in the Parthenon (created by Jeongmin Lee, 2023, Author's Collection)

balancing the weights of opposing forces. Just like in the universe, where centrifugal and centripetal forces maintain perfect balance, our lives are similarly governed by this rhythm of equilibrium. As seen in the case of the MAYA principle and other psychological underpinnings featuring balance, humans have an inherent desire for a middle ground between extremes.

Therefore, in human life, the best solutions often lie in the careful negotiation between opposing forces. Whether we are creators, consumers, or simply observers, respecting this balance can lead to more fulfilling experiences, and with these mindful works about balance, we might be able to sidestep exhausting, sometimes unnecessary tugs-of-war. That is, our creations can include a low-key way not to provoke the strong resistance of the opposite party. Or else they will think you are pushing them too hard and will push you back.

References

Blum, M. (2004). Raymond Loewy: Designs for a consumer culture. *Technology and Culture, 45*(4), 854–855.

Bondarko, V. M., Solnushkin, S. D., & Chikhman, V. N. (2021). Curvature estimation and architecture of the Parthenon. *Journal of Optical Technology, 88*(6), 330–336.

Dosch, M. (2018, September 24). The culture wars and Richard Serra's tilted arc. In *Smarthistory*. Accessed January 23, 2024. https://smarthistory.org/seeing-america-2/tilted-arc-sa/

Edmonds, D., & Warburton, N. (2010). *Philosophy bites*. Oxford University Press.

Hanoch, Y., & Vitouch, O. (2004). When less is more: Information, emotional arousal and the ecological reframing of the Yerkes-Dodson law. *Theory & Psychology, 14*(4), 427–452.

Hunt, R. R. (1995). The subtlety of distinctiveness: What von Restorff really did. *Psychonomic Bulletin & Review, 2*, 105–112.

Iyengar, S. S., & Lepper, M. R. (2000). When choice is demotivating: Can one desire too much of a good thing? *Journal of Personality and Social Psychology, 79*(6), 995–1006.

Lopez, R. (2017, August 7). The story behind the 'controversial' Picasso sculpture that became a symbol of Chicago. In *The Art Newspaper*. Accessed January 23, 2024. https://www.theartnewspaper.com/2017/08/07/the-story-behind-the-controversial-picasso-sculpture-that-became-a-symbol-of-chicago

Mothersbaugh, D. L., Hawkins, D. I., & Kleiser, S. B. (2020). *Consumer behavior: Building marketing strategy* (14th ed., p. 567). McGraw-Hill Education.

Thaler, R. H., & Sunstein, C. R. (2008). *Nudge: Improving decisions about health, wealth, and happiness*. Yale University Press.

Thompson, W. (2000). "The symbol of Paris": Writing the Eiffel Tower. *French Review*, 1130–1140.

Warburton, N. (2011). Hegel. In *A little history of philosophy*. Yale University Press (Chapter 22).

Zajonc, R. B. (2001). Mere exposure: A gateway to the subliminal. *Current Directions in Psychological Science, 10*(6), 224–228.

Chapter 2
Whispers of Change: Nudge for the Better

"Do we even have such a thing as free will?"

"We don't? Seriously?"

Believe it or not, like it or not, a storm in a teacup is brewing around this question. There is a controversy as to whether humans possess free will or not.

Some might argue that *free will* is an inherent right of a human being, a domain untouched by any higher powers or pre-determined fate.[1] Although it gave our creator a lot of divine headaches, here we are—still a creation armed with our own will. Our creator guaranteed that our minds and souls are our own. Don't we enjoy the fact that, in our discretion, we can tickle Him pink and raise a stink, too? It's akin to how we view the actions and decisions of our children. Human volition can be a source of tremendous power and potential, creating a fire in the belly for self-actualization.

On the flip side, there's a whole other camp called *determinism*.[2] It says that there is no such thing as human free will and that the exercise of it is an illusion. A pretty sobering view, isn't it? In this view, our precious "free will" is a puppet at the mercy of factors beyond our control: everything we do has already been determined by the environment or biology. Even though there is a soft determinism, which allows for some degree of human agency, in the eyes of hard determinists, human free will is just a luscious framing, nothing more than an appealing garnish on the plate of life. Environmental factors, in particular, can make us feel helpless because it is not in the power of an individual to manage them. For instance, we know that the parenting environment we grew up in affects our lives over the long haul.

Apart from this macro influence, the environment also throws its weight behind small thoughts and decisions in our daily lives. Consumer behaviorists know it well, but we don't. For example, according to an experiment done in a wine store, German wines sold better when German music was played, and French wine sold better

[1] Fischer et al. (2007).

[2] McKenna and Coates (2021).

© The Author(s), under exclusive license to Springer Nature Singapore Pte Ltd. 2024

J. Lee et al., *The Psychology Behind Design*,
https://doi.org/10.1007/978-981-97-3426-9_2

when French music was played.[3] When informed about this, the wine buyers went into denial mode. Tough pill to swallow, maybe. It must have been difficult to accept that even a trivial environmental factor like background music can stick its nose in their free will decisions.

In this tussle between Team Free Will and Team Determinism, there exists the third team, called *compatibilism*.[4] This savvy faction parks itself smack dab in the middle, asserting both sides have a point. Sounds paradoxical? But compatibilists call it balance and harmony.

Interestingly, Sigmund Freud also utilized a bit of compatibilism. You might object to it.

"Freud? It makes no sense! Didn't he claim our thoughts and actions are directed by our subconscious, etched by childhood experiences?"

Well, yes and no. He clearly emphasized the power of our subconscious and past experiences. However, we can also see that Freud's goal of psychoanalytic therapy was to help the patient realize problematic subconscious force and overcome it. In other words, the effects of his psychoanalytic therapy are the resolution of conflict and the strengthening and maturing of the ego[5]—a viewpoint that, in a way, aligns with the principles of compatibilism that the future is not solely pre-determined by the past. Without this belief, it's Freud's therapy that makes no sense. Thus, even though compatibilism is not a view directly addressed by Freud, we can still say that he borrowed some of its concepts in his therapy.

As a member of Team Compatibilism, I'm prone to proclaim that this compatibilism can be applied not only to the matters of free will vs. determinism but also to the cogs of all life's polarities (we already dealt with it in Chap. 1). Life is not a black-and-white affair, and most things that exist aren't simply all good or all bad, top to bottom. Depending on the vantage point, every situation can be both sides of the coin. Even lying, for instance, can be double-faced—it's a sin for a child, a fault for an adult, but an art for a lover, and, in some scenarios, a tactical maneuver.[6]

Let us look into a traditional Chinese fable. A mother living adjacent to a graveyard found her son playing funeral games. Having high hopes for her son, she thought it was not a good place to raise him, so she moved near a marketplace, only to find him mimicking traders. Since commerce was rather looked down upon then, she moved again to the residence near an academy. Now, her son started to imitate the behaviors of scholars and became interested in studying. She settled there, and her son grew up to be the celebrated scholar, Mencius.[7]

This age-old fable does underscore the weight of the environment, but it also begs the question: would every child living near that academy have become a scholar? Wasn't Mencius' voluntary will a part of the factor that made him study harder? That is, much as we certainly live under the magnetic pull of environmental factors, our

---

[3] North et al. (1997).

[4] Campbell (1997).

[5] Brenner (1994).

[6] On January 30, 2023, extracted and revised from https://upjoke.com/accomplishment-jokes.

[7] Kim and Okazaki (2017).

personal choices can't be entirely dismissed. Let's face it: most of our behaviors are not passive reactions but active responses to the forces that carry weight with us.

Determinists say that humans hold this hocus-pocus regarding free will because maintaining our civilization depends on this belief, and losing it will bring chaos. Suppose they are right. Are you really curious about what this new world might look like? Under a world steeped in determinism, people would be faster to dodge responsibility for their own actions than a cat avoiding a bath. So, tread lightly and don't let excessive curiosity lead you astray. Determinism can be Pandora's box.

While we're at it, let me drop another wisdom bomb. Picture this: when your lovely wife drinking wine says, "I love you so much. I don't know how I could ever live without you," just enjoy the moment. Don't be overcurious and needlessly ask, "Is that you or the wine talking?" She might say, "For now, it's me talking to the wine."[8] Remember, "Curiosity killed the cat!".

Owl of Minerva Behind the Scene

In this chapter, we will delve deeper into the abovementioned compatibilism in the form of a "nudge," which has been briefly mentioned in the previous chapter. It is a behavioral economic theory that espouses directing people's decisions without forcing them.

Nudge puts the compatibilist view into practice for the solutions of real-world agendas, reconciling environmental power with human free will. It has become well-received among policymakers and entered the limelight with its adoption by the Obama administration. Michelle Obama herself wielded the power of the nudge, using it to inspire Americans to embrace healthier habits in her "Let's Move! Program." Shall we unveil the covert art of nudging with the guidance of our wise owl?

Nudge: A Gentle Poking, Not a Hard Kick on the Side

Nudge was devised to set up a choice environment that enhances people's welfare.[9] It is the brainchild of Richard Thaler and Cass Sunstein, who based their ideas on a variety of psychological and economic principles. They proposed that skillfully designed environmental stimuli can lure us toward personally fulfilling and socially commendable choices, like a healthier lifestyle, more savings for retirement, or the noble act of organ donation. In this respect, it goes along with the environmental power on free will.

However, the nudge is no overbearing tyrant. It also cooperates with human free will. That is, it respects the sense of self-control and self-efficacy, which are essential for human well-being, life satisfaction, and survival.[10] This delicate balance between

[8] On January 21, 2023, extracted and revised from https://vincarta.com/blog/wine-jokes.

[9] Thaler and Sunstein (2008, 2021).

[10] Bandura (1997).

environmental power and human free will allows us to feel like we are still the captain of our ships. Hence the name "nudge" comes—a gentle poking, not a hard kick on the side.

Therefore, the bottom line of nudge is not to intrude into people's right to choose. It means there should always be other alternatives from which people can choose. However, savvy framing always works with them, too. It skillfully frames those options so that the beneficial one gets the spotlight. We know good framing can be quite convincing, capable of turning the mundane into the magnificent. With clever framing of linguistic brilliance, even humble scissors can transform into cutting-edge technology, and a mere jackhammer can emerge as a groundbreaking innovation.[11]

So, the beauty of a nudge lies in its guarantee of free will. Well, perhaps not free will in its purest form. Take, for instance, the multi-storied department stores, where every item yearns to catch shoppers' eyes. Thus, they prefer customers to use the escalator rather than the elevator. On this account, escalators are usually located at the place to be seen and approached easily, and elevators play hide and seek in obscure corners. Two options seem to be provided equally, but in effect, customers are robbed of the convenience of using the elevator. An impressive part is that this inconvenience is set at just the right level so customers do not grumble about it. Such is the artistry of a masterful nudge. It leaves us oblivious to a subtle arrangement.

In short, we can say that nudge is an art of understated persuasion. From promoting healthier lifestyles to encouraging financial prudence, nudges operate under the radar, making their impact without triggering resistance. Ultimately, nudges remind us that the gentlest of pushes can often lead to significant changes, all while keeping our sense of free will intact.

Ease Wins: The Nudge with Effortless Choices

There are many nudging strategies to make the desirable option win the case. The *default strategy* is one of them. It has already been mentioned in Chap. 1, but as it is a very efficient nudging method, let me discuss it more and show some more examples, too.

The default option is the primary option that will be automatically adopted if we don't take any action. It means that, unlike the default option, choosing the other option is made to require additional effort. The psychological underpinning is that people don't want to be nagged with everyday choices and usually reconcile with the option that doesn't badger them anymore unless they have an apparent disfavor against it. Thus, the default strategy thrives, for it whispers gently, "Choose me or bear the burden of effort."

We can see the potency of the default strategy in organ donation registration rates by country. In countries such as Austria, France, or Spain, organ donation is the default option, and if you don't want it, you must explicitly "opt out" of it. In

---

[11] On January 21, 2023, extracted and revised from https://upjoke.com/innovation-jokes.

Fig. 2.1 Square-shaped toilet paper (created by DALL.E, 2024, Author's Collection)

"opt-in" countries, it is the opposite. According to Standford SPARQ, in "opt-out" countries, more than 90% of people registered to donate their organs, and in "opt-in" countries, fewer than 15%.[12] See the amazing difference! It is a brilliant testament to the profound impact of a well-crafted decision environment, which can even produce more mature citizenship.

Square-shaped toilet paper (like the one in Fig. 2.1) can be another example of nudging people to behave desirably by badgering them with undesirable alternatives. Instead of the round tube that we're all used to, the core of this toilet paper roll is a square. Shigeru Ban, a renowned architect and designer, actually designed this product—Squared Toilet Paper (2000). At first glance, you might think, "What's the big deal?" However, the nudge theory is all about subtly influencing people's behavior. Here, the desirable user behavior is to use a minimum amount of toilet paper for the environment. Courtesy of its endearing square-like shape, it doesn't spin around wildly when you pull on the paper. That is, rolling is difficult. And this inconvenience gets in the way of using more than necessary. Isn't it delightfully devilish! Despite its inconvenience, it doesn't rob us of the right to choose. We can still choose to use more. However, chances are that while we have to roll it slowly, we might have second thoughts, which probably guide us toward the path of least resistance and toward better behavior.

Next, besides the default strategy, let us discuss another nudging strategy that makes the desirable behavior easier to embrace—"*tapping into existing schemas*." *Schema* is the cognitive "structure" honed over time by repeating behaviors.[13] It's like a blueprint or a plan for something in our environment. For example, the schema of a car encompasses its concept as a motorized, four-wheeled vehicle, designed

[12] Scheiber (accessed 2024).

[13] Van der Veer (2001).

for road travel. It typically includes features like seats, engine, wheels, and steering mechanism. Let's consider another example—the schema for a "chocolate cake." It might include the knowledge that chocolate cakes are sweet, contain chocolate, are black, are usually baked, and often are eaten at celebrations.

Schema helps us understand the world around us and guides us effortlessly through the intricacies of life. Therefore, it is easier to recognize new information if it fits into existing schemas. If it doesn't, it requires additional cognitive resources, a mental stretch beyond our comfort zone. So, the nudge strategy capitalizing on our existing schemas can make the desirable behavior a seamless endeavor.

Designers also use schemas that can nudge consumers to figure out the proper user behavior quickly. That is, designs that tap into an existing schema will be easier to use. For example, a desk lamp with a dish-like base (like the one in Fig. 2.2) gives you a hint that it is more than just a lamp. With the help of our existing schema regarding dishes, we can quickly figure out that it is also intended to keep sundry things (like phones, keys, watches, glasses, etc.). Renowned designer Naoto Fukasawa actually created the table lamp with a dish-like base ("A Light with a Dish," 2003). A good design spares consumers the laborious task of reading manuals. The design itself elicits proper behavior intuitively, and Fukasawa is famous for designing such products.

Fig. 2.2 Desk lamp with a dish-like base (created by DALL.E, 2023, Author's Collection)

Fig. 2.3 Bulla Bulla display design in IKEA store, Gwangmyeong, South Korea (photographed by Jeongmin Lee, 2020, Author's Collection)

Another design example applying a proper schema is IKEA's "Bulla Bulla" technique, a display design method of piling a large number of items inside a big see-through bin (Fig. 2.3). It creates the impression of volume and, therefore, inexpensiveness. That is, products in the bin match consumers' schema that more volume means lower price. Of course, it is for inducing impulse buying.

As we can see, nudging strategies like the default option and tapping into existing schemas work because they understand the human tendency to follow the easy options—that is, the path of least resistance. Nudging techniques like these, therefore, can be ingenious tools for subtly influencing human behaviors.

We Sorely Need Others: The Social Nudge

Now, let's move to the *social nudging strategy*. We humans are social animals by nature, and the social self is an essential component of the self-concept. Rightly or wrongly, willing or not, we seriously need responses and recognition from others in developing our self-concept. Therefore, we soak up social influences like a sponge. We even get social pressure from those who have already died, called "tradition!" In this respect, the *desire for social recognition* can touch off certain behaviors.

With the rise of social networking, a spark of this social craving turned into a great ball of flame. Savvy businesses fan this flame and avail themselves of this hot social phenomenon: they prompt customers to share snapshots of their store visits on social media. That's why flagship stores of famous brands are equipped with

Fig. 2.4 Left—Seoul House of Dior, Christian de Portzamparc, 2015, Seoul, South Korea/Right—Desserts at Cafe Dior (Left: Berk Ozdemir/Shutterstock) (Right: photographed by Jeongmin Lee, 2017, Author's Collection)

charming photo spots and allow customers to take pictures only with smartphones, not with other cameras.

Take the Seoul House of Dior (Fig. 2.4), for instance. Here, we encounter meticulously curated details. Every inch of this store oozes charm and timeless elegance, enticing us to take pictures. It is like walking into a living art gallery as it is garnished to the brim with artworks by renowned artists. Even the desserts at Cafe Dior bear the mark of stylish craftsmanship (see Fig. 2.4 right). Moreover, the place is steeped in brand lore shared by the staff. All these are tip-top ingredients that make up lovely SNS postings, and customers can have the chance to show off their "Been there, done that" story.

Another social tactic for nudging people is *providing information about others as a point of comparison*. For instance, an electricity bill bearing information about the average usage of similarly sized neighboring houses might nudge you to dial down your energy consumption, encouraging friendly competition. In addition, have you ever noticed the "best-seller" tags in brand stores or the "popular choice" labels on restaurant menus? These are also social nudges that provide information about choices of others. They're like friendly neighbors pointing you toward safe, tried-and-true decisions—the ones you'll likely adopt, too. Why wander into uncharted territories when the road most traveled promises satisfaction? So here's to our social nature. May it always lead us to good choices!

The psychological underpinning of social nudging can be explained by the *social comparison theory*.[14] Humans have an inherent drive to evaluate themselves—our worth, decisions, behaviors, opinions, and accomplishments. But here's the kicker:

[14] Gerber (2018).

we lack absolute measures of what's truly good and bad. Therefore, one of the key ways to do this self-assessment is by weighing ourselves in contrast to others.

There are two moves to this comparison urge—*upward social comparison* and *downward social comparison*. The former is comparing ourselves to those we deem better than ourselves, and the latter to those we deem worse. An upward social comparison can be double-edged. It can ignite a "get-up-and-go" spirit, propelling us toward self-improvement, should we be on track. But beware! Conversely, it can also summon negative emotions, leading to gloom and undesirable behaviors. Humans are indeed social animals and perform social comparisons every time and everywhere, even when it is not appropriate.

Thus, we sometimes need a healthy dose of downward comparison. It can give our self-esteem a well-deserved pat on the back, a sprinkle of self-flattery once in a while. We sometimes do this unconsciously, too: isn't it a common reaction that everyone driving faster than us is a maniac, and those driving slower are idiots?[15] That's your brain doing its daily rounds of downward comparison. Furthermore, if you are smart enough, you can cleverly confuse upward and downward social comparisons and turn the awkward circumstance into a win–win situation: when your boss asks you who is stupid, you or him, tell him that he doesn't hire stupid people.[16] So, folks, don't feel ashamed when making downward comparisons because even an old adage tells us the necessity of them in our lives—"Better be first in a village than second at Rome."

We live in an era of social media where the desire for social recognition strongly influences our behaviors. Therefore, the world of social nudging can be a fascinating aspect of human psychology. However, we should also be careful about the potential downsides of social media influence, such as the pressure to conform. Also, constant social comparison, whether upward or downward, can have mental health implications. Therefore, as we navigate these social seas, let's use our social nature wisely, making choices that not only feel right but also bring out the best in us.

Tickling the Choice: The Emotional Nudge

Next, let's discuss the *emotional nudging strategy*. We know well it's important to decide rationally. People put the accent on this because we also know well that emotion wins over rationality quite often. Therefore, sometimes, a dash of emotion can outperform a full measure of intellect.

Taking advantage of *fun and humor* is a standout formula for emotionally nudging people. After all, everyone enjoys a good laugh, and we can't help but love a person with a sense of humor. They can nudge us to do what we usually wouldn't do. For example, forgiving someone who hurt our feelings is usually hard. Nonetheless, I might forgive my partner who forgot my birthday but tried to compensate with this

---

[15] On January 30, 2023, extracted and revised from https://laffgaff.com/funny-sms-text-jokes/.

[16] On January 30, 2023, extracted and revised from https://upjoke.com.

Fig. 2.5 Piano stairs in subway station, Nanjing, China (Imaginechina Limited/Alamy Stock Photo)

handsome wisdom instead: "Forget the future, you cannot predict it. Forget the past, you cannot change it. And forget the present… I didn't get you one."[17]

Now, let's see how design can incorporate fun and humor. Take, for instance, the famous Piano Staircase from Volkswagen's Fun Theory campaign, which was installed in the Stockholm subway. It made the piano sound so luring that people started taking the stairs instead of the escalator, which is the healthier option. The number of stair users increased significantly.[18] Figure 2.5 shows a similar piano staircase installed in a subway station in Nanjing.

The urinal at Schiphol Airport with a fly drawn in (Fig. 2.6) is another example. It was designed to save on toilet cleaning costs. That is, by giving a shot in the arm to men's hunting instinct, it makes them aim precisely at the fly. Urine leakage outside the urinal decreased by 80%.[19] Wow, 80%! That's a clean sweep with a pinch of humor!

An emotional nudge uses *subconscious instincts*, too. Consider this tale of instinctive curiosity: you walk down the street and encounter a sleek advertisement. This isn't just any ad; it sports a peephole, shaped like a liquor bottle and with a well-known liquor brand name emblazoned beneath it—something like the one in Fig. 2.7 (left image). Now, here's the rub: we humans can hardly resist the siren call of a mysterious hole located at eye level. It beckons, whispering, "Come, take a look." So, you do, driven by that primal itch to uncover secrets. But here is the climax of this scenario. As you peer through this intriguing spyhole, what do you find? Not the expected other side of the wall, but your very own reflection on a CCTV screen,

[17] On January 30, 2023, extracted and revised from https://upjoke.com/confused-jokes and https://upjoke.com/wisdom-jokes.

[18] Maultsby (2020).

[19] Lidwell et al. (2010).

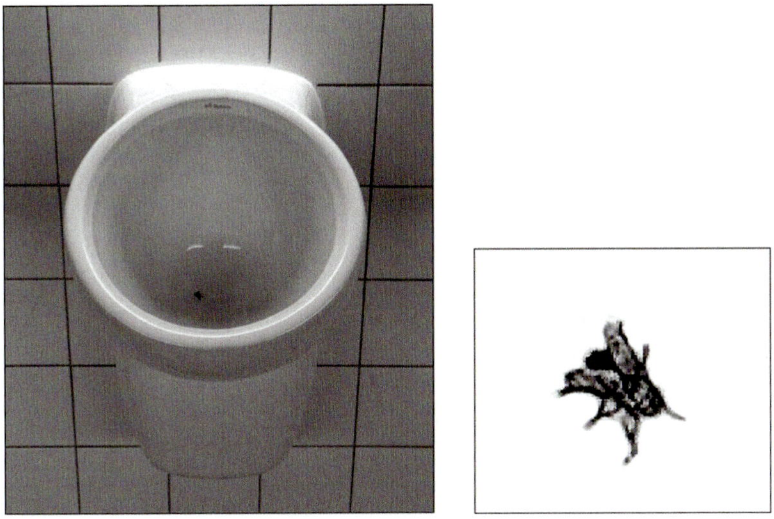

Fig. 2.6 Urinal at Schiphol Airport, Amsterdam, the Netherlands (Daniel Duart/Avalon.red/Alamy Stock Photo)

caught red-handed spying on yourself (Fig. 2.7 right)! You're not just watching an ad; you're part of a scene, the observer turned observed.

This was the scenario of an ad for Absolut Vodka—"Absolut Voyeur" (Whybin TBWA, Pyrmont, 2005). The ad featured a black rectangular frame with an Absolut bottle-shaped peephole placed at eye level, which was a decoy that tempted passersby to look into it. Who, after all, can resist a covert glance through a strategically placed spyhole? The ad also featured the word "ABSOLUT VOYEUR." This design deftly

Fig. 2.7 Advertising design example utilizing human's subconscious desire regarding peephole (created by DALL.E, 2023, Author's Collection)

employs viewer participation: customers become a part of the ad itself, effectively turning into voyeurs. Thus, by nudging passersby to engage with the ad, this ad makes the viewer more likely to remember the product and potentially influences their purchasing decisions.

Obviously, fun and humor are mirthful motivators and can turn the mundane into delightful. Who knew the design world could sport such a clever sense of humor? These smart, playful tweaks make us chuckle in the daily round of our lives.

Wise Whispers: The Rational Nudge

Then, you might ask, "What about nudging with reason?" Nudges aren't shy about tapping into our intellectual understanding, either, and there are *rational nudging strategies*. For example, using *perceptual salience*, nudge design can inform us of what the desirable behavior is. The "Yellow Carpet," installed before the school zone's crosswalk, is a good example (Fig. 2.8). Its bright yellow color is hard to miss and draws immediate attention to the area, signaling to both pedestrians and drivers that they are entering a zone that requires additional caution. Thus, the yellow carpet acts as a psychological speed bump. Drivers may intuitively slow down. For children, the color can be a signal that this is a safe place to wait for crossing. The carpet doesn't force anyone to act in a certain way; instead, it is a soft persuasion that encourages voluntary compliance with safety norms.

For another example of using people's intellectual understanding, let's cast our mind back to the COVID-19 era. Back then, we frequently encountered those floor marks of the feet, reminiscent of Fig. 2.9, guiding us to maintain social distance. It's heartwarming to see how we responsibly positioned ourselves on these markers, showing care not just for our own safety but for others as well. It was, in its own way, a communal care, subtly choreographed by those unassuming footprints.

Fig. 2.8 Yellow Carpet in school zone, Seoul, South Korea (photographed by Jeongmin Lee, 2023, Author's Collection)

Fig. 2.9 Floor marks of the feet for social distancing during the COVID-19 pandemic, IKEA store, Gwangmyeong, South Korea (photographed by Jeongmin Lee, 2020, Author's Collection)

Hopping onto the subway, we encounter another design example of a cerebral nudge. The "OrangeHeart" in Fig. 2.10 nudges passengers toward more socially considerate seating habits. That is, it is a clever intervention to address the issue of "manspreading." To prevent this undesirable behavior, OrangeHeart provides a visual prompt for where passengers should place their feet. It's like a gentle tap on the shoulder reminding them, "Hey buddy, the subway isn't your living room. No manspreading, please!" Furthermore, the use of a heart shape can also be seen as playful. Such joyous guidance often feels less intrusive and more welcoming. So, this winsome nudging that is as disarming as it is intelligent can do a lot more good than a hard-core warning.

When it comes to rationally nudging people, design can also awaken the sleeping beauty in us—the *conscience*. One of the World Wildlife Fund (WWF) advertising campaigns utilizes a paper towel dispenser as a creative visual metaphor. The dispenser features a transparent map of South America on its front, and the paper towel is green in color. This ad consists of three sequential images showing the paper towels at different levels—full, partially used, and nearly depleted, illustrating the impact of paper consumption on the environment. This is to show that the green portion of South America decreases as the paper towels are dispensed. At the top of the dispenser, a message reads, "save paper—save the planet" alongside the WWF logo. Thus, this design can kindle people's feelings of guilt because it shows the result of our irresponsible behaviors—destroying the forest of the world. Suddenly, reaching out for that second sheet of paper in the public restroom doesn't feel so inconsequential anymore, does it?

Fig. 2.10 OrangeHeart, ING Life, 2015, South Korea (used with permission of Joongang Daily, 2015. 12. 6.)

So, it's clear that a little brainy nudge can go a long way. The above designs cleverly appeal to our intellect and conscience. It's like having a wise friend who doesn't nag but gently guides with a knowing wink.

More Design Insights Added to the Scene

Now, let me invite you to another scene—the intriguing world of *affordance*. It is a term that is closely related to the nudge but is a bit different.

Even though nudge was devised by Thaler and Sunstein to improve public policies and systems, marketers and designers have been playing a similar tune for a long time under other names. In the design field, it has been called "affordance." It is a term coined by psychologist James J. Gibson and refers to features of an object that make people perceive doable actions related to that object.

The Armstrong Bin in Fig. 2.11 is a good design example. It has an accordion-style body, hinting at its capability for compression. Better still, it has a lid with a noticeable footprint impression on it. It's as if the bin is inviting you to step on it because the footprint is a universal signal that says, "Go ahead, step on me!" So, when you push down the lid with your foot, the bin compresses, making room for more trash. The design with good affordances makes using it correctly a reflexive act, letting us off the hook of reading the dull manual. Its design features are a wordless manual, rendered in elegant, unspoken instructions.

Let me tell you another amusing nugget about affordance—OTT programs. If Netflix asks, "Do you want to watch a 7-h movie?" you would probably say, "Are you insane?" If it asks again, "How about a series with seven 1-h episodes and watching them all in one sitting?" you might say, "I am in!"[20] That's the subtle charm of affordance. It can even make the implausible seem easily doable.

---

[20] On May 25, 2023, extracted and revised from https://upjoke.com/movie-jokes.

Fig. 2.11 Armstrong Bin, Sukwon Park, Sungwoo Park, Hyunsoo Kim, Young Min Yoon, and Seunghee Son, 2009 (used with permission of iF Design, Germany)

However, unlike the nudge, which guarantees free choice, affordance sometimes resorts to involuntary methods. That is, the design might grant only one option. It is usually for a good purpose, though, and more honestly, for a good marketing purpose as well. For instance, who can pull the door with no doorknob? (preventing errors). Drivers have no choice but to reduce their speed if the road with many pedestrians is intentionally made winding (safety purpose). Also, in many museums, the traffic is directed such that the viewers must go through the museum shop at the end of the tour (marketing purpose).

Lastly, let's look into the case in Fig. 2.12. On the surface, it seems to be a nudge design case with no physical constraints mentioned above. It's a scene from the early stages of the COVID-19 pandemic, where social distancing circles were painted on the lawn of Domino Park. You could, theoretically, seat yourself outside the circle. However... Who would dare?! Sometimes, the psychological and social expectations can be just as binding as the physical ones.

Let's wrap up this nudge narrative, shall we? Nudging is powerful, but you hardly notice it's there. It's not about forcing our choices. Instead, it's like a friend who whispers a hint. That is, it elegantly balances the environmental influence and human free will. Throughout this exploration, we've seen nudges in various forms, from the nudge with effortless choices to the social, emotional, and rational nudges, and they demonstrate their versatility in encouraging positive behavioral changes. But we should also acknowledge that it also raises ethical questions about manipulation and the extent to which it respects individual autonomy. That's why we should be prudent consumers and citizens so that we can be positively influenced by it, not the other way around. Despite its possible problems, we can say nudges can achieve what force and directive might not. So, let's appreciate the gentle wisdom leading us to a path of betterment.

Fig. 2.12 Domino Park, 2020, Brooklyn, USA (John Nacion/NurPhoto SRL/Alamy Stock Photo)

References

Bandura, A. (1997). *Self-efficacy: The exercise of control*. Worth Publishers.

Brenner, C. (1994). The mind as conflict and compromise formation. *Journal of Clinical Psychoanalysis, 3*(4), 473–488.

Campbell, J. (1997). A compatibilist theory of alternative possibilities. *Philosophical Studies, 88*, 319–330.

Fischer, J. M., Kane, R., Pereboom, D., & Vargas, M. (2007). *Four views on free will*. Wiley-Blackwell.

Gerber, J. P. (2018, January 2). Social comparison theory. In *Encyclopedia of personality and individual differences*. Accessed January 23, 2024. https://www.researchgate.net/profile/J-Gerber-2/publication/322209458_Social_Comparison_Theory_entry_for_Encyclopedia_of_Personality_and_Individual_Differences/links/5a4baab00f7e9b8284c2d3e8/Social-Comparison-Theory-entry-for-Encyclopedia-of-Personality-and-Individual-Differences.pdf

Kim, J., & Okazaki, S. (2017). Short-term 'intensive mothering' on a budget: Working mothers of Korean children studying abroad in Southeast Asia. *Asian Women, 33*(3), 111–139.

Lidwell, W., Holden, K., & Butler, J. (2010). *Universal principles of design: 125 ways to enhance usability, influence perception, increase appeal, make better design decisions, and teach through design*. Rockport Publishers.

Maultsby, C. (2020, December 8). The fun theory. In *Norse News*. Accessed January 23, 2024. https://shsnorsenews.org/1647/columns/the-fun-theory/

McKenna, M., & Coates, D. J. (2021). Compatibilism. In E. N. Zalta (Ed.), *The Stanford encyclopedia of philosophy* (Fall 2021 ed.). Accessed January 23, 2024. https://plato.stanford.edu/archives/fall2021/entries/compatibilism/

North, A. C., Hargreaves, D. J., & McKendrick, J. (1997). In-store music affects product choice. *Nature, 390*, 132.

Scheiber F. (accessed 2024). *'Opt out' policies increase organ donation*. Accessed January 23, 2024. https://sparq.stanford.edu/solutions/opt-out-policies-increase-organ-donation

Thaler, R. H., & Sunstein, C. R. (2008). *Nudge: Improving decisions about health, wealth, and happiness*. Yale University Press.

Thaler, R. H., & Sunstein, C. R. (2021). *Nudge: The final edition*. Penguin Books.

Van der Veer, R. (2001). Remembering Bartlett. *Culture & Psychology, 7*(2), 223–229.

Chapter 3
Without Charlie's Angels, We Can Be Happier: The Comparison Conundrum

Does the sparkle of Charlie's Angels really work wonders in every aspect? Any doubts? Well, let's dive into the intriguing and sometimes shady world of human psychology, shall we?

According to one experiment, watching these celestial heroines can cause a social problem.[1] Between two groups of male dormitory residents, one relished an episode of Charlie's Angels while the other didn't watch it. Then, they were asked to rate the attractiveness of an average female. The group that reveled in crime-fighting beauties rated this female subject "less" attractive. The study concluded that exposure to highly attractive individuals could adversely affect the perceived attractiveness of average individuals. In other words, people can become less appreciative when exposed to an upward comparison—as it were, the seemingly remarkable lives of others. We humans just can't resist getting hooked on the comparison game. So, when you come down to it, without Charlie's angels, we can be happier.

At any rate, sadly enough, we evaluate our worth by comparing ourselves with others. We are like fence-peepers, constantly sizing up our neighbors' lawns to see who's got the greener grass, and the problem is, "The grass is always greener on the other side."

Let me show you the prowess of comparative nature, which even permeates our perception. Behold two squares at the center in Fig. 3.1 (upper image). Both of them share an identical size (lower image Fig. 3.1), yet intriguingly, the left one appears to diminish a bit as if plagued by self-doubt amidst its burly neighbors. This is one of the famous perceptual illusions called the Ebbinghaus illusion.[2] Figuratively speaking, it can be compared to the shrunken feeling we get when encircled by ultra-cool, impeccably dressed individuals. The ever-present human inclination to compare has proven so mighty that it even baffles our eyes!

---

[1] Kenrick and Gutierres (1980).

[2] Massaro and Anderson (1971).

© The Author(s), under exclusive license to Springer Nature Singapore Pte Ltd. 2024

J. Lee et al., *The Psychology Behind Design*,
https://doi.org/10.1007/978-981-97-3426-9_3

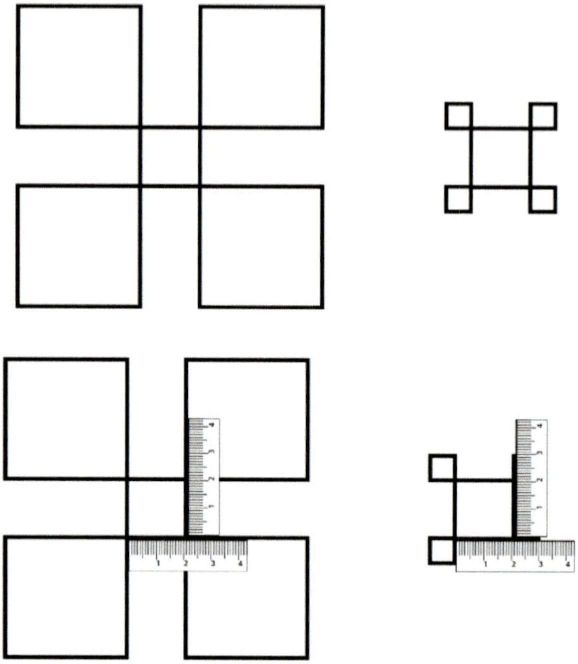

Fig. 3.1 Ebbinghaus illusion (created by Jeongmin Lee, 2023, Author's Collection)

Fig. 3.2 Victoria's Secret, Royal Fantasy Bra, 2013 (FashionStock.com/Shutterstock)

Marketers know this insatiable human nature so well that they pull strings on us every day with savvy comparison game plans. Ever heard that tempting catchphrase "affordable luxury"? It entices us to long for a piece of the luxury that fortunate others enjoy. The annual extravaganza of Victoria's Secret's million-dollar "Fantasy Bra" (Fig. 3.2), often incorporating precious gems and rare metals, was also a strategic marketing tactic. When such astronomical price tags bombard our senses, the other high-priced wares of Victoria's Secret seem far less daunting. It's hard not to be entrapped. So, please beware of the comparison trap, for it lurks around every corner!

Fig. 3.3 AVIS: "We try harder" Campaign, 1962 (used with permission of Avis Budget Group)

Be that as it may, our tendency to compare has a sunny side too: it works not only as a drag but also as an uplifting energy. It's akin to electricity. When wielded wisely, it enhances our lives. When mishandled, we are in for a shock. Likewise, when harnessed well, comparative energy can fuel our personal growth, spurring us to advance further because we need to observe high fliers for inspiration. But it serves us well only if we can acknowledge those up-and-comers as catalysts bringing out the best in us. And those who can graciously tip their hats to their rivals while simultaneously leveling up are a rare and commendable breed.

One of those rare cases was the triumphant advertising campaign of AVIS. AVIS astutely capitalized on straightforward admission as a second-fiddle, crafting a campaign, "We try harder" (Fig. 3.3). Their message declared, "When you're only No. 2, you try harder. Or else." This is the case that a positive attitude toward social comparison acted as a dynamic nourishment.

In far too many instances, though, we wind up trapping ourselves in the comparison game, looking askance with a sour mind. Jealousy, that irritating downer, has a talent for tiptoeing into our lives. Be it in the realms of the heart, friendships, or work, it can be a real bummer. So, as a protector of our self-esteem, we occasionally need someone who would consider us a high flier, that is, a downward comparison. As the saying goes, "Better to be a big fish in a small pond than a small fish in a big pond." Or, if you prefer, divert your comparing mind like this: "My wife is not only lovely but also smarter than me! She did a much better job of picking a spouse than I did."[3]

Therefore, in the pursuit of happiness, we need a protector, the vigilante who can tame the green-eyed monster in us. While we may not be able to eradicate it altogether, we can certainly show who the boss is. To tone down this pesky presence,

[3] On April 24, 2023, extracted and revised from https://upjoke.com/jealous-jokes.

we must first admit that we harbor this annoying, albeit natural, human emotion (Don't worry, you're in a crowded club!). Doing so will rouse our inner sage, who enlightens us with this wisdom, "The grass isn't greener on the other side. It's greener where you water it." So, if the grass is truly greener on the other side, the fair bet is that the water bill is also higher there.[4]

With this awareness, our guru would give us a magic tip that works wonders to steer our gaze away from the neighbor's bounties to our own luscious lawn—"daily gratitude." It's all about tallying up those itty-bitty wins and blessings, rain or shine, every day at every turn. It works for real, and "penny and penny laid up will be many!" Despite ourselves, we would be surprised to find ourselves too busy celebrating our own bounties to bother with comparisons.

To cultivate this gratitude proneness, we sometimes have to play detective and dig up reasons to be grateful, especially when life feels like a series of bad breaks. Keep in mind that nothing in this world is all good or all bad. Example? When eating an apple and finding a worm, we still can be thankful because there is something worse—eating an apple and finding half a worm![5] These endeavors gradually engineer the "gratefulness" neural networks in our brains, and our sweat will be well worth it. After all, we "can't afford" to let the green-eyed monster cramp our style.

Owl of Minerva Behind the Scene

In this chapter, we will delve into the psychology of comparison. It is a thought-provoking and also bewildering facet of the human mind. Our sagacious owl shall guide us as we explore its depths.

There are a few types of comparison in human psychology—social comparison (the whole "keeping up with the Joneses" thing), perceptual comparison (like sizing up the world's sensory feed), and referential comparison (where we measure a certain thing against a nifty benchmark) are the representative ones. We will delve into them one by one.

Keeping Up with the Joneses: Social Comparison

Let's start with *social comparison*. We already talked briefly about social comparison theory in the previous chapter as the psychological underpinning of social nudging. But here, we will explore it more deeply and discuss its additional roles.

According to *social comparison theory*, we humans possess an undeniable tendency to assess ourselves and, more often than not, figure out how valuable we are by comparing ourselves to others. This suggests that our sense of self-worth is not derived from an absolute benchmark but rather sways within a relative spectrum of ever-changing social comparisons. Sad, isn't it?

---

[4] On April 24, 2023, extracted and revised from https://topfunnyjokes.net/funny-sayings/grass-greener-side.

[5] On January 9, 2023, extracted and revised from http://www.funny-jokes-quotes.com/daily-life-situations.html.

Humans engage in a dualistic attitude of self-appraisal, a social seesaw oscillating between upward and downward comparisons. When we are on track and on target toward our own goals and aspirations, *upward social comparison* (measuring ourselves against those who excel) works as a constructive booster. However, when we veer off course, this same comparison can work as a dispiriting drag, causing jealousy or depression. Similarly, *downward social comparison* (measuring ourselves against those deemed less successful than us) isn't always a bad habit of a smart alec. It sometimes works as a mental guardian that helps us maintain a sound level of self-esteem. A somewhat bittersweet but handy psychological gadget!

All these double-sided values of psychological phenomena remind me of this wisdom again: everything in this world is neither good nor bad in absolute terms. Take a keyring, for example. It is a nifty little gadget and also lets you lose all your keys at once.[6] Or, consider educational standards for parenting. We spend the first 12 months of our children's lives teaching them to walk and talk. Then, in the next 12 years, we are telling them to sit down and shut up.[7] How challenging parenting is!

Akin to human character, brands also possess personality, so they also activate social comparisons, often manifesting in the form of *comparative advertisements*. Usually, secondary players in the market bring such campaigns into operation. Frontrunners have little need for that. They already bask in the limelight. Thus, if we find ourselves partaking in upward comparison, it inadvertently reveals our subconscious recognition as the number two. A case in point is Samsung Galaxy's successful ad campaign in 2012, wherein they claimed the Galaxy S3 to be "the most amazing iPhone yet." As further evidence, have you ever seen an iPhone ad that talks about Galaxy?

Likewise, to carve a niche in a market dominated by the cola giants, 7-UP launched the famous "Uncola" campaign in the 1960s, highlighting everything cola wasn't.[8] It was like telling the world, "Hey, we're not them, and that's cool!" This campaign harnessed a social climate of the time that was questioning traditional norms and values. That is, it positioned 7-UP as an "alternative brand for alternative consumers" who were aligned with the values of rebellion and the youth culture of the 1960s. In essence, this campaign effectively utilized social comparison to create a distinct brand identity that resonated with people looking to express their individuality and nonconformity through their consumption choices.

The "Uncola" ads were also a vivid reflection of this strategy and of the psychedelic era. They were pop art masterpieces featuring bright, colorful, and often surreal artwork. Artworks like "UnCanny In Cans" (by John Alcorn), "Like No Cola Can" (by Milton Glaser), and "The Light Shining Over The Dark" (by Pat Dypold) used whimsical and vibrant designs to capture the spirit of the times. Through their creative and unconventional visuals, they could successfully present 7-Up as a unique,

---

[6] On April 25, 2023, extracted and revised from https://upjoke.com/gadget-jokes.

[7] On April 25, 2023, extracted and revised from https://en.paperblog.com/funny-antithesis-sentences-figure-of-speech-examples-1609941/.

[8] Kardes et al. (2014).

rebellious brand. The quick-witted marketing move even spawned an "Uncola" cup molded in the likeness of an inverted Coca-Cola bottle. Talk about turning the soda world upside down!

Now, it should be noted that people around the globe do not all play the same tune when it comes to comparative ads.[9] As such, a comparative ad campaign scoring impressive success in the U.S. may involuntarily provoke a backlash in some countries.[10] It often depends on the values of individualistic, "me-first" societies versus collectivist, "we-first" societies. Cultures with individualistic values openly demonstrate a competitive spirit, and comparative ads go down smooth. On the other hand, people in more "we-first" cultures regard outright competitive gestures as affronts, especially if they make someone "lose face." Historically, comparative ads have been met with disfavor in these societies.

So, let's tip our hats to the quirky world of social comparison. It's a realm where our inner values constantly swing, pushed by the winds of societal benchmarks. And those wily comparative ads always nudge us to pick sides in a brand battle royale. But let's remember that in the kaleidoscope of social comparisons, sometimes, it's just cool to march to the beat of your own drum.

Contextual Mind Games: Perceptual Comparison

Next, let's move on to the second comparison psychology—*perceptual comparison*.

Now and then, our penchant for comparisons works subconsciously and makes our minds fall prey to imprecise, illogical judgments. The *context effect* is one of them. Human judgments are heavily influenced by the context in which an item or experience is viewed, causing the same thing to sway from hero to zero.

The context effect has partners—the *assimilation effect* and the *contrast effect*.[11] See Fig. 3.4. What do you see in the upper row? You see a group of alphabets. Then, what do you see in the lower row? A group of numbers, right? However, did you notice that the "B" in the upper row and the "13" in the lower row are identical forms? Yet, according to the context, our minds perceive them differently, as an alphabet and as a number. This is the "assimilation effect." It shifts our perception of a certain subject closer to its point of comparison. In other words, a specific stimulus is comprehended in the same context as other stimuli presented together.

Researchers found that even the degree of "comfort" felt on a store floor can influence how we judge the quality of products in that very store.[12] It means a store floor's "coziness" factor can form a context for the product's worth. That's why posh brands pull out all the stops to create not just top-notch products but also store designs with high aesthetics. Take Gentle Monster, a sunglass brand, for example.

---

[9] Mothersbaugh et al. (2020).

[10] Jeon and Beatty (2002).

[11] Sherif et al. (1958).

[12] Meyers-Levy et al. (2009).

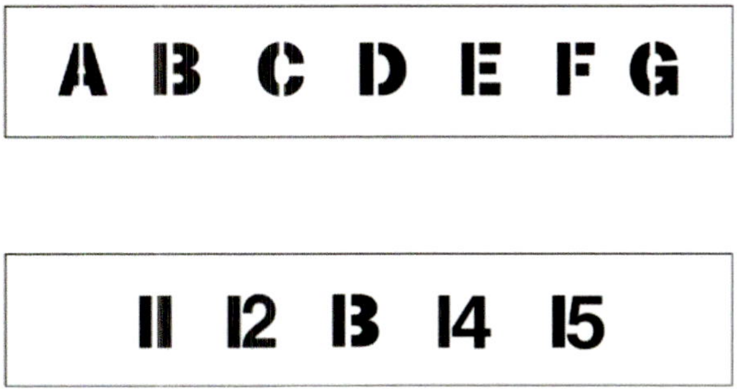

Fig. 3.4 Assimilation effect (created by Jeongmin Lee, 2023, Author's Collection)

Fig. 3.5 Assimilation effect: Gentle Monster showroom, Seoul, South Korea (photographed by Jeongmin Lee, 2017, Author's Collection)

Their showrooms are designed like modern art galleries (Fig. 3.5). Why? When you walk into a space that feels like an art gallery, you cannot help but see the products on display as wearable artistic masterpieces. Covertly clever!

Conformity, a group persuasion of sorts, is another gripping psychological phenomenon related to assimilation. It shows the human desire to blend with others surrounding them. Have you ever felt the urge to fit in with cool kids? Or maybe you've found yourself nodding along with the crowd even when you don't really agree with them. Well, that's the power of conformity at work.

In the acclaimed "Asch conformity experiment," Solomon Asch devised a method to prove how strong this desire can be.[13] He presented a group of eight subjects with a simple task—matching a target line with the most similar one out of options A, B, or C (Fig. 3.6). A piece of cake, right? But here is the twist: there was only one real

[13] Asch (1963).

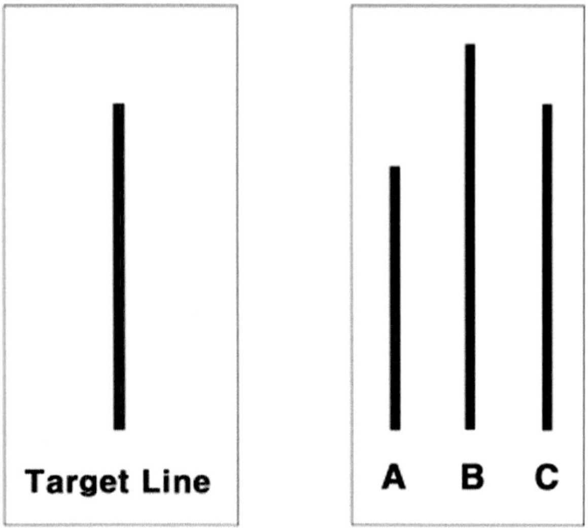

Fig. 3.6 Asch conformity experiment (created by Jeongmin Lee, 2023, Author's Collection)

participant in the group, and the rest were stooges who had already agreed on the wrong answer. It was up to our unsuspecting participant to be the voice of reason. As each person answered aloud, the real participant was placed at the end of the row, amplifying the pressure to conform. Asch also tested a control group with no stooges.

The results? A whopping 75% conformed at least once, while 25% stood their ground. But in the control group, less than 1% goofed up. It's clear that the desire for conformity influenced by group pressure is a powerful force that can make us do some pretty silly things. Why did the participants conform so readily? It turned out that they didn't want to be labeled "peculiar," preferring to blend in. Even more interesting is that some truly believed the group's answers were correct.

As expected, designers and marketers put this art of group persuasion into action. Have you ever seen an ad design with a bunch of good-looking people having a blast as a group using a target product (something like Fig. 3.7)? The ad furtively whispers, "These cool buddies think this brand is the bee's knees. If you're part of their tribe, you'll too!".

Let me share with you some interesting assimilation cases. Some famous sports stars' names perfectly match their passions, pursuits, and outstanding achievements. Usain Bolt, the remarkable sprinter who truly lives up to his last name; Margaret Court, the great tennis player whose name is engraved on the tennis court for the Australian Open; and Josh Outman, the celebrated baseball pitcher whose name is just too perfect for words.[14]

Now, let's talk about the "contrast effect," another partner for the context effect. It is like the rebellious sibling of the assimilation effect, so it propels the perception of a certain thing further away from its point of comparison. The contrast effect

[14] On April 25, 2023, extracted and revised from https://upjoke.com/peculiar-jokes.

Fig. 3.7 Example of beer ad utilizing the effect of conformity (created by DALL.E, 2023, Author's Collection)

is also responsible for some of the common optical illusions. Take, for instance, the aforementioned *Ebbinghaus illusion* in Fig. 3.1, where size perception fell prey. Another mind-bender is the *brightness contrast*, which plays tricks on color perception. In Fig. 3.8, take note of the two gray squares in the middle, one against a white background and the other against a black one. Because of the contrast effect, the gray square surrounded by white looks darker, while the one against black looks lighter. But they're the exact same shade of gray. If you're skeptical, try covering the backgrounds and see what happens.

The poster design of "127 Hours" in Fig. 3.9 shows a masterful play of brightness contrast, creating a strong visual impact that underscores the film's intense subject matter. "127 Hours" is a survival drama film that tells the true story of Aron Ralston, an adventurer and mountain climber who becomes trapped by a boulder in an isolated canyon in Utah. The poster has a distinct division between the bright, almost glowing section and the dark section, and the dark area looks darker in contrast with the bright background and vice versa. The brightness suggests hope and life, while the darkness

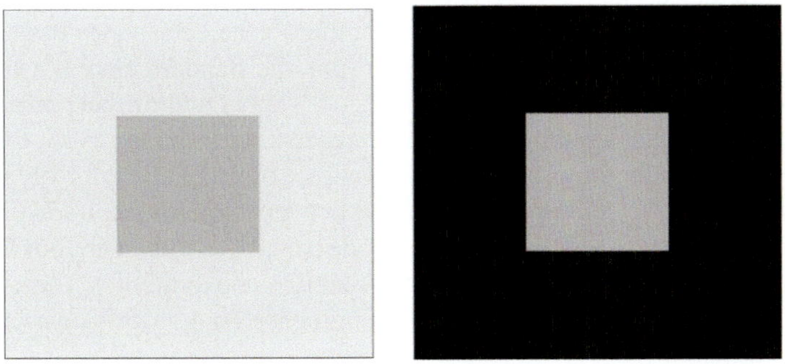

Fig. 3.8 Contrast effect: Brightness contrast (created by Jeongmin Lee, 2023, Author's Collection)

Fig. 3.9 "127 Hours" poster design (FlixPix/Alamy Stock Photo)

looms as a threat. Therefore, this contrast conveys the feeling of the protagonist's predicament, all the while hinting that the audience will witness his attempts to overcome extreme challenges.

In addition to assimilation and contrast effects, the intriguing *compromise effect* also weaves its way through the contextual mind game.[15] Imagine walking into a store, faced with a variety of options to compare. Most of us tend to go for the middle option, especially when we are not sure about which product is the best bang for our buck. This is what experts call the compromise effect. It feels just safe enough while giving us a sense of balance.

Let's take a look at examples we're all familiar with. You know the tactics of online streaming services or software subscriptions: there's the bare-bones basic plan, the all-out premium plan, and, right in the sweet spot, the standard plan. It's no surprise that a lot of us end up choosing the standard plan. It's about finding that perfect balance between cost-saving and getting enough features to keep us happy. Now, think about your last visit to a coffee shop. Faced with the choice of small, medium, or large sizes, many of us go for the medium. The decision between paperback, trade paperback, and hardcover editions is another case. The trade paperback often wins our hearts as it strikes that harmonious balance between affordability and durability. These everyday scenarios showcase the compromise effect's influence on our decisions.

[15] Simonson and Tversky (1992).

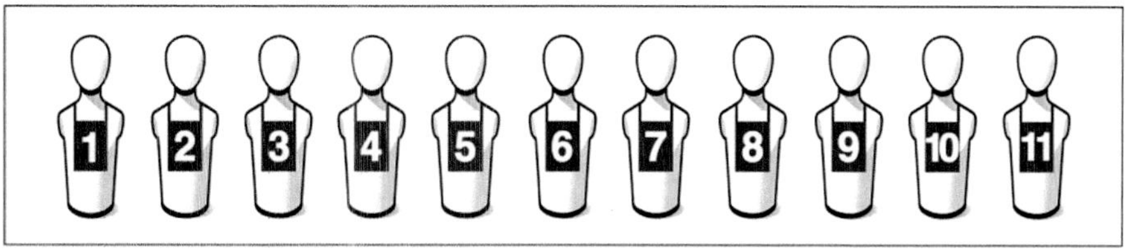

Fig. 3.10 Example of choice options for center-stage effect (created by Jeongmin Lee, 2024, Author's Collection)

Marketers, those clever strategists, often use this effect to their advantage. By placing a product they want to sell right between the priciest and the cheapest options, they make it shine as the perfect choice. That is, the priciest and the cheapest options are intentionally inserted to form the context for the target option so that it looks like a middle option. It's a smart play on our natural tendency to find equilibrium, a concept we discussed back in Chap. 1. Therefore, this phenomenon can be understood not only as the phenomenon of comparison psychology but also as the phenomenon of psychological equilibrium, a balancing act between opposites.

The *center-stage effect* is a physical version of the compromise effect. It highlights how a physical placement influences consumer preference and choice: amidst an array of options, humans are instinctively drawn to the option nestled physically at the center.[16]

This effect sprang to life in the acclaimed Netflix series "Squid Game," an idiosyncratic drama where competitors play children's games with life-or-death stakes. In the scene where players select their turns for the unknown 5th game, there are podiums arranged in a neat row, each with a number marking the fate of its chooser (something like Fig. 3.10). As the selection begins, the numbers in the center get snapped up first, while the ones at the fringes languish till the end. This shows the "center-stage effect" at play. The players instinctively think the middle numbers are somehow safer—a fallacy choreographed by the puppeteers of the game. In fact, it is the last number that holds the golden ticket. Moreover, the design of this scene is cleverly minimalistic—a space in all white and nothing in it. It strips away distractions. Thus, the audience's gaze is arrested, not by flamboyant set pieces, but by the raw display of human psychology under pressure.

As we can see, our minds are like magicians, conjuring tricks of perception that leave us both amused and bemused. From the assimilation effect to the contrast effects and compromise effect, we're constantly involved in the mind game of perceptual comparison. In the end, our mind loves a comparison, even in the perceptual world.

[16] Valenzuela and Raghubir (2009).

The Pricey Persuasion: Referential Comparison

Now, let's discuss the third comparison psychology—*referential comparison*.

Marketers of Victoria's Secret knew a thing or two about manipulating *reference dependence*, a concept from the renowned *prospect theory*.[17] We will deal with this theory in more detail in Chap. 8, but here, in regard to referential comparison, let's discuss one of its important concepts, the *reference point*. It is the psychology behind Victoria's Secret's "Fantasy Bra" (see Fig. 3.2). That is, when deciding how much something is worth, we don't just look at the raw numbers, but instead, we compare it to a reference point. And our judgments shift as these reference points change.

For example, a $3000 handbag might seem like a total splurge for someone used to buying $100 bags. But for an affluent spender accustomed to designer goods, a $3000 bag can be just another day at the office. Similarly, consider the classic "half-empty" versus "half-full" cup illustration. While one person may see it as half-empty, another sees it as half-full according to their usual perspective. And out of the blue, a third party, say an engineer, might chime in and tell you the glass is twice as big as necessary, using an entirely different reference point.[18] It's fascinating how our perception can change so drastically depending on the reference we use.

Now, let's get back to that Fantasy Bra. By showing us a crazy-high price tag on a piece of lingerie, Victoria's Secret effectively changed customers' reference points for the cost of luxury underwear. And the prices for other clothing lines of Victoria's Secret might not seem so bad anymore.

Many other marketing and design examples employ this consumer psychology on the quiet. Ever wondered why those high-end stores parade their priciest items first? That's no mere coincidence. They're just setting the stage, so the less expensive items inside look like a good bargain. Let's consider the same phenomenon on a larger scale. Have you ever noticed that high-end department stores tend to put ultra-luxurious brands on the first floor? By showing us the most expensive stuff right off the bat, they effectively set our reference point for what's "normal." Suddenly, those $200 shirts on the second floor seem much more reasonable by comparison.

Designers take advantage of reference dependence to create a memorable customer experience, too. When crafting a climax in an experiential space, setting up emotional lows as a reference point can make emotional highs feel even more exhilarating. Leading customers through a dark, unsettling area before revealing the main attraction is a good example of this creative approach.

A little bit of brain science could be so cool, isn't it? So, here's the deal with referential comparison: what's expensive to some is not so pricey to others, according to each one's usual reference point and according to the previous experience that sets the temporary reference point. It's all about the art of comparison. So, next time you're out shopping, remember this little brain trick, and it might just be your shield against those sneaky comparison traps, saving your wallet from an unnecessary surprise.

---

[17] Kahneman and Tversky (1979).

[18] On April 25, 2023, extracted and revised from https://www.humorthatworks.com/database/funny-work-jokes-to-get-you-through-the-day/.

More Design Insights Added to the Scene

Lastly, let me explain a bit more about perceptual comparison, in particular, the contexts that can forge *color assimilation* and *color contrast*.

In Fig. 3.11, you see two pictures with the same shade of gray lines. But, in our eyes, those gray lines appear slightly different. In the left image, assimilation occurs, and thin gray lines blend in with the black background, resulting in a darker appearance. In the right image, the wide gray column boldly distances itself from the black background, creating a contrast effect. This daring shift makes the gray column seem brighter than it actually is. Take the Netflix logo (Fig. 3.12), for example. That fiery "N" with a strong red color stands out against the mysterious black background thanks to color contrast. The powerful "N" is shouting, "Look at me. I'm blazing bright!" And we can't help but be captivated.

Then, you might wonder which condition sparks each effect, color assimilation or color contrast. To find the answer, let's go over a helpful analogy. What happens in human relationships also occurs in color relationships: the meek join forces to gain strength, whereas the audacious engage in confrontation, confident in their self-sufficient prowess. Similarly, in the realm of colors, assimilation unfolds in meek, thin stripe designs, and contrast does in bold, large figures juxtaposed side by side. Simply put, subtle lines join hands while formidable figures vie for dominance. What a fascinating phenomenon!

Now, let's wrap up our journey through the intriguing world of comparison psychology. It's clear that human minds are adept at playing the comparison game in myriad ways. From social comparisons to perceptual and referential comparisons, we navigate a world where marketers and designers can cleverly steer our decisions through this comparison game. On the other hand, it's also true that comparison can be our active sidekick in place, which helps us explore and navigate this complicated world efficiently, like a handy Swiss army knife on hand. It may not always be precise, but it might be a time-saver. Well, perhaps this might be a silver lining of

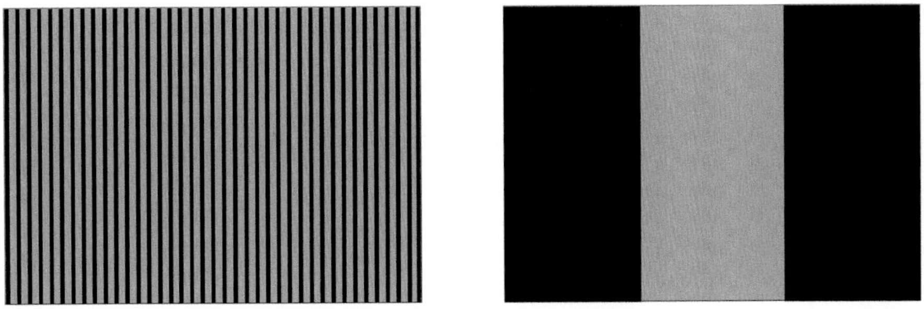

Fig. 3.11 Color assimilation versus color contrast (created by Jeongmin Lee, 2023, Author's Collection)

Fig. 3.12 Netflix logo (Dayat Amir/Shutterstock)

our comparing minds. So, let's remember that while this psychological savvy can be a handy tool to enrich our understanding of the world and ourselves, it can also be a double-edged sword. We'd better be aware of its pros and cons so that we won't be led by the nose at least.

References

Asch, S. E. (1963). Effects of group pressure upon the modification and distortion of judgments. In H. Guetzkow (Ed.), *Groups, leadership and men: Research in human relations*. Russell and Russell.

Jeon, J. O., & Beatty, S. E. (2002). Comparative advertising effectiveness in different national cultures. *Journal of Business Research, 55*(11), 907–913.

Kahneman, D., & Tversky, A. (1979). Prospect theory: An analysis of decision under risk. *Econometrica, 47*(4), 263–291.

Kardes, F., Cronley, M., & Cline, T. (2014). *Consumer behavior* (2nd ed.). Cengage Learning.

Kenrick, D. T., & Gutierres, S. E. (1980). Contrast effects and judgments of physical attractiveness: When beauty becomes a social problem. *Journal of Personality and Social Psychology, 38*(1), 131–140.

Massaro, D. W., & Anderson, N. H. (1971). Judgmental model of the Ebbinghaus illusion. *Journal of Experimental Psychology, 89*(1), 147.

Meyers-Levy, J., Zhu, R., & Jiang, L. (2009). Context effects from bodily sensations: Examining bodily sensations induced by flooring and the moderating role of product viewing distance. *Journal of Consumer Research, 37*(1), 1–14.

Mothersbaugh, D., Hawkins, D. I., & Kleiser, S. B. (2020). *Consumer behavior: Building marketing strategy* (14th ed., p. 48). McGraw-Hill.

Sherif, M., Taub, D., & Hovland, C. I. (1958). Assimilation and contrast effects of anchoring stimuli on judgments. *Journal of Experimental Psychology, 55*(2), 150–155.

Simonson, I., & Tversky, A. (1992). Choice in context: Tradeoff contrast and extremeness aversion. *Journal of Marketing Research, 29*(3), 281–295.

Valenzuela, A., & Raghubir, P. (2009). Position-based beliefs: The center-stage effect. *Journal of Consumer Psychology, 19*(2), 185–196.

Chapter 4
The Bragging Spectrum from Wealth to Altruism: Signaling by Consumption

"It makes a statement about me."

What do you think is this "it" thing that makes a statement about me? It's a Toyota Prius, a hybrid car. Let's rewind the clock to 2007. The New York Times article revealed that 57% of Prius buyers purchased their vehicles for the status symbol, followed by 36% for economic motivation.[1] What about those who had the planet's best interest at heart, lower emissions, you may ask? They accounted for a mere 25%—quite a plot twist results for the survey that allowed multiple answers.

This result reveals that many Prius owners wanted to make their prosocial behaviors publicly exposed. "I really want people to know that I care about the environment," said one of the respondents, who seems to be quite the spokesperson for this faction. So, how did these folks drive? One hand on the wheel, the other patting themselves on the back.[2]

Now, fast forward to the electric vehicle age, and the scenario has changed. More people have become interested in environmental value, giving Mother Nature more of that well-deserved care. According to a survey in 2022 that allowed multiple answers, 51% of current EV owners answered "reducing my impact on the environment" as an important factor when purchasing an electric vehicle.[3] But still, there's more to the story. According to another survey in 2018, 70% of electric car owners still bought them to polish their societal image.[4]

Let's take Tesla as an example. Sure, Tesla has earned a reputation for being a leading environment-friendly brand. Nonetheless, they are not just silent, emissions-free wonders but a clear billboard that shouts, "I can afford this luxury." Unlike

---

[1] Maynard (2007).

[2] On September 10, 2022, extracted and revised from http://www.jokes4us.com/miscellaneousjokes/greenjokes.html.

[3] Battery electric vehicles and low carbon fuel survey. Consumer Reports, April 2022.

[4] Song et al. (2022).

© The Author(s), under exclusive license to Springer Nature Singapore Pte Ltd. 2024

J. Lee et al., *The Psychology Behind Design*,
https://doi.org/10.1007/978-981-97-3426-9_4

Prius, Tesla, with its high-tech wizardry and equally extravagant price tag, is parked firmly in the luxury brand zone. Therefore, its rising popularity isn't solely fueled by a green heart but also by that age-old urge to keep up with the Joneses…or, in this case, outshine them.

The difference between Prius owners and Tesla owners, then? Their external displays may seem different on the surface: one's signaling a prosocial message while the other's flashing a "look-at-my-wallet" symbol. But deep down, they play the same game: social signaling through conspicuous consumption. They both wanted to "show off" their social image through the consumption of automobiles. Why, you ask? It is because such signaling helps one climb the social ladder, which in turn bestows benefits exclusive to the upper elite. And nothing says "I'm here, notice me" louder than the car you drive. It's the most conspicuous product category for this public announcement.

Be that as it may, in the stage of signaling "prosocial" behaviors, we can observe an intriguing aspect of human nature, a puzzling paradox: humans can be pretty self-centered even when acting altruistically. Let's talk more about this thought-provoking psychological phenomenon, shall we?

We know the age-old human habit of showing off status. People usually do it by displaying ostentatious items that are prohibitively expensive for most. Yet, after a sufficient amount of wealth-bragging, they progress to the next upgraded level—altruistic and prosocial signaling. There can be an ulterior motive behind such actions, though. It endows them with so-called social benefits—the approval and the respect of others.

This social motive exercises its authority even as people consume things. For example, my acquaintance, an uptown man, loved to drive his fancy supercar. But he showed up to parent-teacher meetings in an electric vehicle to play the "responsible parent" card. Therefore, "consumption behaviors perceived by others" is a significant factor in consumer psychology today. Don't get me wrong, though. I don't intend to make a sweeping generalization. There undoubtedly exist individuals who remain indifferent to bragging about their status. Noble and admirable as they are few in number.

Today, many celebrities and social leaders express concerns about important social issues. They donate a lot, too. However, there might be an ulterior motive. If this holds true, is there any reason to admire their altruistic demeanors, even if they aren't pure or genuine? The answer is an unequivocal "yes."

First and foremost, choosing to sacrifice for a significant social cause is no walk in the park. Indeed, it's quite a challenging decision. For example, the environmental crisis and its dire consequences are literally around the corner. Jay Leno wittily said, "According to a new UN report, the global warming outlook is much worse than originally predicted. Which is pretty bad when they originally predicted it would destroy the planet." Nevertheless, for most, behavior patterns have not changed significantly. Amid this situation, it's good to have role models with noblesse-oblige. The world desperately needs eco-ambassadors with good exterior behaviors, so long as their interior motives are not harmful. We need more of this good-natured behavior sprinkled liberally across all other meaningful societal matters.

Secondly, even those ingenuine ulterior motives can be altered, and people can be converted from mere show-offs to bona fide altruists. In psychology, it's well-acknowledged that our external actions hold the power to change our internal attitudes and emotions.[5] This implies that the distinction between external behaviors and internal thinking isn't so crystal clear. In age-old Asian philosophies, antithetical concepts don't have a cut-and-dry boundary between them and inevitably influence each other—yin-yang, anode–cathode, negative–positive, centrifugal-centripetal, good-evil, reality-dream, and of course, interior-exterior. Behavioral psychology proposed a similar concept regarding the relationship between outer behaviors and inner attitudes.

Thus, when you come down to it, we'd better embrace and respect those prosocial ostentations because those behaviors can generate not only beneficial social results but also benevolent human minds eventually. After all, Nike hit the nail on the head when it proclaimed, "Just do it!" Actions do indeed pave the way for intentions, so quite often, the will follows the deed!

Owl of Minerva Behind the Scene

This chapter's central theme is "social signaling through conspicuous consumption," which means "consumption behaviors perceived by others." We will deal with two aspects of it—"status signaling" and "prosocial signaling." Owl of Minerva will also tell the psychological and visual stories behind them.

Whisperer Versus Shouter: Status Signaling

Let's start our exploration with *status signaling* and its psychological underpinnings.

People consume products with two distinctive motivations—"*utilitarian benefits*" like sturdy boots and "*hedonic benefits*" like glittering sandals. Utilitarian benefits mean you are "satisfied," whereas hedonic benefits mean you are "delighted."[6] To illustrate, let's take a stroll into high-end fashion outlets. If you are reluctant to buy their products, saying the item isn't positively necessary, the polished salesperson will reply, "We don't sell things that people need."[7] Here, need is an outlaw, and desire, the ruling authority. Clearly, "delight" wields a more persuasive charm than "satisfaction."

However, things are not that simple. There's a third player sneaking onto the stage, "anger." If hedonic sandals aren't comfy enough, their sparkle dims too. That is, without a certain level of utilitarian benefits fulfilled, hedonic benefits won't show off their talents because negative emotion caused by anger almost always overthrows any positive emotions. This psychological phenomenon can be related to *negativity*

[5] Bem (1972).

[6] Chitturi et al. (2008).

[7] On September 10, 2022, extracted from Reader's Digest Canada, https://www.readersdigest.ca/culture/70-funniest-jokes-readers-digest/ (Joe Caputo).

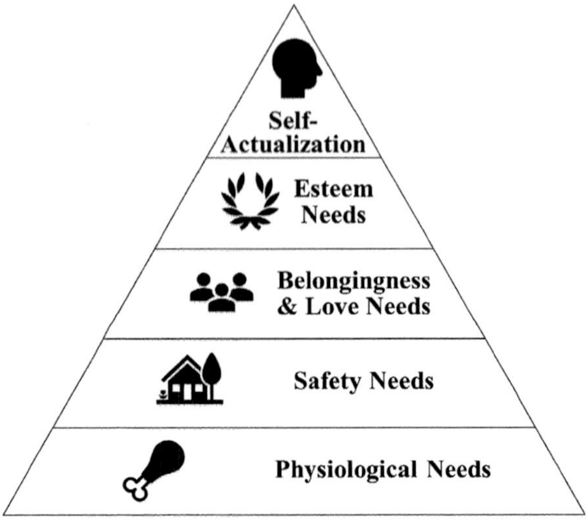

Fig. 4.1 Maslow's hierarchy of needs (created by Jeongmin Lee, 2023, Author's Collection)

bias[8] or *loss aversion*[9]: our brains are much more inclined to evade negative results than to acquire positive ones. It's in our genes. Why this obsession with negativity, you ask? Picture yourself living in the wild. Between looking for delicious fruits and steering clear of a looming predator, which would be more vital for your survival?

Maslow's hierarchy of needs makes it clear.[10] See Fig. 4.1. At its foundation lie the physiological needs and safety needs, the building blocks of human existence. Once those boxes are ticked, we begin to level up, moving through layers of friendships, affirming nods, and heartfelt moments (belongingness and love needs, esteem needs). The final destination? The penthouse suite of this tower culminates in self-actualization, realizing our true potential.

So, it emphasizes that only when the lower basic needs are satisfied, humans do pursue higher needs. That's why essential utilitarian benefits should be fulfilled first before the hedonic benefit flaunts its flair. However, it also hints at another aspect: once we're done with the basics, we'll surely hunt for upper desires. One of the ways that we pursue these upper delights, especially social needs, is through so-called *conspicuous consumption*—a fancy way of saying that our consumption behaviors are show-offish, carrying a whole lot of *signaling* power to others.

For conspicuous consumption, the crucial thing is "how others view it." The age-old human itch to "outdo the Joneses" drives the narrative here. Most humans have the desire to be better than others. Therefore, if a particular trait that someone possesses garners public desirability, rest assured that it will be put on a billboard. We've all chuckled at this joke before: "How do you know if someone is a vegan or

[8] Rozin and Royzman (2001).
[9] Kahneman and Tversky (1979).
[10] Mothersbaugh et al. (2020).

Fig. 4.2 Grill designs of BMW (photograph by Jeongmin Lee, 2023, Author's Collection)

has run a marathon?—They'll let you know!"[11] They want to quote-unquote "signal" it to others. And visual design, that is, *product visibility*, can be the secret weapon for turning up the volume of these broadcasts. Consumers who wish to stand out from their average peers will delve into products with high visibility pertinent to the quality to show off.

Hence, it's the designer's important mission to ensure that their design provides unfailing product visibility for status signaling. How can designers accomplish this mission? One of the popular strategies is creating the *family look*—a unique and well-known design trademark of the luxury brand. Take Ferrari, for instance, with its signature side door design. Regardless of the model, you can be sure it's a Ferrari. The svelte rear design of Jaguar or BMW's distinct grill (Fig. 4.2) is also impossible to miss. Similarly, the quilted leather design of the Chanel bag, the straps of Gucci bags with green and red stripes, and the Louis Vuitton monogram are also creating the family look of the brand. It allows customers to identify the high-end brand instantly.

Regarding this product visibility, especially the "salience of logos" in luxury brands, there is an intriguing research finding: the patricians' penchant differs from the parvenus'.[12] Patricians do not need to shout out their status from the rooftops. Everyone's already in the know. For example, if someone introduces herself as Ms. Vanderbilt, the aura of her name defies further descriptions. The product designs that these people prefer don't show off the logo clamorously (Fig. 4.3, left). Yet, they know the understated charm of each brand and savor these quiet signals of exclusivity. And honestly, they don't care whether those outside their circle recognize it or not.

This is not the case with the parvenus. They wish to flaunt their freshly minted wealth, so they are drawn to designs where the big, bold logos shout rather than whisper (Fig. 4.3, right). Namely, they prefer the transparent display that clearly shows their newfound status. For this reason, even if the target of luxury brands is the parvenus, the target for their ads had better encompass the middle class as well—the onlookers who appreciate the show. After all, it's a bit pointless to show off something to someone who doesn't know that something is expensive.

As we can see, once our basic needs are comfortably met, much like completing a basic level in a computer game (nobody stops there!), we humans usually level up to the high-stakes game of conspicuous consumption. Here, we find ourselves driven

---

[11] On April 10, 2023, extracted and revised from https://runningbrite.com/top-55-marathon-jokes/.

[12] Han et al. (2010).

Fig. 4.3 Gucci bags (Left: FashionStock.com/Shutterstock) (Right: Andersphoto/Shutterstock)

not just by what we need or even what we want, but by how we wish to be seen in the eyes of others. So, our consumption choices at this level are less about filling a void and more about painting a picture of who we are or who we aspire to be. It's about signaling status.

Altruistic Bragging: Prosocial Signaling

Next, let's talk about *prosocial signaling* through conspicuous consumption.

It was Aristotle who first said that humans are social animals. Since then, no one dared to gainsay this fact. After all, not only mentally but also physically, humans couldn't have lived through wildlife's ordeal without acceptance in a group. We're designed to be social.

In this social theater, the "give and take" rule governs." This rule permeates even the affairs of altruistic behaviors. The "give" side? Good deeds come with a cost, whether a pinch or a pound of sacrifice. The "take" side? They're a ticket to a higher social status, offering the perks that come with a high-status person.[13] The greater the sacrifice, the higher the social elevation. Consequently, people with this social desire yearn to brandish a vibrant neon symbol that broadcasts their prosocial conduct to the world around them.

As mentioned above, the "family look" strategy performs an excellent role in status signaling. Then, how about the trade dress for prosocial signaling in design? For example, the eco-chic crowd also wants to signal their concern for the environment, and having that green stamp on their possessions is very important for them.[14] Savvy businesses have taken note of this, launching products that are as much ego-enhancing as they are eco-friendly.

[13] Hardy and Van Vugt (2006).

[14] Lee et al. (2015).

Fig. 4.4 Freitag bag (photograph by Jeongmin Lee, 2022, Author's Collection)

Case in point? Freitag is the design inspiration for prosocial signaling, especially product visibility for *green cue prominence* (Fig. 4.4). Crafted from recycled truck tarps and seat belts, this upcycled chic screams to the world, "I'm an eco-warrior!" You might be thinking it should be cheap because it is made from recycled materials. Think again! It isn't cheap, and that's part of the charm. Remember the "give and take" rule? The higher the cost, the higher the bragging rights! Thus, unconsciously, the price is one of the traits that make Freitag owners proudly flaunt their bags while riding their bikes.

So, just as a Ferrari or a BMW can be spotted from a mile away for status signaling, eco-chic products like Freitag bags passionately broadcast their wearer's environmental consciousness. It's not just about being green; it's about being "seen" to be green. Therefore, let's not forget the important role of design in shaping customers' social scripts. It helps them perform well in the great play of prosocial signaling.

From Pretense to Genuine: How Actions Reshape Beliefs

Now, let me explain psychological theories about why we still look up to those who display altruistic prosocial behaviors even when we suspect their hidden motives. In the earlier episode, it was presented that, according to behavioral psychology, even those ingenuine ulterior motives can be altered, and people can be converted from mere show-offs to bona fide altruists.

The psychological theory that can resolve this paradox is the *cognitive dissonance theory* by Leon Festinger.[15] It's the mind games our brain plays behind the scenes—the subconscious rationalizing process. Festinger said, "Humans are not a rational animal, but a rationalizing one."

We customarily think that our internal thoughts and feelings are the puppet masters pulling the strings of external behaviors. No room for doubt? Well, to our surprise,

[15] Festinger (1957).

it works the other way around, too! Our outward actions are powerful enough to rearrange our inner attitudes and emotions, showing that sometimes the puppet can control the puppeteer. This is what cognitive dissonance theory says.

Among many factors that stir up cognitive dissonance, which is a kind of mental unrest, there is *attitude-discrepant behavior*. It is an outer behavior that doesn't exactly line up with an inner attitude. For example, if you happen to say that you're an environmentalist (outer behavior) when you actually are not (inner attitude), it is a situation of attitude-discrepant behavior. Of course, this mismatch causes cognitive inconsistency, hence psychological discomfort.

When our minds detect such inconsistency, the process of mental cleaning up is automatically launched. We, humans, are armed not only with a biological immune system but also with a mental immune system. Just like our biological immune system reflexively fights off physical invaders, our mental immune system also reflexively springs into action when mental chaos comes in. What's more, this happens while you're conveniently unaware.

Among several ways to restore mental peace (that is, cognitive consonance), an easy path is changing the inner attitude to match the outer behavior. Like a shot arrow and spilled water, it's difficult to undo our behavior, which is already done. Then, the only thing that we can still fiddle with is our inner attitude and thoughts. So subconsciously, we start to reshape them to match outer actions, all to restore that harmonious tune in our psyche.

An experiment by Leon Festinger in 1959 proved this effect.[16] He recruited college students and made them do an obviously boring and repetitive task. The plot thickens as the experimenter then asks these students to lie to the next unsuspecting student that this task was fun. In return for this lie, one group was paid $1 and the other $20 (quite a big buck then). Later, he asked the subjects what it was like to do the task. Surprisingly, the participants who were paid $1 reported more enjoyment than those who were paid $20. What made this difference? Unlike the $20 group who could easily justify their lie with a fat paycheck, the $1 group could neither claim the defense of a pretty penny nor say they were a born liar. So what did they do? They staged a subconscious rationalization, convincing themselves that they enjoyed the task. How quick-witted our minds are!

This study is often cited as a classic example in psychology to demonstrate how cognitive dissonance can lead to an inner attitude change. So, what's the moral of this theory, you ask? If we continuously engage in external prosocial behaviors, our subconscious mind starts to believe that we genuinely like those behaviors.

The *self-perception theory*, developed by Daryl Bem, also backs up the influence of external behaviors on inner attitudes and emotions.[17] We know we should often play detective with others' inner thinking, using their external behaviors as clues. For example, we often interpret others' smiles and frowns as clues to their thoughts. But here's the kicker. According to self-perception theory, we apply the same detective skills to ourselves! So, we often figure out our own feelings and attitudes by

---

[16] Festinger and Carlsmith (1959).

[17] Bem (1972).

watching what we do. This happens especially in situations where internal cues are weak, ambiguous, or uninterpretable. While the old-school views suggest that inner attitudes lead and actions follow, self-perception theory suggests it's a two-way street: our actions can also be the ones starting the conversation and shaping our attitudes.

In addition, there is the *IKEA effect*. The IKEA effect in consumer psychology, pertaining to its famous do-it-yourself (DIY) design strategy, can be simply translated as "the more sweat poured, the more value inflated, unconsciously." For example, when customers put a lot of effort into assembling DIY products, they endow these products with a more exaggerated value—a kind of love story between the customers and their self-assembled masterpieces. The same happens with all other things that customers pour their exertions into. It is natural that we support our painstaking endeavor with a more magnified worth.

Now, with these theories in our hands, let's get back to prosocial behaviors with suspicious ulterior motives. How can these people become bonafide altruists that we can truly respect? According to the above theories, their volition can be changed in line with their action. Thus, let's just do it! For example, even though you might chuckle at the irony when you find yourself in a small ATM room with its air conditioner humming 24/7 and a sign politely asking you to refrain from printing a receipt in the name of "going green,"[18] remember the mantra, "Just do it!" Those tiny altruistic actions, when accumulated, have the power to reshape your inner beliefs and eventually transform you into a genuine upholder for the environment.

Engagement Wins Hearts: User Participation

Let's turn our spotlight to see how this effect (external behavior reshaping inner belief) plays out in real-world design examples. Design methodologies such as *participatory design*, *customizing design*, and *user-led design*, which cleverly orchestrate user engagement behaviors, are under our spotlight. These strategies invite customers to invest their efforts into the design, allowing for the inner cultivation of preferences toward that design.

A participatory mural project is a good example (Fig. 4.5). Here, villagers are invited to dip their brushes and add their touch to create a better environment for their town. Not only does it turn them into beaming artists, but it also makes them happily roll up their sleeves to maintain their joint masterpiece, treating it with love and care.

Bruce Mau Design (BMD) proposed a user-involving logo design for OCAD University in Canada. Instead of going the old-school, top-down route, they chose a more "let's get everyone involved" method. First of all, BMD worked with the OCAD University community and had a series of workshops where students, faculty, staff, community members, and alumni were invited to share their stories, experiences,

[18] On September 10, 2022, extracted and revised from https://www.conserve-energy-future.com/best-environmental-jokes.php.

Fig. 4.5 Student art (mural) project, Subang Jaya, Malaysia, 2019 (Sweeann/Shutterstock)

and ideas. The end result? The final logo design projects a concept of ever-changing CI, a CI as a living organism rather than a static monument. It represents the image of a dynamic and multivalent future for the institution. Can you imagine the logo of a famous brand changing every year? Pretty wild idea, right? BMD ventured with this task by blending invariable components with a variable part.

The logo has a base of black and white pixel "windows" (three square frames of different sizes with the university's name in them). Two of these boxes remain steady as invariable elements. But the biggest box? It undergoes a yearly transformation. That is, every year, graduating student medal winners are invited to design an image, which can be included in this largest box, providing the university with a set of logos for that year and making sure the logo always has something fresh to show off. This whole thing represents OCAD's never-ending zest for innovation. Plus, as the logo is continuously updated in the future, the university will form a "Living Library of Identities," where each year's logo tells a bit of the story about the trends and ideas shaping our world over time. Kind of like a yearbook, but way cooler. Isn't that a delightful cherry on top?[19]

Next, let's take a look at customizing design. You can think of it as a fashion equivalent of a restaurant kitchen where the designer is the sous-chef, prepping all the necessary ingredients, and the customer is the head chef crafting the final dish. You can choose the design elements you like and make your own design. "Nike By You" (Fig. 4.6) is a good example. You get to pick everything—the colors and materials. The coolest part? You can even add your personal messages. This could be your name, your favorite number, or a special date. It's like signing your own masterpiece that you can wear and show off to the world. This creative participation process makes you like these personal shoes all the more.

The user involvement story doesn't stop there. It evolved further from humble self-assembly, via participatory or customizing design, all the way to the user-led process of designing brand-new products. Take "LEGO IDEAS," for instance. On its homepage, consumers can play the role they want—the creative designer or the

[19] OCAD University (2011).

Fig. 4.6 "Nike by you" inscription at Nike store, Jewel Changi Airport, Singapore (Sorbis/ Shutterstock)

discerning voter. If you submit a design and rack up over 10,000 votes, it can enter the expert review stage to be considered as an actual LEGO set. Make it through that stage, and voila! You become a LEGO Fan designer! You will have your name on it as a creator and earn a royalty for each set sold.

All these brand-related activities (external behaviors) foster a unique sense of ownership, pride, and, of course, preference in the participants (inner attitudes). Therefore, the magic of user participation in design is not just a buzzword; it can be a transformative experience. In addition, this isn't just about creating products; it's about crafting stories and experiences that resonate on a personal level. In this participatory age, everyone has a brush, and the canvas of design is vast and ever-evolving.

More Design Insights Added to the Scene

Lastly, shall we chat more about the *negativity bias* (a similar term in economics, *loss aversion*) mentioned earlier? Imagine your boss telling you that you are workshy when you are late to work, that you are anxious when you are early, and that you are obsessional when you are on time.[20] Baffled? Don't worry. It's not just a case of your boss waking up on the wrong side of the bed. It is a natural human inclination to look for negative information, the bitter over the sweet. While your boss might be a bit more grumpy than most, we all have this bias hidden away in the nooks and crannies of our minds.

[20] On September 10, 2022, extracted and revised from https://jurassic-lifetech.crocodile.dyndns.tv/us/blog/hide-and-seek/201303/top-10-psychology-jokes.

Shall we check whether we really do or not? Think about the movie intro image that presents the production company. Which company's intro pops into your head first? Isn't it the one with a roaring lion? That is MGM's. Despite 20th Century Fox, Columbia Pictures, Paramount Pictures, or Universal all having unique identifiers, don't they seem harder to recall than MGM's? It's because MGM's packs a punch with a predator, a hint of danger. That is, the negativity bias is the reason behind this fast recall. Negative experiences of the same amount as positive ones have a much greater impact on our minds and memory. Hence, the intro with a roaring lion remained stronger in your head and could be retrieved more easily, while other benign ones got the short end of the stick.

Albeit more subtly, IKEA uses the same psychological trick in their promotional designs. You might have seen their captions saying, "Because sometimes you forget things," "Because sometimes we're all fingers and thumbs," or "Because sometimes you change your mind." Due to accentuation on our shortcomings or mistakes, we cannot help eyeing them and their service information.

At last, we've finished our journey through the realms of conspicuous consumption, social signaling, and their psychological underpinnings. We've seen how our consumption behaviors are not just mere acts but powerful statements about who we are or who we aspire to be. Furthermore, just like the cognitive dissonance theory, self-perception theory, and IKEA effect suggest, our external actions can lead to genuine changes in our internal mindsets. So, if you find yourself making a choice that signals something to the world, remember it might just be the start of a real transformation within you. Isn't it wonderful that what starts as a superficial act can lead to meaningful growth?

References

Bem, D. J. (1972). Self-perception theory. In *Advances in experimental social psychology* (Vol. 6, pp. 1–62). Academic Press.

Chitturi, R., Raghunathan, R., & Mahajan, V. (2008). Delight by design: The role of hedonic versus utilitarian benefits. *Journal of Marketing, 72*(3), 48–63.

Festinger, L. (1957). *A theory of cognitive dissonance*. Stanford University Press.

Festinger, L., & Carlsmith, J. M. (1959). Cognitive consequences of forced compliance. *Journal of Abnormal and Social Psychology, 58*(2), 203.

Han, Y. J., Nunes, J. C., & Drèze, X. (2010). Signaling status with luxury goods: The role of brand prominence. *Journal of Marketing, 74*(4), 15–30.

Hardy, C. L., & Van Vugt, M. (2006). Nice guys finish first: The competitive altruism hypothesis. *Personality and Social Psychology, 32*(10), 1402–1413.

Kahneman, D., & Tversky, A. (1979). Prospect theory: An analysis of decision under risk. *Econometrica, 47*(4), 263–291.

Lee, J., Jung, B., & Chu, W. (2015). Signaling environmental altruism through design: The role of green cue prominence in hybrid cars. *International Journal of Design, 9*(2), 79–91.

Maynard, M. (2007, July 4). Say hybrid and most people will hear Prius. In *The New York Times*. Survey by CNW Marketing Research of Bandon. Accessed January 23, 2024. https://www.nytimes.com/2007/07/04/business/04hybrid.html

Mothersbaugh, D., Hawkins, D. I., & Kleiser, S. B. (2020). *Consumer behavior: Building marketing strategy* (14th ed., pp. 366–367). McGraw-Hill.

OCAD University. (2014, January). *OCAD University graphic standards guide*. Accessed June 15, 2024. https://www.ocadu.ca/sites/default/files/legacy_assets/documents/2011-ocadu-graphic-standards-guideline.pdf

Rozin, P., & Royzman, E. B. (2001). Negativity bias, negativity dominance, and contagion. *Personality and Social Psychology Review, 5*(4), 296–320.

Song, M., Chu, W., & Im, M. (2022). The effect of cultural and psychological characteristics on the purchase behavior and satisfaction of electric vehicles: A comparative study of US and China. *International Journal of Consumer Studies, 46*(1), 345–364.

Chapter 5
Eyes Wide Open: How Visuals Shape Minds

Do We Absolutely Need Art in Our Lives?

You may misconstrue me as a philistine for questioning such a matter of course. Do not jump the gun, though. The trick of this inquiry isn't the question as a whole. The little word "absolutely" is the mischief-maker here. No doubt, we all nod in agreement at the notion of art enriching our lives. But do we "absolutely" need it? If that's the case, do you have a compelling reasoning ready at hand?

"Hmm…."

I'm pretty sure many would share your hesitation.

Having said that, in fact, I'm firmly anchored in the camp claiming the absolute need for art. Art is not just nice but "absolutely" necessary in our lives. So, are you ready to lend an ear to this view, or at least, are you curious about what my grounds for the argument are? Let's not make pomp and ceremony around this nuanced and rather philosophical subject. Instead, allow me to lay out two simple footings supporting my stance.

The first footing stands on the "inborn" needs of human beings. If we can propose that art is the best vehicle for satisfying one of the innate human yearnings, then we could decree its incontrovertible necessity, couldn't we? By the word "art" here, I'm casting a net wide enough to snag not only polished works of professional artists but also the humble yet invaluable creative endeavors of everyday folks.

As mentioned in the previous chapter, Maslow organized human needs in a hierarchical pyramid, pronouncing that lower physical needs should be satisfied before we can pursue higher psychological needs. Be that as it may, he also asserted that these needs span both ends of the spectrum, inhabiting within our innate desires. The physiological drives for sleep, food, and sex are universally accepted as non-negotiable human needs that should be absolutely satisfied. Riding the same wave, our desire for self-expression, one of the mental needs, is another inborn urge. And we all know that art has been a powerful channel to satisfy this desire throughout human history, even though it's not the only channel.

© The Author(s), under exclusive license to Springer Nature Singapore Pte Ltd. 2024
J. Lee et al., *The Psychology Behind Design*,
https://doi.org/10.1007/978-981-97-3426-9_5

Nevertheless, some might argue that psychological needs are less vital for human survival and weaker than their physical counterparts, so they shouldn't be put on the pedestal of absolute necessity. However, if you take a closer look, you can observe that there's a pecking order even within physiological needs. Sleep sits on the throne, with hunger as its close courtier. Once the urgency of these needs is quelled, we then turn to pacify sexual urges. Despite its lower rank, nobody will dare to challenge the absolute necessity of sexual gratification in our lives. By sexual desires, I mean not only sex for the sake of continuing our species but also sex for sheer pleasure.

The same goes for psychological desires. Despite their delayed debut on the hierarchical stage, expressive cravings are still fundamentally innate desires of human beings. We can observe this fact in the artistic endeavors of toddlers. As soon as they get their chubby fingers around a crayon, they radiate joy as they surprise unsuspecting parents with unauthorized wallpaper murals. They've created something on their own, releasing their expressive energy, and their toothy grin says it all. It's the same satisfied smile that comes with a belly full of mother's milk.

The second footing for my argument opposes the conventional value judgment. The once prevalent belief had posited that the utilitarian and rational prowess outweighs the hedonic and emotional one for human survival. But what if emotion is a hidden kingmaker that helps rational thinking perform its best as a king of the survival island? This may not be as wild a conjecture as it appears since research has proven this. In an experiment where users were asked to evaluate the utilitarian functionality of the design, people perceived an aesthetically pleasing design as much easier to use.[1] That is, subjects' rational reactions to functionality are significantly steered by their emotional responses to aesthetics. The rational left brain and the emotional right brain aren't as independently minded as you might think. Indeed, these cerebral chums often whisper secrets to each other and plot strategies together, according to brain research.[2]

So, in a nutshell, hedonic pleasures grease the wheels of rational thinking, helping it solve utilitarian problems more efficiently.

Now, let's return to our original brain-teaser: "Do we absolutely need art in our lives?" I hope you and I are singing from the same hymn sheet now. We absolutely do because sooner or later, all innate human desires, expressive urges included, will inevitably orchestrate our behavior. Plus, let's not forget that the hedonic talent is as much a part of the rational staging. It's pulling strings backstage, after all.

Ending note: Kurt Vonnegut said, "*To practice any art, no matter how well or badly, is a way to make your soul grow. So do it.*" In the same vein, I dare to say that anyone can don the hat of an artist. Here is an amusing but unfailing tip to do art.[3]

---

[1] Kurosu and Kashimura (1995).

[2] Banich and Belger (1990).

[3] On September 19, 2022, extracted and revised from https://www.lcps.org/Page/227975 (Connie J. Sun, 2012).

Step 1: Call yourself an artist.
Step 2: Do art.
Step 3: Don't apologize!

Owl of Minerva Behind the Scene

Our scholarly friend, the owl, wants to tell us more about the psychology shrouded in the scene of art, aesthetics, visuals, and creativity in our lives. There's an array of art forms—visual arts, music, literature, dance, and so on. Yet here, we will fix our gaze on the visual aspects, given that the matter in hand for this book is consumer psychology and design. So, shall we begin with the superiority of visual perception?

Bossy Vision Is in the Driver's Seat: Visual Dominance

A picture is worth a thousand words.

Should I delve into a detailed lecture about this saying? Or… perhaps I can just show you a "picture" (Fig. 5.1).

About 70–90% of information transmitted to our brain is visual. Don't get me wrong, though. Each of the five senses undoubtedly plays a role critical for human life and survival. But in this sensory ensemble, it's the vision that has taken up the conductor's baton. This isn't just some hasty conjecture. Just take a peek at the number of sensory cells each sense brings to the table. Taste, not bad, sporting about ten thousand. Hearing, decent with about fifteen thousand. Smell, now that's impressive, about ten million. But vision? A whopping hundred million plus![4]

Fig. 5.1 A picture is worth a thousand words (created by DALL. E & Jeongmin Lee, 2023, Author's Collection)

[4] Goldstein (1996), Gleitman et al. (1995).

With this numerical imbalance, the result of their match is like being pre-chalked on the scoreboard. For instance, when we receive visual and auditory information simultaneously, visual information is perceived dominantly over auditory one. This is known as the *visual dominance effect*.[5] A commonplace experience? Ever been to a cinema with a surround sound system? Regardless of the strategic placement of speakers, you're pretty convinced the characters are lending their voices right from the big screen, where your eyes are riveted.

Visual dominance occurs in our memory, too. We recall the information with pictures far better and for longer than text-only information. This phenomenon is called the *picture superiority effect*. John Medina noted that when you just read words, you might remember only 10% of the information after three days. But if the words come with a related picture, you're more likely to remember 65% of the information after three days.[6] That's a 6.5 times better memory boost! It's no wonder the logo designs that readily spring to our minds are logos like Nike, Starbucks, or Apple. Text-only logos don't easily pop up unless they are repeatedly exposed to us every day. That is why this book also tries to include as many images as possible so that the impact of text information can be strengthened.

In addition, pictures make it easier to grab attention. Hence their prevalence in advertisements. However, it is also worth noting that "to go beyond is as wrong as to fall short." Images in ads, when overused, can hurt the recognition of the brand name and its selling point. Humans are mere mortals, not supercomputers, with limited cognitive bandwidth. It means dealing with the right amount of information is essential for our mental health.

You want a case in point? If your significant other ever pops the question, "How would you describe me?" you may reply, "ABCDEFGHIJK." However, please sweeten the moment with just the right amount of information—"Adorable, Beautiful, Cute, Delightful, Elegant, Fashionable, Gorgeous, Hot," leaving "IJK" as a mysterious charm. Trust me, no one wants to step on a landmine with an overloaded wit, "I'm Just Kidding."[7] So, in our cognitive system, it really holds true that "You may go farther and fare worse."

Likewise, in advertising design, if there is an overdose of a strong image, it risks overshadowing another element. This overshadowed underdog should never be the brand name or the sales pitch. Yet, the design world is fraught with such foot-in-mouth moments lacking finesse. Designers are well aware of this collateral damage, so they sometimes put the brand name or the advertising copy in a way that these key messages are impossible to overlook.

One of the design strategies for this purpose is applying the *law of good continuation*, one of the Gestalt principles.[8] Human visual perception favors stimuli arranged in a smooth, seamless contour over those with abrupt or jagged edges. For

[5] Sinnett et al. (2007).

[6] Medina (2008).

[7] On June 8, 2023, extracted and revised from https://upjoke.com/abcdefghijk-jokes.

[8] Chang et al. (2002).

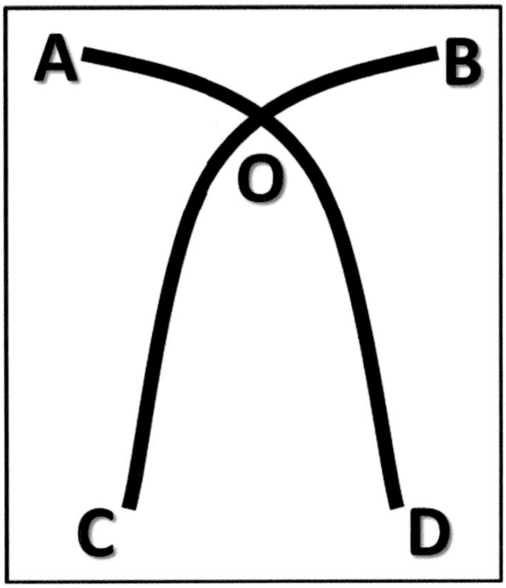

Fig. 5.2 Gestalt principle: Law of good continuation (created by Jeongmin Lee, 2023, Author's Collection)

example, in Fig. 5.2, if you are asked to discern two lines, I bet your eyes instantly connected lines AD and BC instead of taking a detour via AOB and COD, which are apparently another option.

This law of good continuation is one of the designers' favorite recipes, especially when it comes to guiding our attention to an essential element in ads. Have a gander at the ad design example in Fig. 5.3. Notice how the brand name is written in delicate print and subtly tucked away in the cozy corner of the scene. However, it still manages to attract our attention, thanks to the eye-catching images arranged in a smooth, continuous sequence. The brand name is located at the end of this arresting sequence.

Fig. 5.3 Law of good continuation: Ad design example (created by DALL. E, 2023, Author's Collection)

So, let's remember not only that a picture, indeed, speaks volumes, much more than a text can, but also that overloading an image can be as counterproductive as underutilizing it. In a nutshell, we should use visual power wisely, appreciating its strengths while being mindful of its potential to overshadow other information. After all, the world of design is not just about seeing but about seeing right.

Judging a Book by Its Cover: Aesthetic Bias

We've talked about the power of visual stimuli until now. This time, let's talk about the power of visual aesthetics in human minds. The wise saying of our forefathers solemnly teaches us, "Never judge a book by its cover." At the same time, they whisper in our ear, "What looks good tastes good." These are the paradoxes that fiddle with our perceptions of beauty.

Those adages are related to the psychological phenomenon called the *What-Is-Beautiful-Is-Good (WIBIG) effect*. We, humans, have a habit of linking physical attractiveness with positive inner qualities like intelligence, honesty, and good character. History may keep debunking this folly, but most people remain unswayed, ensnared by this visual dominance. Sadly enough, according to Daniel Hamermesh and Jeff Biddle, people with below-average looks earn 5–10% less than people with good looks.[9] No wonder "love at first sight" still happens even though it has been shown time and again that this can turn into a Halloween surprise. People assert, with conscious conviction, that beauty is only skin deep, while their subconscious minds whisper in an undertone that beauty penetrates deep. So, yes, beauty is indeed skin deep, but only when you look really, really hard. It also reminds us that we should be careful about the fact that this bias can have negative social implications, such as discrimination based on appearance.

This WIBIG effect doesn't stop at personal aesthetics but infiltrates the realm of design, too. That is, according to Donald Norman, people think that aesthetic things work better functionally as well.[10] He termed it the *attractive things work better effect*. It can also be called the *aesthetic-usability effect*.[11] This principle suggests that the aesthetics of design not only spark joy in the user but also quietly buff up the product's functionality. For instance, the nicely designed Starbucks stores, like the one in Fig. 5.4, not only help customers feel better but also make coffee taste better. As you can see, when this WIBIG effect is applied to designs, not humans, the side effects are not harmful but rather beneficial.

In an experiment proving this effect, subjects assessed the usability of ATM interface designs.[12] All interfaces were functionally identical but differed only aesthetically. The outcome? People thought that the aesthetically designed interface was

9 Hamermesh and Biddle (1993).

10 Norman (2002).

11 Lidwell et al. (2010).

12 Kurosu and Kashimura (1995).

Fig. 5.4 Starbucks Fukuoka Dazaifu, Kengo Kuma and Associates, 2011, Fukuoka, Japan (photograph by Jeongmin Lee, 2015, Author's Collection)

easier to use. That is, subjects were strongly affected by the aesthetics of the design even when they evaluated its functional aspects. Quite the optical illusion!

So yes, many indeed judge a book by its cover. Even so, it also makes a virtuous cycle: people can be prompted to a closer reading by its beautiful cover, thus facilitating a more accurate understanding. Expressly, "*What is beautiful is good and more accurately understood*."[13] The beautiful keep your eyes on the ball.

Therefore, we can safely say that emotional aesthetics do influence people's rational judgments. There is a covert affair between affective and cognitive systems. Sad when applied to humans, glad when applied to things. That's where designers come in.

Positive Affect Colors Our Creativity: Divergent Thinking

Then, why does this "attractive things work better" phenomenon take place? According to Donald Norman, feeling happy or positive makes people more lenient with minor difficulties and problems related to the things they interact with.[14] It also makes people think in more creative and flexible ways to find solutions to those problems. Let's look into these two aspects that lie behind the "attractive things work better" phenomenon.

Firstly, the positive affect incurred by an aesthetic design makes us overlook minor difficulties in using that design because feeling happy makes us generous and forgiving. That is, when users are in a good mood, they gladly and unconsciously make light of mild complications of the design so those are no longer problems in their minds. It's like when you pull a classic gag on your unsuspecting teacher. "Would you scold me for something I didn't do?" She'd probably reply, "No, of course not." Then, "I didn't do my homework." She may just laugh and let it go. Laughter, the best happiness booster!

---

[13] Lorenzo et al. (2010).

[14] Norman (2002).

Secondly, positive affect catalyzes what's known as *divergent thinking* in the brain, the cradle for creative sparkles.[15] It means that when users are in a good mood, their brains become more springy with various ideas, and this out-of-the-box prowess can help them find creative solutions to design problems more efficiently. Therefore, you'd better not be angry or depressed in your creative pursuits. That is misdirecting your brain power.[16]

With this, you may ask, "Then, what about those negative feelings we're all too familiar with?" If humans also possess them, those sour sips must have a purpose, too. A survival instinct, perhaps? Quite right you are! Negative affect fires up *convergent thinking*, which makes us zero in on the problem at hand. Namely, it fosters a laser-focus mode of the mind that helps us grapple with the imminent difficulties of life. It also drives us to carry out the given task and get the job done. Truly, all that comes from God comes in very handy.

Let's get back to the positive affect and talk about *Brainstorming* that relies on it. It's a group discussion technique intended literally to bring storms into members' brains, that is, "divergent thinking." There are four golden rules: "Focus on quantity," "Withhold criticism," "Welcome wild ideas," and "Combine ideas." Among these, take note of the second—"Withhold criticism." It protects members against the negative vibes—a bodyguard helping unleash the cheeky, spunky, and confident spirit within the group. It also helps members be more receptive to wild ideas. This is why an environment that tolerates occasional trips and falls matters much for fostering creativity. That is, not being afraid to fail is a crucial step for creativity.[17] So, pump up the happy, let people tumble, and then watch creativity abound. They will bring forth creative ideas you never thought of.

Let's have a little fun with examples. Imagine we are brainstorming, which allows any wild ideas, about survival strategies in the following situation.

"You're riding a horse. You're being chased by a lion, and there's a giraffe in the way in front of you."

What will be your suggestion for escaping this dangerous situation? The wildest idea I got was, "Get off the carousel."[18]

Let's ratchet up the tension for round two—the following dire situation.

"I've lost control. I don't see an end. There is no escape. I don't even have a home anymore."

What will be your solution? How about "Time for a new keyboard!".[19]

Design example? Google does provide the feel-happy stuff with its non-conventional office designs, conveying the impression of luxury resort hotels

---

[15] Campion and Levita (2014).

[16] Quote from Julia Margaret Cameron: "When we are angry or depressed in our creativity, we have misplaced our power." On September 19, 2022, extracted from https://jokes-and-riddles.com/quotes/creativity-quotes/.

[17] Chamorro-Premuzic and Reichenbacher (2008).

[18] On September 20, 2022, extracted from Reader's Digest Canada, https://www.readersdigest.ca/culture/70-funniest-jokes-readers-digest/.

[19] On June 8, 2023, extracted and revised from https://upjoke.com/control-jokes.

Fig. 5.5 Google Campus (Left: Ian Shipley ARC/Alamy Stock Photo) (Right: Christian Offenberg/Alamy Stock Photo)

(Fig. 5.5). They call their working place "Google Campus," where employees enjoy fascinating designs. Please don't be naive to think that Google's stunning campuses exist merely to keep their staff feeling pampered and special. Companies rarely pour money into a pit with no gold at the bottom. Google campuses are meticulously designed to steam up their members with creative power. It's a win–win strategy, anyway.

Therefore, we can say that an aesthetically pleasing design can transform user frustrations into forgiveness. Furthermore, the positive affect it causes also makes the creative juices in us flow more freely. Like Google Campuses that make its workers' creativity bloom, aesthetic spaces are creative catalysts, proving that a happy mind is a fertile ground for innovation. So, let's embrace the power of aesthetic vibes in design more enthusiastically.

However, it should also be noted that in design projects, being aesthetic is not always the "be-all and end-all." Sometimes, there is a profitableness of "non-aesthetic" design, too. Consider this situation that is different from Google's case: what if the company doesn't want to promote the freewheeling creativity of its workers, and what if wild ideas in the workplace can bring about disaster? Think about a nuclear power plant control room. Extreme focus and strict adherence to manuals are the orders of the day. To stimulate this kind of "convergent thinking," you'd need an ambiance that whispers "keep calm" rather than screaming "wild and free." The designs for such a place should not include elements that attract workers' attention too often, as seen in the quiet, neutral interior design of Fig. 5.6. This design says, "Nothing to see here, folks. Just carry on with the important stuff." And sometimes, that's just what the doctor ordered.

Fig. 5.6 Zwentendorf Nuclear Power Plant control room, Austria (Vadym Kulykov/Radiokafka/Shutterstock)

"Think Different" in Apple Stores: Ceiling Height and Priming

Now, besides design aesthetics, let's talk about another design element that can boost human creativity—the *ceiling height*. Quite unexpected, isn't it? Let me show you a familiar design example—the Apple store.

Like Google campuses, Apple stores are also architectural hymns to creativity, this time, of customers (Fig. 5.7). The high-profile features of these tech temples include a bodacious ceiling height, a roomy interior with no pillars, and a full-glass facade with a huge Apple logo. Collectively, these elements evoke the feeling of openness and free rein. So, the store design whispers in customers' ears—"Go wild. You're free here." These features have become the trademark of Apple Stores all over the world.

Especially, the loftiness of its ceiling is not mere visual indulgence. It employs a cognitive effect called the *cathedral effect*[20]: high ceilings stimulate our abstract and creative thinking, while their lower counterparts ground us in concrete, detail-oriented thoughts. In other words, the high ceiling of the Apple store makes our brains step in tune with the creative and unconstrained experience that we are going to have there. Therefore, the next time you wander into an Apple Store, remember to think big and let the sky-high ceiling do the rest.

An experiment gives credence to this effect.[21] When subjects were placed in rooms with high or low ceilings and asked to solve anagrams, a fascinating pattern emerged. The "high-ceiling" group deciphered the anagrams about "freedom" faster than the

[20] Lidwell et al. (2010).

[21] Meyers-Levy and Zhu (2007).

Fig. 5.7 Apple store, Santa Monica, USA (Mirko Vitali/View Apart/Shutterstock)

"low-ceiling" group, while the opposite happened with the anagram regarding "confinement." Furthermore, in high-ceiling rooms, subjects tended to focus on commonalities among product features, whereas in low-ceiling rooms, they emphasized specific, distinct features. It suggests that people in high-ceiling rooms might use more abstract, creative approaches to problem-solving, while those in low-ceiling rooms might focus on details.

This result puts a bug in your ear. If you are aiming to pull some dazzling insights for your new proposal, work in a spacious, high-ceilinged room. Prepping for an exam thick with devilish details? Best find yourself a cozy, low-ceilinged cubbyhole. Along the same line, places that should serve as cradles of innovation and creativity, such as R&D centers, need to bask under high ceilings. In contrast, meticulous task-oriented spaces, like security offices, need solace under the lower ceilings. Flagship stores, which want customers to linger and experience the store at their pleasure, had better luxuriate in elevated ceilings. Meanwhile, convenience stores, whose primary doctrine is the no-fuss, rapid shop-n-go, had better have low ceilings.

IKEA, with its Swedish knack for design, employs this ceiling-height trick in its store design. Shopping areas are designed with an open ceiling to add additional height to the space, fueling customers' creative visions for their homes (Fig. 5.8, left). Interestingly, there is one little nook in its expansive store that clings to the charm of a lower ceiling—the checkout area (Fig. 5.8, right). It's a cozy little box stimulating the accuracy of tallying up.

In its store design, Apple waves another magic wand—the *priming effect*. It says that exposure to one stimulus influences the response to a subsequent stimulus. In the case of the Apple store, the priming stimulus is the huge logo emblazoned on the full-glass facade (see Fig. 5.7), and it stimulates customers' creative mode of mind. The magic potion? Their long-championed mantra, "Think Different." This ad slogan has been linking Apple with a certain avant-garde ethos. Thus, the sight of

Fig. 5.8 Left—IKEA store, Goyang, South Korea/Right—IKEA store, Giheung, South Korea (photograph by Jeongmin Lee, 2019 (Left) and 2020 (Right), Author's Collection)

that bitten apple logo became to flip a switch in customers' brains, priming an out-of-box mindset. As it turns out, this isn't just Apple's wishful thinking. Research backs it up, too: using the Apple logo as a priming stimulus boosted people's creativity for real.[22] The group shown the Apple logo had a higher creativity test score than the group shown the IBM logo. Well done, Apple, in many ways indeed!

So, we can say that the Apple store is a masterclass in design psychology. From the lofty ceilings echoing the cathedral effect to the iconic logo serving as a creative trigger, every element is a nudge toward thinking bigger and bolder. It's a strong reminder that our surroundings influence our thoughts more than we realize.

Function First, Glamor Later: The Product Lifecycle

Lastly, let me explain the "product life cycle" in relation to "Maslow's hierarchy of needs." We discussed this need hierarchy in the previous chapter (see Fig. 4.1) with regard to social signaling, but here, we will review it with respect to the design's developmental cycle and its relationship with design aesthetics.

Maslow said that human needs form a hierarchical order, and one must check off the boxes of physiological and safety requirements before seeking social or self-related aspirations. Then, you may be scratching your head, wondering, "How does this relate to design?" To get that, let's look into the *product life cycle*.

[22] Fitzsimons et al. (2008).

As in human mortal life, products, too, go through a life cycle. It is born into the world as a trailblazing newcomer. It then rides the wave of growth, where sales spike like a teenager's growth spurt. The mature stage follows, a time when it basks in its heyday glory. But all good things must come to an end, and so it does in the twilight years of decline, passing on the scepter to the next generation of sprightly new products.

Look no further than the rise and fall of the cell phone for a textbook example. From its birth, triggering a mobile revolution, its growth spurt marked by nifty tech advancements and a shrinking size, to its prime awash with a myriad of attractive designs, and finally, its decline nudged by the advent of the flashy smartphone.

We, consumers, play different roles at each stage of this product life cycle. Initially, we are a pragmatic bunch. A product that works well is all we care about. So, businesses wisely put their money on cutting-edge tech, not on an aesthetic design that also cries for money. Therefore, at early stages, designers also sweat over supporting functions. Aesthetics? It's a luxury customers can ill-afford yet. However, as the product strides into its mature stage, technology loses its comparative edge—no more dazzling eye-opener. That's when we, consumers, swap our practical hats for fancier ones. Now is the designers' turn to take center stage and let their creative flag fly high.

These shifts in the design's role during the product life cycle all hark back to Maslow's hierarchy of needs. Just as humans first address basic needs before reaching for higher needs, products also need to tick off the functional boxes before they can strut their aesthetic stuff. However, the time will surely come when customers want to gratify their social or self-actualization needs in their consumption. Only then are people willing to pay extra for aesthetic designs. So, if you find yourself sighing over the dull design of an early stage product, just remember that you are not quite ready to pick up the expensive tab for the designer dazzle yet.

Now, let's wrap up our journey through the influences of visual elements on human psychology. We have delved into how visual stimuli command our attention, shape our perceptions, and impact our decision-making processes. The dominance of visual information was emphasized, and how visually appealing designs can enhance usability, satisfaction, and creativity was also examined. Therefore, let's advocate for a thoughtful and balanced approach to leveraging its potential in design, marketing, and communication.

References

Banich, M. T., & Belger, A. (1990). Interhemispheric interaction: How do the hemispheres divide and conquer a task? *Cortex, 26*(1), 77–94.

Campion, M., & Levita, L. (2014). Enhancing positive affect and divergent thinking abilities: Play some music and dance. *The Journal of Positive Psychology, 9*(2), 137–145.

Chamorro-Premuzic, T., & Reichenbacher, L. (2008). Effects of personality and threat of evaluation on divergent and convergent thinking. *Journal of Research in Personality, 42*(4), 1095–1101.

Chang, D., Dooley, L., & Tuovinen, J. E. (2002). Gestalt theory in visual screen design—A new look at an old subject. In Selected papers from the 7th World Conference on Computers in Education (WCCE'01), Copenhagen, Computers in Education 2001: Australian Topics. Australian Computer Society (Vol. 8, pp. 5–12).

Fitzsimons, G. M., Chartrand, T. L., & Fitzsimons, G. J. (2008). Automatic effects of brand exposure on motivated behavior: How Apple makes you "think different." *Journal of Consumer Research, 35*(1), 21–35.

Gleitman, H., Fridlund, A., & Reisberg, A. (1995). *Basic psychology* (4th ed.). W. W. Norton & Co.

Goldstein, E. B. (1996). *Sensation & perception* (4th ed.). Brooks/Cole Publishing Company.

Hamermesh, D. S., & Biddle, J. (1993). Beauty and the labor market. Accessed January 10, 2023. https://www.nber.org/papers/w4518. https://doi.org/10.3386/w4518

Kurosu, M., & Kashimura, K. (1995). Apparent usability vs. inherent usability: Experimental analysis on the determinants of the apparent usability. In Conference Companion on Human Factors in Computing Systems (pp. 292–293).

Lidwell, W., Holden, K., & Butler, J. (2010). *Universal principles of design: 125 ways to enhance usability, influence perception, increase appeal, make better design decisions, and teach through design.* Rockport Publishers.

Lorenzo, G. L., Biesanz, J. C., & Human, L. J. (2010). What is beautiful is good and more accurately understood: Physical attractiveness and accuracy in first impressions of personality. *Psychological Science, 21*(12), 1777–1782.

Medina, J. (2008). *Brain rules: 12 principles for surviving and thriving at work, home, and school.* Pear Press.

Meyers-Levy, J., & Zhu, R. (2007). The influence of ceiling height: The effect of priming on the type of processing that people use. *Journal of Consumer Research, 34*(2), 174–186.

Norman, D. (2002). Emotion & design: Attractive things work better. *Interactions, 9*(4), 36–42.

Sinnett, S., Spence, C., & Soto-Faraco, S. (2007). Visual dominance and attention: The Colavita effect revisited. *Perception & Psychophysics, 69*(5), 673–686.

Chapter 6
The Self-centric Universe: It's All about "Me"

"The universe doesn't revolve around you!".

Sounds familiar? Galileo Galilei, who supported the heliocentric model against the geocentric view of the time, vainly tried to say this to the people who decided not to listen to him. Do you know what Galileo and today's parents have in common? Just as Galileo struggled to convince a disbelieving public, modern parents often face their own uphill battle in persuading their teens with the similar parenting anthem—"The world doesn't revolve around you!" In Galileo's case, he was the one brandishing the scientific fact, not the other party. However, when our adolescents brazenly declare, "You're just as self-centered as I am!" ironically, they might unknowingly echo the findings of scientific studies.

Let me elaborate. The study titled "When Change in the Self Is Mistaken for Change in the World" examined the concept of how personal changes can lead to a mistaken belief that the world around us has changed.[1] That is, when individuals meet with changes themselves, such as becoming parents or undergoing financial changes, they often misattribute these changes to the external world and perceive the world differently. For instance, new parents might perceive the world as more dangerous, or individuals with financial changes might see society as having altered freedom levels. Why did they feel this way when the reality wasn't? It's because their situation made them extra sensitive to the related societal conditions, turning them into walking, talking radars for that matter. In their view, it's the world, not them, that underwent a makeover.

Now, hold your judgment on these sensitive folks, for so many people commonly experience something known as "perceptual vigilance": we pay attention to what's highly relevant to us and ignore the rest. Ever heard, "Hear what you want to hear,

---

[1] Eibach et al. (2003).

© The Author(s), under exclusive license to Springer Nature Singapore Pte Ltd. 2024

J. Lee et al., *The Psychology Behind Design*,
https://doi.org/10.1007/978-981-97-3426-9_6

see what you want to see?"[2] We often do that. Therefore, we easily find ourselves in a memory mismatch where our recollection of an event and someone else's seem to be reading from different scripts. Somebody will even read "Fine for littering" as "really fine for littering" if one holds trash in one's hands.[3]

Before you ask why we are such self-absorbed creatures, let us remember that humans are not all-powerful entities with infinite intellect. We must prioritize our attention since our modest cognitive prowess simply won't allow us to be Mr. and Ms. Know-it-alls. So, cheers to our selectively attentive minds for keeping us alive and well!

It means we are naturally inclined to think, "The world does and should revolve around me," despite reality's protests. No need to blush! You're in excellent company within this self-centered society of mere mortals. After all, the most worthy and meaningful being to me is "me."

Since "self" holds such a crucial spot in our lives, we possess a subconscious yearning to uphold a healthy level of self-esteem. When we're incessantly in situations that drain this vital reservoir, and when it starts dipping too low, the warning signal blares, and our subconscious summons the ego-defense team—self-rationalization and self-elevation.

Humans are true masters of rationalization, especially when it comes to shielding their self-esteem. It's understandable and, from time to time, unavoidable. Occasionally, well-made ones are pretty ahead of the game so that even we can be persuaded by what we made up. It's a so-called D.E.N.I.A.L. stage, that is, "**D**on't **E**ven **N**otice **I** **A**m **L**ying."[4]

One study showed a surprising result—the rationalizing power of physical cleansing.[5] Believe it or not, physical cleansing could help us wash away our guilt. In this study, participants were asked to recall an immoral behavior from their own past. Following this, some participants were given an antiseptic wipe to use, while others were not. The study then measured the participants' feelings of guilt and their willingness to volunteer for another project, a prosocial behavior often motivated by guilt. The result? Participants who didn't wipe their hands felt guilty about their past actions and were more likely to volunteer for another project. In contrast, those who used the antiseptic wipe felt less guilty and were less inclined to volunteer, suggesting that the act of physical cleansing reduced their feelings of guilt.

Doesn't this sound familiar? In the Bible and in many other literature like Macbeth, there are scenes of washing hands to wipe out the guilt or to declare one's innocence toward some bad conspiracy. But does it literally ease our guilt? Well, color me surprised! The astonishing resourcefulness of the human mind in cooking up justifications never ceases to amaze us.

---

[2] Williams et al. (2016).

[3] On May 8, 2023, extracted and revised from https://punstoppable.com/trash-can-puns.

[4] On May 8, 2023, extracted and revised from http://www.jokes4us.com/peoplejokes/funnyacronyms.html.

[5] Lee and Schwarz (2011).

We also have the "I deserve to be bad" justification. Remember James Bond's "License to Kill"? Much like a secret agent with a special permit, our subconscious sometimes grants us a "License to Deviate" from our usual standards under special circumstances. That is, if we perform a virtuous act, we are more prone to follow it up with a naughty action. It happens because doing good deeds has filled our self-esteem reservoir, and subconsciously, it's okay to let it fall a little. Not surprisingly, it is called the "licensing effect."[6]

Let's take a peek at our everyday life showcasing this phenomenon, shall we? When you've filled your cart with organic goodies, it's easy to convince yourself that a pinch of junk food is simply the cherry on top. Ever felt like you deserved a sizzling T-bone steak and an ice-cold beer after a strenuous workout? And let's not forget the eco-warrior who occasionally opts for the convenience of disposable items. The list can go on. They might believe their good efforts earn them a "get-out-of-jail-free" card for the off-and-on slips. We, humans, seem like a delightful cocktail made of the angel and the devil—shaken, not stirred!

To defend self-esteem, humans mobilize not only self-rationalization but also self-elevation. Example? Have you ever scratched your head, wondering why reality TV shows are all the rage? Sure, it's really fun to peek into someone else's private affairs, but oddly enough, "me" meddles here again. As we immerse ourselves in these on-screen reality scenarios, we can't help but think, "If that were me, I'd have done this or that and emerged victorious!" This make-believe self-satisfaction gives our self-esteem a nice little lift.[7] Intriguing, isn't it? A peculiar, vicarious, yet oh-so-convenient and user-friendly channel to recharge our self-worth batteries!

See? It's all about "Me," I tell you! In some sense, we are all narcissists holding the lightbulb in place while waiting for the world to revolve around us and change the bulb.[8]

Owl of Minerva Behind the Scene

If we were to pinpoint a buzzword that truly captures the very soul of today's consumer culture, I'd bet my bottom dollar on "Me" (the "Self"). We, the folks of the twenty-first century, are so absorbed in ourselves that we don't even notice the irony and hypocrisy of our go-to gripe—"I am not telling you what to do, so do not tell me what to do."[9] Why is this hypocritical? See? You don't notice!

So, welcome to the age of "me, myself, and I," where retail therapy is all about pampering numero uno! We are smack dab in the middle of an era where "What's the deal for me?" is the paramount query on shoppers' minds while swiping their cards. Let's take a closer look into this self-focused human proclivity. Here, our wise owl won't be an ethics teacher, though, telling it just the way it is.

---

[6] Khan and Dhar (2006).

[7] Kardes et al. (2014).

[8] On May 8, 2023, extracted and revised from https://www.psychologytoday.com/intl/blog/hide-and-seek/201303/top-10-psychology-jokes.

[9] On May 10, 2023, extracted and revised from https://www.boredpanda.com/ironic-jokes/?utm_source=google&utm_medium=organic&utm_campaign=organic.

Design's Journey from Mass to Me: A Brief History

In this era of "self-discovery," a whole lot of self-talk is going on. Remember the "Share a Coke" campaign? It was a smashing hit, and the key ingredient was simply common names put on Coke bottles, providing the sheer delight of spotting one's own name amidst an ocean of beverages (Fig. 6.1). It was more than enough to make anyone feel like a child in a confectionery wonderland. This astute marketing project unveiled a simple reality: when it comes to forging bonds with consumers, making it personal is the spellbinding solution.

Let's look into the brief history of this phenomenon in design. Remember Maslow's hierarchy of human needs? The basic needs are at the bottom, then climbing up to self-actualization. The *history of design* shares a similar progress. During the Industrial Revolution and the Industrial Era in the twentieth century, design was all about getting essential things done—helping material production solve physiological and safety needs, which had not been sufficiently addressed in human history. And with mass production as the name of the game, there wasn't much room for diversity or individuality. Then, times shifted, and we stepped into the post-industrial era, a period of more diversity and smaller-scale production to suit consumers' more refined appetites. Today, even one production tailored to the taste of an individual consumer is being realized, helping everyone express themselves through their purchases. In short, self-actualization, the highest desire in the need hierarchy, is in full swing in design today.

Fig. 6.1 Share a Coke Campaign, 2010s (Chayut Orapinpatipat/Shutterstock)

Fig. 6.2 Custom Converse (Michael Doolittle/Alamy Stock Photo)

In this era of the self, companies are striving to cater to individual preferences. That is, we entered the realm of *one-on-one marketing*, where customers are lavished with tailor-made treats that make them feel like royalty. We dealt with the customizing design in Chap. 4 with regard to cultivating preferences through "user participation." Here, let's talk about it in relation to fulfilling "self-actualization."

Custom Converse is a good example (Fig. 6.2). On their homepage, customers can engage in a creative process where they customize their own shoes. These sneakers are ready to morph into whatever your heart desires. Colors, logos, text, materials—you name it, they've got it. Whether you're stitching in a date to commemorate a special event or just screaming your eccentricities through shoelaces, every element is a verse in your own poetry. Moreover, it's not merely a shoe anymore. It's a megaphone for your soul—a form of self-expression that communicates one's personality, values, and aesthetics to the outside world.

The customization craze is now reaching new heights, diving into realms previously thought impossible to customize. Home appliances, electronics, and even automobiles are joining the party. Take Samsung Bespoke (home appliance brand), for instance. It opens a door for a more personalized touch to your living spaces (Fig. 6.3). Bespoke is your palette, and your home is the canvas. Imagine a kitchen where your refrigerator isn't just a chilly box but a statement piece, reflecting your favorite shade of cerulean or that sleek city loft vibe you adore. In essence, Samsung Bespoke brings a pinch of soul to the stainless steel heart of home appliances, making them less of a household necessity and more of a personal choice. It is truly an era of consumption "for me" and "by me."

In this brief history of design's evolution, it's clear that we've journeyed from the simple assembly lines of the industrial era to a world where our morning coffee cup can bear our name. That is, we are living in an era with a vibrant tapestry of personalized experiences, where design is performing a powerful medium for self-expression.

Fig. 6.3 Samsung Bespoke (photograph by Jeongmin Lee, 2023, Author's Collection)

Actual Myself and Other Myselves: The Four-faced Self

Before we delve into the psychological theories underpinning this selfhood phenomenon, grasping a few essential terms regarding the "self" is key to getting the hang of the story.

Let's start with *self-concept*, or, as it's more casually known, *self-image*. This is our mental scrapbook, filled with snapshots of who we think we are—our values, looks, quirks, talents, likes, etc. It's our collage of self-awareness.[10]

Now, this self-concept can be broken down into four categories. First, there is the *actual self-concept*—how I see myself, warts and all. Second, we have the *ideal self-concept*—how I think I am ideally to be, the superhero version of myself. Third, there is the *social self-concept*—how I think others perceive me (sometimes it's spot-on, sometimes not so much). And finally, we have the *ideal social self-concept*—the dazzling persona I hope others see when they lay their eyes on me.

Another vital terminology related to self is *self-esteem*[11]—the degree to which I think positively about myself. It is an inner cheerleader giving me a pep talk about how awesome I am. But beware, this cheerleader is run by an esteem-battery, and this battery can run low. Therefore, it needs regular recharging to keep us in the groove. Do you know what the scariest Halloween outfit is? A smartphone-shaped costume with a 1% battery warning.[12] How much more scary is a barely charged esteem-battery!

---

[10] Sirgy (1982).

[11] Orth and Robins (2014).

[12] On May 10, 2023, extracted and revised from https://punsandoneliners.com/randomness/charge-jokes/.

Self-concept and self-esteem are crucial factors in human life. They're the puppet masters, pulling the strings on a whole bunch of human behaviors. That is, many human behaviors are carried out to protect or enhance them. Moreover, they are also the invisible hand behind our spending sprees. For example, when life hands us lemons, we try to relieve stress by chatting, binging, sleeping, exercising, etc., or many times, finding solace in the aisles of retail indulgence. The products we buy can give our self-image and self-esteem a snazzy makeover. So, we might unconsciously try to boost our inner cheerleaders as we swipe our credit cards.

Art of Dodging Guilt: Rationalization

Now, let's probe into psychological theories underpinning our self-related behaviors.

Edward Tory Higgins proposed the *regulatory focus theory*.[13] It is about two goals that regulate human behaviors—*promotion* and *prevention*. The "promotion" goal aims to obtain positive outcomes, while the "prevention" goal strives to avoid negative outcomes. This promotion-prevention paradigm can also be applied to human behaviors related to the self. We call upon this tag team when we need to do something for the self.

First, let's look at human behaviors with a "prevention" focus aimed at shielding the self from further bruising. The most popular playbook humans use for this purpose is *rationalization*. Hold on to your hats because we're all guilty of these shenanigans. As mentioned in the episode section, humans are the true mavens of self-justification, and we're not afraid to use it.

One of the psychological phenomena related to rationalization is the *self-serving bias*.[14] It's our crafty habit of giving ourselves a hearty pat on the back when things go right but pointing fingers when things go wrong. We love taking credit for our successes, chalking them up to our skills or abilities. Even the saying goes, "Every man is the hero of his own story." So, one might even describe himself as "I'm great at multitasking. I can waste time, be unproductive, and procrastinate all at once."[15] Very creative! On the other hand, when we fail, it must be due to luck, circumstances, or that guy over there. Did you notice that luck plays a vital role in success, only according to those who have failed?[16]

It is a familiar everyday experience cause we've all done it, from the highest boss to little you and me. We are lucky if we are not to become scapegoats cause we know "To err is human, to blame it on someone else shows management potential."

---

[13] Brockner and Higgins (2001).

[14] Miller and Ross (1975).

[15] On May 11, 2023, extracted and revised from https://onelinefun.com/life/.

[16] On May 11, 2023, extracted and revised from https://fitcaptions.com/good-luck-puns/.

Let's peek at some mundane examples. Remember being a student? High grades were all due to our sheer brilliance and studious ways. Low grades? It must be those cruel exams or clueless teachers. Now, let's hit the road. We dodge an accident and feel like driving maestros, but when we crash, it's suddenly the road's fault or that other lousy driver. In the workplace, we revel in the glory of a successful project, but when it goes downhill, we blame a lack of resources or those unhelpful teammates. Need more examples? Trust me. The list is virtually endless!

People employ these self-protective behaviors to keep pesky emotions like guilt and remorse at bay, all in the name of keeping our self-esteem shiny and bright. However, in terms of interpersonal consequences, this little habit may result in conflicts and strained relationships. We know it's not the best, yet we'll likely hit the replay button again tomorrow. Why? Think about the battle—protecting my self-esteem versus other people's feelings. Which contender would you bet on? Some are heavyweights in this arena, while others are lightweights. Nonetheless, we are all in this wild rationalization rodeo together.

Let's move into another mind-bending phenomenon related to rationalization—the *licensing effect*. Remember we talked about the "I deserve to be bad" feeling? That little "get-out-of-jail-free" card we earn by previous virtuous deeds? In the fascinating research of Uzma Khan and Ravi Dhar, subjects were divided into two groups, and only one group engaged in activities like volunteering or imagining donating to charity. These activities were intended to boost their self-esteem. The result showed that after such activities, participants were more likely to make choices that were self-indulgent, like choosing luxury items over necessities.[17] Performing good deeds makes people feel moral superiority, and they seem less guilty about spending on luxury items, as they have already proven their altruism.

So, our self-esteem batteries get recharged when we do nice things, and then we subconsciously believe we've earned a "license to go astray," a guilt-evading pass to dabble in some mischief. Namely, people use their past ethical behaviors as a means to "justify" some not-so-angelic endeavors in the future.

As you can see, the licensing effect makes us act inconsistently with our overall moral principles. It lurks around every corner. Here are some everyday experiences. Healthy eating: people following a strict diet may allow themselves a "cheat day" and indulge in unhealthy foods.[18] Good work performance: employees working hard and receiving positive feedback might feel entitled to slack off on the next task. Volunteering: after volunteering their time to help others, people may feel entitled to prioritize their own needs over others, even when it might not be fair or considerate. And, in the earlier episode, I already mentioned "junk food consumption accompanied by organic food purchases," "indulgence after strenuous exercise," and "petty eco slips back of strong environmentalism." See? It's everywhere! There is even a famous "American Weight Loss Plan": order a Big Mac with "Diet" Coke.[19]

[17] Khan and Dhar (2006).

[18] Prinsen et al. (2019).

[19] On May 11, 2023, extracted and revised from https://upjoke.com/coke-jokes.

Fig. 6.4 Toms store, Kuala Lumpur, Malaysia (Air Elegant/Shutterstock)

Now, savvy marketers have caught on to this, too. They use the licensing effect in *cause-related marketing*. You've seen those ad designs that tug at your heartstrings, encouraging you to donate to a good cause by purchasing their products. (PRODUCT)RED, a licensed brand that helps fight HIV/AIDS in African countries, partners with companies like Apple, Starbucks, and Nike. A portion of the profits from (PRODUCT)RED-branded items goes to The Global Fund to fight AIDS, Tuberculosis, and Malaria. This initiative allows consumers to support the cause through their purchases. The shoe company TOMS was also known for its "One For One" campaign (2006–2019) (Fig. 6.4), where the company had promised that for every pair of shoes sold, another pair would be donated to a child in need. This initiative, launched in 2006, quickly gained widespread attention and praise for its socially responsible approach. It not only addressed a social issue but also allowed consumers to be a part of the solution simply by purchasing a product they needed.

Wait! Don't confuse cause-related marketing with social marketing. *Social marketing* is about promoting the welfare of people or society without any direct benefits for a company. On the other hand, cause-related marketing ties a company and its products to a worthy cause to boost sales or polish its image, all while supporting that cause. It's a win–win-win situation anyway: the company gets a sales boost, the organization a donation boost, and the consumer a self-boost!

We've seen the artful alleys of rationalization for protecting our self-esteem. Besides these, in the episode section, I already talked about the *rationalizing power of physical cleansing* and the experiment proving this effect. In the same study, there is another fascinating experiment.[20] It involved participants performing a role-playing task where they conveyed a malevolent lie either by voicemail (using their mouth) or by email (using their hands). After this, the participants were asked to evaluate several consumer products, including mouthwash and hand sanitizer. The

[20] Lee and Schwarz (2011).

results showed that participants who lied using their mouths exhibited a preference for mouthwash over hand sanitizer. Conversely, those who typed the lie with their hands preferred the hand sanitizer. Additionally, participants were more inclined to pay a higher price for the product that cleansed the body part they used to commit the lie. These results indicate a psychological connection between the mode of lying and the subsequent preference for cleansing products.

As you can see, we're all masterful artists at dodging guilt and dressing up our actions in the best possible light. So, what's the take-home message? Perhaps it's that while we're all champions at self-preservation, a dash of self-awareness might not hurt. Knowing our tendency to rationalize and self-justify, we might just catch ourselves in the act and perhaps chuckle at our all-too-human antics.

Art of Elevating the Self I: Self-expression

Next, let's look into the world of "promotion-focused" behaviors in regulatory focus theory, which we take to produce positive outcomes in elevating the self.

The top formula is *self-expression*. Today's consumers opt for products reflecting their self-portraits—items that cheer who they are. Take Chanel No. 5, for instance. It's not just the bewitching scent that reels customers in but also the little self-image boosts it delivers on the side. What they are really purchasing is a slice of symbolism (Fig. 6.5).

This boils down to a simple truth: we don't just shop for stuff because it's practical or useful but buy goods for hedonic purposes as well. Sometimes, these pleasure-seeking feelings overpower utilitarian considerations and become the reason to choose or not to choose some products. For example, many people choose a simple, no-frills bathroom scale over the high-tech model that measures not just their weight but also body fat, bone mass, and water percentage. They might subconsciously think, "I don't need to be depressed every day in four ways. Thanks, but no thanks. I'll stick to my single scoop of reality."[21]

Self-expression in consumerism is a bit like a mirror game where *self-image congruency theory* comes into play. Consumers compare their self-image with the image of the brand.[22] When the reflections match, they're swept off their feet, and satisfaction, purchase/repurchase intention, positive word-of-mouth, and brand loyalty increase. To get it more easily, let's take the classic Armani-Versace comparison.

The magic of Armani's wardrobe (Fig. 6.6) lies in its neutral hues, like beige and gray, coupled with simple, timeless, and intelligent silhouettes. It's the go-to label for powerhouse businesswomen and stars flexing their talent, not just their looks. The message they send? "I'm smart, capable, and brimming with intellectual confidence."

---

[21] On May 11, 2023, extracted and revised from https://www.readersdigest.ca/culture/70-funniest-jokes-readers-digest/.

[22] Sirgy (1982).

Fig. 6.5 Marilyn Monroe illustration (Fashion illustrations/Alamy Stock Photo)

Fig. 6.6 Armani (FashionStock.com/Shutterstock)

Fig. 6.7 Versace (FashionStock.com/Shutterstock)

Meanwhile, Versace designs (Fig. 6.7) are characterized by psychedelic prints, sensual silhouettes, bold color clashes, and splendor—sophisticated yet intense style. It was called "luxurious decadence" because it fed the yearning to flaunt sensuality, luxury, passion, and opulence, the perfect match for consumers craving more freedom in the face of social taboos.

So, the dazzling world of promotion-focused self-expression is a realm where shopping bags are brimming with reflections of our inner selves. Whether it's the understated elegance of Armani or the bold, unapologetic splendor of Versace, it's less about the practicality of the items and more about the stories they tell and the roles they let us play in our everyday theaters.

Art of Elevating the Self II: Aesthetic Alchemy

There are more psychological phenomena regarding "promotion-focused" self-elevation—the power of aesthetics and the extended self.

First, let's discuss the *influence of aesthetics on self-esteem*. In the previous chapter, we discussed the power of aesthetics with regard to the perception of design's usability (utilitarian functions). In this chapter, we will talk about its role in promoting the self (hedonic functions).

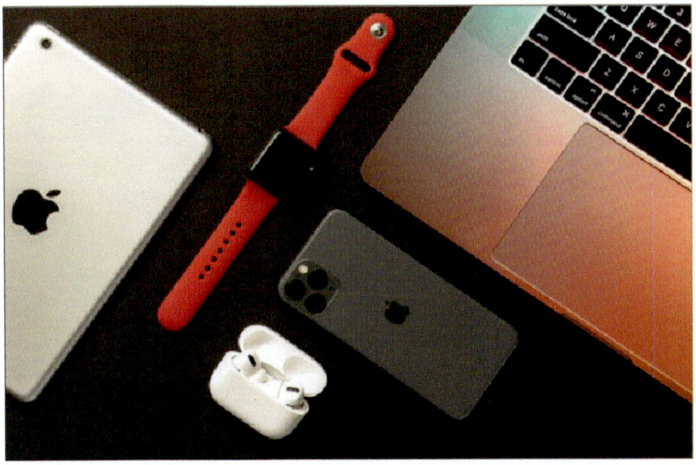

Fig. 6.8 Apple products (Shahid Jamil/Shutterstock)

We all know that aesthetic design promotes consumption and increases satisfaction. But it can have a more fundamental impact on human life, boosting self-esteem. Researchers did some digging about it. One study found that when assessing opinions about capital punishment, subjects who went through a self-affirmation process were less defensive, more open, and potentially more rational about opposing views than those who did not go through that process.[23] Inspired by this study, Townsend and Sood experimented with whether choosing an aesthetic design could have the same self-affirming effect.[24] It turns out that it did. Subjects with an aesthetic design selection process were more open-minded and level-headed about different opinions as if they'd gone through the self-affirmation process.

Now, with this strong proof, designers might be able to convince CEOs that investing in the aesthetics of the design is just as important as investing in the technical and functional aspects. That's what Steve Jobs did when he scouted Jonathan Ive as the chief design officer (CDO) of Apple Inc., who, with his many hit designs, proved Jobs was right (Fig. 6.8).

Art of Elevating the Self III: Extended Self

Lastly, let's follow up on the concept of the *extended self*, which is also related to "promotion-focused" self-elevation. It is a unique self that exists outside our minds and bodies. That means we don't limit weaving the fabric of our souls within

[23] Cohen et al. (2000).

[24] Townsend and Sood (2012).

Fig. 6.9 Extended self: A car (HBRH/Shutterstock)

ourselves. We extend it to the world around us—people, external objects, and environments, with which we interact or share emotional bonds. This phenomenon, known as the extended self, was conjured up by Russell Belk.[25] According to Belk, the moment we seize control of external objects, they become an extension of our very being. So, it's no wonder we often define ourselves partly by our prized possessions. However, non-material elements, like relationships, experiences, or creative pursuits, also play a significant role in forming an extended self. The existence of extended self makes it clear that our sense of self is woven together by myriad factors, making us the intriguing, complex beings that we are. As aforementioned, we even have four different types of self-concepts.

Take, for instance, the automobile. For many individuals, the automobile often represents an extension of their personal identity. Many people love their cars so much that they become part of who they are. Sometimes, people attach human names to personify them, even carrying on a conversation with their vehicles (Fig. 6.9).

As mentioned earlier, design aesthetics are closely related to self-elevation. In addition, aesthetically pleasing objects have a knack for becoming extended selves. It is a natural human tendency to be more attached to things that lift our spirits. There's more! We also have a soft spot for lovely anthropomorphic designs. These objects look like they could come to life and strike up a conversation. Take, for instance, the charming Anna G. Corkscrew by Alessandro Mendini (Fig. 6.10). Inspired by Mendini's girlfriend stretching, this delightful gizmo seems to dance as we uncork our bottle. With her arms moving up and down, she playfully interacts with us, and we can't help but grin at her teasing. Plus, giving her a human name, "Anna," makes it even easier to be personified. Unsurprisingly, it was such a hit that multiple versions, even a boyfriend version, Alessandro, were released (Fig. 6.10, left three items). We will talk more about the psychological effect of design anthropomorphism later in Chap. 13.

---

[25] Belk (1988).

Fig. 6.10 Alessi Anna G. Corkscrew, Alessandro Mendini, 1994 (Malcolm Park/Alamy Stock Photo)

There you have it! We have reached the end of our exploration into the psychology of the self. It has revealed that the things we choose, be they fragrant perfumes or sleek cars, do more than serve practical purposes. They echo our inner narratives. Furthermore, these objects can become extensions of ourselves. So, what's the grand takeaway from this journey? It's that we are constantly engaged in the art of self-creation. Every decision we make, every action we do, and every item we select—they all tell a part of the story about ourselves. Therefore, as we continue to navigate through this self-centric universe, let's embrace the beauty of this process, celebrating the unique and ever-evolving masterpiece that is "myself." After all, our personal narrative is our most powerful and enduring creation.

References

Belk, R. W. (1988). Possessions and the extended self. *Journal of Consumer Research, 15*(2), 139–168.

Brockner, J., & Higgins, E. T. (2001). Regulatory focus theory: Implications for the study of emotions at work. *Organizational Behavior and Human Decision Processes, 86*(1), 35–66.

Cohen, G. L., Aronson, J., & Steele, C. M. (2000). When beliefs yield to evidence: Reducing biased evaluation by affirming the self. *Personality and Social Psychology Bulletin, 26*(9), 1151–1164.

Eibach, R. P., Libby, L. K., & Gilovich, T. D. (2003). When change in the self is mistaken for change in the world. *Journal of Personality and Social Psychology, 84*(5), 917–931.

Kardes, F., Cronley, M., & Cline, T. (2014). *Consumer behavior* (2nd ed.). Cengage Learning.

Khan, U., & Dhar, R. (2006). Licensing effect in consumer choice. *Journal of Marketing Research, 43*(2), 259–266.

Lee, S. W. S., & Schwarz, N. (2011). Wiping the slate clean: Psychological consequences of physical cleansing. *Current Directions in Psychological Science, 20*, 307–311.

Miller, D. T., & Ross, M. (1975). Self-serving biases in the attribution of causality: Fact or fiction? *Psychological Bulletin, 82*(2), 213–225.

Orth, U., & Robins, R. W. (2014). The development of self-esteem. *Current Directions in Psychological Science, 23*(5), 381–387.

Prinsen, S., Evers, C., & de Ridder, D. T. (2019). Justified indulgence: Self-licensing effects on caloric consumption. *Psychology & Health, 34*(1), 24–43.

Sirgy, M. J. (1982). Self-concept in consumer behavior: A critical review. *Journal of Consumer Research, 9*(3), 287–300.

Townsend, C., & Sood, S. (2012). Self-affirmation through the choice of highly aesthetic products. *Journal of Consumer Research, 39*(2), 415–428.

Williams, P., Kern, M. L., & Waters, L. (2016). Exploring selective exposure and confirmation bias as processes underlying employee work happiness: An intervention study. *Frontiers in Psychology, 7*(878), 1–13.

Chapter 7
Survival of the Stingiest: Cognitive Miser

"Guess what! We are all misers by birth!"

Does that sit askew with you? Well, fret not. It isn't our choice. Rather, it's our neurological functions. In addition, more precisely speaking, it's not with monetary resources but with our cognitive resources that our brains are penny-pinchers with. Say hello to a concept known as the "cognitive miser theory."[1] Just as a miser pursues to avoid spending money, our brains love to stockpile cognitive resources and, more often than not, would rather sit on them than spend them.

The penny-pinching tendency of human beings doesn't stop in the cognitive realm. It seems we're frugal on the physiological front, too. Take, for instance, the conditions of astronauts. Staying in space, they experience a decrease in bone density, especially in weight-bearing bones like the spine, hip, and leg bones. Why? These bones no longer need to support the astronaut's weight against gravity. The human body decides maintaining strong bones isn't worth the energy expense, so it stops payments. Without the pull of gravity, even proteins start bailing on their muscles as well. In these terms, astronauts are amazing people. They know all these dangers, and still, they pioneer the unknown world. Anyway, humans are, both in mind and body, natural-born tightwad accountants. Wonderous, right? Smart accountants are always like that—they are the ones who solve a problem we did not know we had in a way we don't understand.[2]

What's this all about, you ask? Well, it's all about survival! We are born misers for survival. It happens because, much to our chagrin, we are creatures of finite resources. So, what does our brain do? It has no choice but to allocate these limited resources as efficiently as possible. The brain distributes a minimum of cognitive investment to those run-of-the-mill tasks. Only then can it spare the mental energy for the things that really matter. Therefore, in addition to "survival of the fittest," here is the "survival of the stingiest!".

---

[1] Fiske and Taylor (1991), Corcoran and Mussweiler (2010).

[2] On July 7, 2023, extracted and revised from https://www.lhh.com/us/en/insights/accounting-jokes/.

© The Author(s), under exclusive license to Springer Nature Singapore Pte Ltd. 2024
J. Lee et al., *The Psychology Behind Design*,
https://doi.org/10.1007/978-981-97-3426-9_7

Disappointed? Yet, With this cognitive miser theory, we have good news, too—we have something to blame for our questionable willpower. Ever wonder why your New Year's resolutions end up as mid-January amnesias? Don't blame your weak self-control too harshly. Fortunately, you can share some of the blame with the finite capacity of human mental bandwidth. Your brain, already buried under the daily information avalanche, might find it hard to juggle energy-guzzling info like a New Year's resolution. I don't mean that we can completely escape from the responsibility of our self-control, but, hey, we are no supercomputers, either.

What's more, we are lucky to have another scapegoat to blame. It turns out that the human brain is quite the creature of habit: it prefers the familiar situation, not the better improvement.[3] Actually, it doesn't just prefer the familiar but is downright clingy, resisting change because the familiar requires much less energy to run. So when we try to introduce a difficult new routine like a New Year's resolution, our brains recognize it as an emergency situation and pull out all stops to return to its status quo. This is the culprit behind the notorious "yo-yo effect." So, if your resolution hits the brick wall, console yourself a bit with the fact that it's your brain's "return to sender" policy in action.

Yo-yos aren't just for diets: they're the modus operandi for all our habits. Think about your emotions, for instance. They, too, have set up camp in the comfort zones in your brain. For example, if you've got a penchant for flying off the handle, your brain thinks of it as your familiar state and easily gets that scene on replay. Breaking this familiar circuit and forming new, better ones will demand sweat, tears, and a bucket-load of patience. How much patience, you ask? Think about using a computer with a very slow internet connection. With this, you can show who you truly are. If you can graciously endure that seemingly endless loading screen, then you have a high probability of forming a new brain circuit, too.[4]

Let's chew over the most infamous real-life example of the brain science for short-lived resolutions—our gym membership. Signing up for several months at a stretch is generally easier on the wallet. Even though we are well aware it's a sly sales pitch, we still fall for it. Why? Because we're pretty convinced that this year's resolution is quite strong. But the gym manager knows better, laying bets on our grand escape come February. We might sigh, saying exercising would be much more rewarding if calories screamed while we burned them.[5]

It happens daily, too—our brave attempts at day after day of diet resolution. We usually sail through the morning quite well, dodging doughnuts with grace. But by late afternoon, we slowly lose our resistance to temptations. This is why things that are important but not so easy to do should be done in the bright-eyed hours of the morning. In this way, you can also finish the workout before your brain realizes what it's doing.[6]

---

[3] Zajonc (2001).

[4] On July 7, 2023, extracted and revised from https://memesbams.com/funny-relationship-jokes/.

[5] On July 9, 2023, suggested by ChatGPT-4.

[6] On July 7, 2023, extracted and revised from https://upjoke.com/workout-jokes.

So far, so good. We have justifiable excuses for our short-lived resolutions, an acceptable dose of excuses and blaming. If it stays in an "adequate" range, it can even be helpful for our mental health. Funny enough, it makes us very creative, too: open up a gym membership and see how many creative excuses you have come up with not to go.[7] Just don't go beyond those reasonable bounds.

Then, does this mean our willpower has a permanent backstage pass, free to avoid the spotlight? Not by a long shot! Our motivation and determination obviously play a big role. That is, if you're really serious about embracing something new, it's like waving a checkered flag at your brain, which then deems it important, assigning much cognitive energy to deal with it. Consequently, a higher possibility of success! Let's take an amusing real-life example of the power of motivation and determination. When the teenager loses a contact lens, he will give up after a brief, fruitless search. But when his mother takes up the cause, she will find the lens within minutes. If he asks, "How did you do it?" she will answer, "We weren't looking for the same thing. You were looking for a piece of plastic. I was looking for $300."[8]

Be that as it may, don't play too much with your willpower. You'd better avoid juggling too many willpower-demanding tasks all at once. For example, when your work piles up, the success of a simultaneous diet plan is almost unattainable. We have science to back up this assertion. In an experiment, participants had to choose between a sinfully delicious, waistline-unfriendly chocolate cake and a virtuous, albeit less thrilling, fruit salad.[9] Before selection, one group had to remember the short string of numbers, and another group had to remember the long string of numbers. The outcome? The group juggling the longer numbers flocked to the chocolate cake—their choice of it was significantly higher than the other group. Their brain, already having a hard time processing the longer numbers, ran low on self-control fuel to resist the seductive call of the chocolate cake. Note that "stressed" is "desserts" spelled backward! Coincidence? Well, maybe not.[10]

So, despite our initial disappointment, we have a good reason not to moan over the fact that we are cognitive misers. After all, it's a natural survival instinct. Yet, let's also keep in mind that if our resolution is desperate enough to persuade our brain, it will cut us a generous budget, helping us create new brain circuits and better ourselves. Some see the glass half full. Others see it half empty. Determined people just start to refill the glass![11]

---

[7] On July 10, 2023, extracted and revised from https://upjoke.com/creative-jokes.

[8] On July 8, 2023, extracted and revised from https://www.readersdigest.ca/culture/70-funniest-jokes-readers-digest/.

[9] Shiv and Fedorikhin (1999).

[10] See Footnote 5.

[11] See Footnote 5.

Owl of Minerva Behind the Scene

Welcome to the chapter about a *cognitive miser*. Psychology characterizes the human mind as having limited cognitive resources and, thus, as an inherent cognitive miser. Let's explore this phenomenon more. Our wise associate, the owl, is well-equipped to elucidate the relevant psychological principles. Let's start with "cognitive miser theory."[12]

A Budget for Survival: Cognitive Miser Theory

Our brain is the ultimate bargain-hunter, constantly rummaging through the easiest, least energy-sucking ways to solve problems. This phenomenon is called *cognitive miser theory*. Like a miser's inclination to circumvent spending money, our brain stashes away mental energy as much as possible. The mental shortcuts that our brains commonly use to save energy encompass schemas, mental models, stereotypes, and heuristics. They are like "ready meals" of the mental world. In those terms, our brain is like a savvy city driver, always knowing the fastest backroads.

Susan T. Fiske and Shelley E. Taylor, who coined this term, suggested the reason behind this phenomenon: people are limited in their capacity to process information. It means that given our limited time, knowledge, attention, and energy, our thrifty brains try to spend our cognitive resources as wisely and efficiently as possible so that the piled-up energy can be used for other important matters.

Our brain's limited capacity and its smart strategy to rise above it can be clearly seen in our short-term memory. *Short-term memory* is a bustling temporary hub for all the incoming data we encounter daily, also known as *working memory*. It can be likened to a computer's RAM (Random Access Memory), where data disappears if not saved to the hard drive (long-term memory).

You'd think this invaluable memory tool would have the storage space of a roomy warehouse, right? To our surprise, its basic capacity is more akin to a tiny wardrobe, a mere "7 ± 2" items at a time. This number is dubbed *Miller's Law* after the psychologist who presented it.[13] Surprised? But here's where our smart brain pulls a rabbit out of the hat. It knows an amazing trick to boost this humble capacity—*chunking*. If we group similar info into neat categories, we can insert a whole lot more into our short-term memory. Therefore, the "7 ± 2" can also refer to the number of chunkings. Now, suddenly, that small wardrobe feels more like a walk-in closet with 7 ± 2 hangers, each holding a chunk of related items. Still and all, it's not a spacious warehouse as ever.

Design whizzes consider this limitation of our memory in their works, of course. Just look at the blueprint of any grand, labyrinthine store like IKEA. With its sprawling square footage, you'd expect it to have more sections than a large jigsaw puzzle. But if you look carefully, the contents are tidily organized into four main

[12] Fiske and Taylor (2020).

[13] Miller (1956).

areas—showroom, restaurant, home furnishing accessories, and self-serve furniture. And the magic number strikes again: each of the showroom area and home furnishing accessories area is further sliced into nine sections, just nudging that 7 ± 2 threshold.

Now, let's turn our attention to *long-term memory*. One comforting fact about our cognitive capacity is this long-term memory, where informative knowledge is held indefinitely. Guess what! Its storage capacity is known to be "infinite." Finally, in this chapter, something is not finite! Even so, there's still a catch. This memory loves to play the not-so-fun game of hide-and-seek. Namely, the *retrieval failure* happens quite often. With long-term memory, more often than not, it's not about how much data we've stored but how good we are at finding them when needed. This is why "accessibility" is the real MVP here.

How do designers put this fact into practice? They incorporate *retrieval cues* in their designs. Let's picture walking into a brand store and seeing images from an advertisement we've seen before (e.g., Fig. 7.1). They aren't just there to look pretty; they're strategic design elements that serve as retrieval cues, whispering, "Remember that awesome ad you saw? That's us!" They're helping customers retrieve all that brand-related information they've tucked away in long-term memory.

As we can see, our brain is very impressive in its knack for efficiency, making the most out of its limited resources. Who knew our brain, with its capacity akin to a tiny wardrobe, could still perform marvels through clever techniques like chunking, transforming that wardrobe into a deceptively spacious walk-in closet? This insight into our brain's workings can have important implications in ensuring designs to help customers so that they can navigate and retrieve information with ease in this complex modern environment.

Fig. 7.1 Lancome store, Hong Kong (Sorbis/Shutterstock)

Heuristics Highway I: Availability Heuristic

Shall we now delve into *cognitive heuristics*? It's a kind of limited information processing—the brain propensity we all have, thanks to our inherent tendency to be cognitive misers. Even though "limited information processing" doesn't sound very satisfactory, heuristics aren't necessarily the villains in our story as much as cognitive miser isn't. They are the brain's way of making quick decisions that don't require a full-blown debate in our heads. In other words, we need this because investing substantial mental effort in every decision of life could result in an imprudent allocation of our finite cognitive resources. Therefore, sometimes, we're the methodical Sherlock Holmes, carefully considering every single clue, and other times, we're more like reality show contestants, making hasty decisions based on limited information.

This indicates the existence of two distinct information processing systems within us—systematic processing and heuristic processing. When we deal with life's big issues entailing high motivation and involvement, we switch on the Sherlock mode and engage in *systematic processing*, considering all possibilities before making a move. But when it comes to those "extra cookie" moments incorporating low motivation and involvement, we rely on our inner reality star, and *heuristic processing* takes over. This heuristic processing is what we're going to explore more due to its relevance to the concept of a cognitive miser.

Heuristics serve as cognitive shortcuts, streamlining our decision-making processes and thereby conserving mental energy.[14] Yet, they're not without "uh-oh" moments. Sometimes, we end up making less-than-optimal decisions. And you'd better check whether you are running the heuristic processing inappropriately even for an important matter. Nevertheless, when it comes to those everyday, low-stakes decisions, we're more likely to let heuristics take the wheel. Heuristics also rescue us when we're drowning in an information overload, under time pressure, or just plain stressed. Given our high-speed lives today, saturated with stress and overloaded information, it's hardly surprising that our reliance on heuristics is on the rise.

There exists an array of heuristics, each with its unique functions. Among those, we will check two particularly intriguing types—the availability heuristic and the representativeness heuristic.

The *availability heuristic* is about the power of readily available information over more accurate information.[15] You can think of it as the "right here, right now" process. Usually, emotionally charged, frequently encountered, or recently exposed information is easy to recall, and it tends to strut onto the center stage of our memory, pushing aside the less flashy, yet more accurate, data. Consequently, they wield a substantial influence on our judgment, more than objective facts.

Any real-world fallout from this? Yes, it is! It can sometimes skew our perception of reality. For instance, people are prone to overestimate the probability of fatalities resulting from accidents or natural disasters (e.g., plane or train accidents,

---

[14] Tversky and Kahneman (1974).

[15] Tversky and Kahneman (1974).

earthquakes, tornadoes, etc.). Why? These attention-grabbing events hog the media spotlight and become more accessible in our memory. And when information is easily accessible, our brains deem it more probable. That's the availability heuristic in action!

Let's examine this heuristic in marketing and design contexts. Ever notice how those heart-wrenching charity ads often have precise details about the person in need? You know, their name, age, and picture, etc. It's no coincidence. This strategy transforms a sea of unknown faces into relatable individuals and alters their abstract and distant plights into concrete and immediate incidents. Suddenly, Bob, 42, with his sorrowful eyes, isn't just another face in the crowd. He's someone you feel like you know. These ads are like a mental sticky note, making you remember, thus increasing your willingness to help.

So, there's the strategy of "real people sharing real stories" in charity marketing campaigns. Sure, a celebrity endorsement can be a shiny appeal and a good way to make it popular, but only some people can identify with celebrities. But all of us can identify with the stories of everyday folks, someone like us. Therefore, this approach makes the cause more relatable and memorable, leveraging the availability heuristic—our tendency to be influenced by what's immediate and familiar.

Consider UNICEF Sweden's "Likes Don't Save Lives" campaign, for instance. It's a reality check with social media engagement. The gist? Tapping a "like" button on social media may feel good and raise awareness. Still, it doesn't quite cut it when it comes to real help—actual donations and volunteering. In one of their ads, we meet Rahim, a ten-year-old orphan living with his younger brother, and he needs more than digital likes. He needs real support. His story serves as a gentle prod, reminding us that real children with real needs are waiting on the other side of our screens, far beyond the realm of social media gestures.

Let's stroll into a retail setting. Have you ever noticed that the sales promo materials, like the one in Fig. 7.2, are usually in loud colors (mostly red)? That's not just to catch your attention. It's also to make the promo stick in your mind and thus make it more "available" next time you decide to shop. You see, the availability heuristic is all around us, working in ways you've probably never even considered.

Related to the availability heuristic, let's look into the *truth effect*. It is the effect of frequently encountered information. However, don't let its name fool you. It's quite the mind-bender. This is our brain's subtle bias toward believing something to be true simply because we've heard it repeatedly, even without putting it under a fact-checking microscope. It's as if our minds decided that quantity equals quality.

How does this happen, you wonder? It happens because, when assessing truthfulness, our brains prefer to pick teams with familiar faces rather than new ones. That is, we often depend on how well the information aligns with our existing knowledge or how familiar it feels. Repetition fosters familiarity, making repeated statements easier to process. Therefore, this effect implies that familiarity and easiness could overpower objectivity, enjoying the cozy predictability of the familiar over the hard work of logic and evidence.[16]

---

[16] Zajonc (2001).

Fig. 7.2 Sale signage: Victoria's Secret store, Chicago, USA (photographed by Jeongmin Lee, 2016, Author's Collection)

The truth effect bears significant implications in fields such as advertising, news media, and political propaganda. Consider how companies often treat us to endless advertising claims, hoping they'll stick to our minds like a catchy jingle. Through constant exposure to slogans endorsing a product as "the best choice," we may begin to accept this assertion as factual, not because we've made any detailed comparison or checked its inherent merit, but simply because we've been told so many times.

IKEA, for example, deftly uses this bias to propagate its core marketing messages—democratic design, sustainability, and low price. The promotional designs for these themes (e.g., Fig. 7.3) are repeated throughout their labyrinthine stores. For instance, graphic design materials spotlighting its proud business philosophy of "DESIGN FOR EVERYONE" (Democratic Design) were displayed more than twenty times at the Giheung store in South Korea. This repetition gently nudges customers to see this claim as believable and convincing. So, if you find yourself buying into a claim after hearing it multiple times, it might be the "truth effect" singing its irresistible song in your ear.

Fig. 7.3 IKEA: Graphic design materials for "DESIGN FOR EVERYONE" (photographed by Jeongmin Lee, 2019, Author's Collection)

Heuristics Highway II: Representativeness Heuristic

Next up on our heuristics stage is the *representativeness heuristic*,[17] wherein people make predictions based on the perceived similarities between specific items and broader categories. For instance, a consumer who holds Samsung Galaxy phones in high regard is likely to extend this positive evaluation to Samsung washing machines, too.

When predicting quality by using the representativeness heuristic, we often rely on *surrogate indicators*. Commonly used surrogate indicators are price, advertising intensity, warranty, brand reputation, and country of origin. It's not always accurate, though. We're taking a leap of faith based on some related cues. That's why it is called "heuristics."

Examples? The abovementioned liaison between Samsung Galaxy phones and Samsung washing machines is the case of using the brand reputation as a surrogate indicator. It's like implying, "Our phones are smart, and so are our washers." Then there's Ricola, wrapping its candies in "Swiss Made" pride (Fig. 7.4). That is, packaging labels like "Swiss Alpine Herbs," "Swiss Herb Candy," or "Product of Switzerland" are subtle hints of Swiss-level precision, quality, reliability, and clean nature, transforming a simple candy into a little piece of Swiss craftsmanship. A surrogate indicator, country of origin, in action! So, if you find yourself impressed by a product because it's "Engineered in Germany" or "Designed in Italy," notice that the representativeness heuristic has just given you a high-five.

With regard to the representativeness heuristic, we can also consider the *peak-end effect* to be under the umbrella of its influence. It is another mental shortcut wherein individuals evaluate a series of experiences (e.g., event design) primarily based on the most intense moment (the peak) and how the experience concluded (the end),

[17] Tversky and Kahneman (1974).

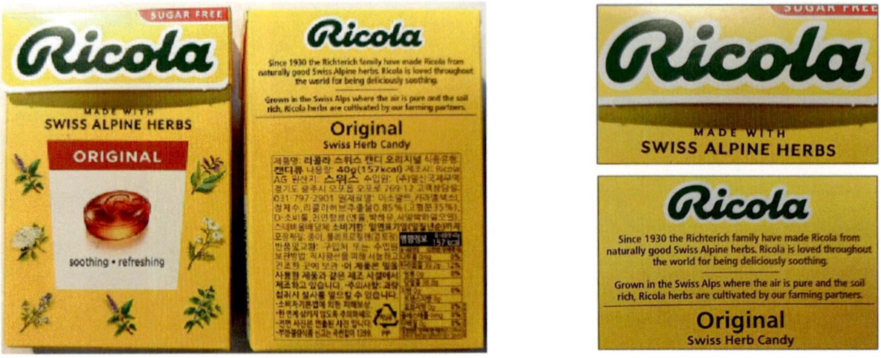

Fig. 7.4 Package design of Ricola (photographed by Jeongmin Lee, 2023, Author's Collection)

rather than assessing every moment within the whole experience.[18] This psychological shortcut could have significant implications for designing customer experiences unfolding over time. With this bias in mind, one can effectively create a certain experience to be more memorable.

Imagine you're watching the opening ceremony of the Olympic Games, with a feast of performances vying for your attention. But when the curtain falls, what parts do you usually remember? The odds are that your memory will pick the most heart-pounding moments and the show-stopping finale. Therefore, your overall satisfaction with the ceremony is likely to be swayed more by these two moments.

Take that awe-inspiring moment that brings the crowd to its feet. That's your peak, which leaves an indelible mark. Then, the grand finale comes into play—the suspenseful unveiling of the Olympic rings and the lighting of the Olympic cauldron. These performances are closely guarded secrets, revealed only at the last moment to ensure that the ceremony concludes on a high note. For example, the Olympic rings performance in the 2018 Pyeongchang Olympics was done with 1218 drones, which was a heart-pounding moment of the Olympic spirit. And speaking of unexpected turns, the 2012 London Olympics had the cauldron fired up not by a renowned athlete but by Britain's next big things—seven young sports prospects aged between 16 and 19, marking a memorable moment in the event's history (Fig. 7.5).

So, even if there were moments that didn't quite get your pulse racing, they don't do much to shape your overall memory and satisfaction with the event. The human brain, being the efficient editor, will cut the footage down to a highlight reel of peaks and ends.

So, it's clear that many times, our brains work less like meticulous librarians and more like savvy, snap-decision makers. It all boils down to our brain's love for cognitive shortcuts. This might not always lead to the best decisions, but hey, in the fast-paced, information-flooded world we live in, who has time for a detailed analysis of every choice? The heuristic heroes in your head are just trying to make

[18] Do et al. (2008).

Fig. 7.5 2012 London Olympics: Lighting of the Olympic Cauldron (Pat Benic/UPI /Alamy Stock Photo)

your high-speed life a tad easier. Remember, though, while these brain quirks are handy, they're not infallible. Don't forget the occasional reality check, too!

Other Brain Games Caused by Cognitive Limitations

Let's shift our focus from cognitive miser theory to other cognitive theories that showcase human cognitive limitations. We will highlight a few of these, especially the ones illustrating the fact that the human brain tries to allocate its limited energy as efficiently as possible.

Firstly, let's delve into the renowned phenomenon, the *Invisible Gorilla*, an all-time classic in psychology. Officially, it is the *selective attention* phenomenon. In a famous experiment on this, subjects were tasked with observing a video.[19] The video had two teams of students, one in white t-shirts and the other in black, passing around a basketball. The subject's job was to count the number of passes made by the white team. No biggie, right? However, during the course of the video, a student dressed as a gorilla entered the scene, remained in the center of the screen briefly, and then departed (Fig. 7.6).

The result? Hold on to your hat! Overall, across all conditions, about half of the subjects failed to perceive the presence of the gorilla. A gorilla out of left field, right in the middle, and they completely missed it! Why did our poor gorilla go unnoticed? It's due to our lack of brain power when we are multi-tasking, so our brain needs to select what to focus on. Therefore, when subjects were too busy keeping track of those important passes, their brains put the gorilla spotting on the back burner. That

[19] Simons and Chabris (1999).

Fig. 7.6 Invisible gorilla experiment (created by DALL.E & Jeongmin Lee, 2023, Author's Collection)

is, the gorilla became a background element to them! Talk about being engrossed in the survival game. You should focus on the enemies, not the background bushes or flowers.

In essence, due to the finite capacity to perceive stimuli simultaneously, humans have no choice but to choose what to pay attention to (foreground elements) and what to ignore (background elements). As a result, they are unable to recognize stimuli other than those specifically attended to. This phenomenon is called "selective attention." It is also called the *cocktail party effect* because selective attention can induce a heightened concentration on your friend's gossip at a noisy party while a big scandal told by an adjacent individual becomes the background noise.

Now, let's connect the dots of this theory to design. Designers must comprehend this fundamental principle, as many designs fail to capture consumers' attention. In the realm of design, grabbing selective attention means that the essential design element should stand out enough to be noticed and remembered amid a sea of other stimuli. Certain attributes such as a "changing stimulus," "negative stimulus," "stimulus distinct from the surroundings," "initial stimulus," and "repeated stimulus" possess the ability to readily attract customers' attention. So, when crafting your next big thing, keep in mind to add a good dose of these attributes. After all, it's a jungle out there, and you don't want your work to be the invisible gorilla!

Let's zoom in on a specific design example—a poster from the "Know the Score" drug awareness campaign in Fig. 7.7. To capture the selective attention of viewers, this design uses a "negative stimulus"—a visual cue that triggers a strong emotional response, which is hard to ignore. It features an unsettling image of a man's face and chest peeled back to reveal the anatomy underneath. It's not your everyday imagery,

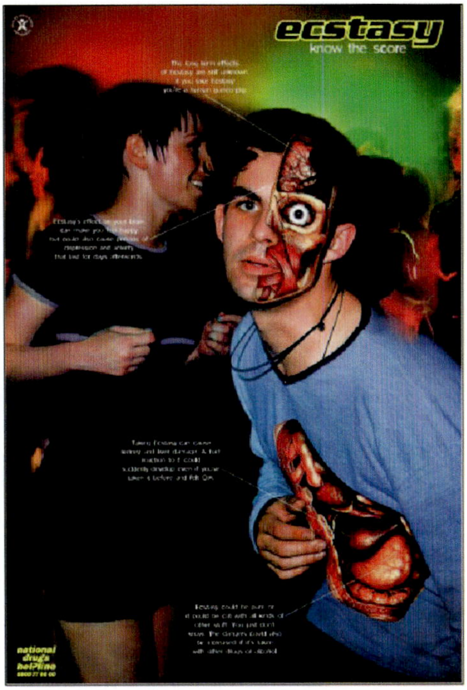

Fig. 7.7 Poster design from the National Drugs Helpline's "Know the Score" drug awareness campaign, 1998 (Contraband Collection/Alamy Stock Photo)

and that's the point. It's like a visual siren. In addition, the use of vivid, contrasting colors and the bright reds of the internal organs against the subdued tones of the party scene further draws the eye. These bold design elements serve as a metaphor for the hidden, internal ravages of drug abuse.

Next, let's stand in front of the Walt Disney Concert Hall (Fig. 7.8). This architecture catches the eye in the city skyline, where its neighboring buildings are all straight lines and square angles. Its contrasting design bends like a group ballet dance. That is, it is the "stimulus distinct from the surroundings." Consequently, it ensures salience in its visual impact. You can't miss it!

Now, let's move to our second theory related to the human brain's limited cognitive energy and its effort for efficient energy allocation—*mental model dissonance*.[20] Humans form *mental models* to run familiar things with minimum cognitive energy. It is a complex concept, but let me simplify it a bit and focus on the procedural character of it.

The mental model is the knowledge in our minds, picturing how specific processes should unfold or how specific things should work. It is formed by past experience and is subject to change. In Chap. 2, we mentioned the "schema," which is related to the mental model. However, they are a bit different. Schema is the general concept or important features of something formed by past experience. For example, the schema of the car is "a motorized, four-wheeled vehicle designed for road travel with seats,

[20] Wilke et al. (2007).

Fig. 7.8 Walt Disney Concert Hall (Los Angeles Music Center), Frank Gehry, 2003, LA, USA (photographed by Jeongmin Lee, 2016, Author's Collection)

engine, wheels, and steering mechanism." On the other hand, the mental model of the car can be the procedural knowledge of "how to drive a car." Any deviation from familiar mental models or schemas can be pretty challenging because it requires a lot more mental energy. Still, the mental model can be changed, and over time, people can adjust themselves to new mental models. But schemas are difficult to change.

Let's take a real-life example. Consider a person learning how to drive a car. Their mental model of driving a car includes understanding how the steering wheel, pedals, and mirrors work, as well as the rules of the road. So, you learned all of those and became a good driver. Then, when you go to a foreign country where the driver's seat is located on the other side, and the rules of the road are also different, you will be quite confused at first, causing your brain to mutter, "Hold on, that's not right!" That feeling of discomfort is none other than "mental model dissonance." Don't worry, though. As you gain experience, your mental model of driving a car adapts, allowing you to become a better driver in that country, too. But your schema of the car itself? It doesn't change that much, even in that country.

This kind of discomfort caused by mental model dissonance can also happen when companies try to introduce a new, unfamiliar method or process for using their products. When pre-existing mental models of customers clash with this new one, it can induce confusion, frustration, and, at times, even anger. Marketers know this peril and present a savvy solution to this problem—the "transition period." So, when introducing a novel process, they usually keep the old one running in tandem for a while. This way, consumers can adjust to the new format at their own pace.

A good example of this approach is the interface design change for social media. They usually let you use the old version for a while. Another example is the handling of the famous brand's catalog format change. When companies decide to switch from their paper catalog to a snazzy digital version, they don't suddenly pull the rug from under their customers. They usually keep printing paper versions for a while until customers become comfortable navigating the digital seas. This careful, patient approach showcases their respect for the fact that customers need time to adjust their mental models.

The third theory related to the human brain's limited cognitive energy and its effort for efficient energy allocation is the *order effect*. It's our brain's quirky knack for remembering information: when humans are presented with a sequence of information, they remember what was shared at the beginning and at the end, while the information delivered in the middle tends to be less remembered. Don't confuse the "order effect" with the "peak-end effect" mentioned earlier. Even though they are pretty similar, the latter happens when we evaluate the sequential "experiences," while the order effect is about the memory and impact of the sequential "information."

Let's bring this theory to life with the story of Tom. Tom possesses four strengths (smart, diligent, punctual, active) as well as four weaknesses (insidious, impulsive, stubborn, jealous). Now, here's the trick. When honestly talking about all his strengths and weaknesses, you can still paint him as a hero or a zero by the order in which you list these traits. If you want to fluff up his image, you might say, "Tom is smart, diligent, insidious, impulsive, stubborn, jealous, punctual, and active." But if you're feeling a little mischievous, you could say, "Tom is insidious, impulsive, smart, diligent, punctual, active, stubborn, and jealous." In addition, here's a pro tip: the words positioned earlier in the list tend to exert a greater influence than those appearing later. As such, showcasing the most desirable traits first is typically advantageous.[21] No wonder why every candidate wants to be in the first position on the ballot.

Why does the order effect exist? As mentioned above, our memory has short-term memory and long-term memory. The stuff you hear first could have time for the treatment to get into the long-term memory suite. This phenomenon, known as the *primacy effect*, is an equivalent of "first come, first served." The information checks in early and makes itself comfortable for a long stay. On the other hand, the final pieces of information are remembered more as they still linger in short-term memory, which keeps the info accessible for a quick recall. This is known as the *recency effect*.[22]

Applying this understanding to practical design can be quite fruitful. For your design (e.g., advertising design), ensure that you put the important content at the beginning and final segments. Our brain will recall that information much better. Avoid putting them in the middle, as they risk getting lost in the Bermuda Triangle of memory.

More Design Insights Added to the Scene

Before we end our journey into the concept of a cognitive miser, let me explain the *interference effect*. It might not be directly related to the concept of the cognitive miser or the efficient allocation of our limited cognitive resources. Still, it is caused by our limited mental energy.

---

[21] Lidwell et al. (2010).

[22] Glanzer and Cunitz (1966).

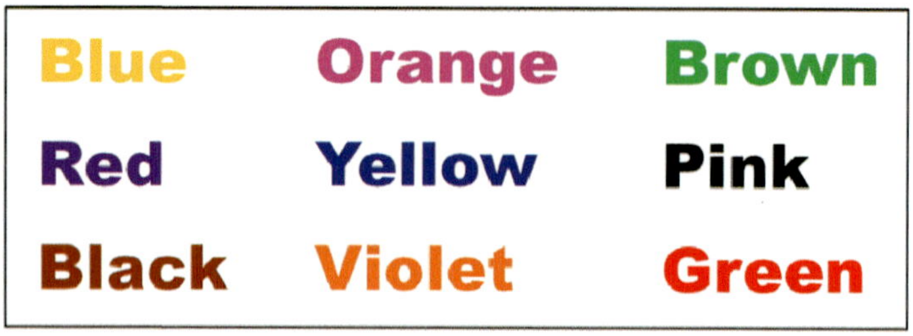

Fig. 7.9 Stroop task (created by Jeongmin Lee, 2023, Author's Collection)

Cognitive interference is fundamentally induced by the simultaneous presence of additional information. That is, it happens due to concurrent information stepping on each other's toes, all vying for our attention at the same time. Because we don't have abundant mental energy for the problems requiring a multi-task operation, quite often, we can't sort them out accurately.

The culprits behind this effect are typically "similarity" and "discordance." You can think of *interference by similarity* as two mischievous twins.[23] Similarity makes them look alike, getting them mixed up. To prevent this, designers often make different bits of information with potential confusion visually stand out from one another. For example, think of a multicolored pie chart versus a monochrome one. In the case of mischievous twins? They can have different hairstyles.

On the other hand, *interference by discordance* refers to the psychological confusion that occurs when two pieces of information presented together clash with each other, sending mixed messages. A famous study concerning this effect is the Stroop task experiment, rooted in the *Stroop effect*.[24] In this experiment, the control group gets the cushy job. They just have to read the texts printed in different colors, ignoring the colors of the texts. Meanwhile, the experimental group has to name the colors of the texts (which differ from the word's meaning) instead of reading the texts. For example, they had to say "yellow" for the text "Blue" written in yellow color. Sounds easy, right? Try it yourself with the stimulus in Fig. 7.9. First, read the texts, then name the colors of the texts, and compare the reaction times.

You got the result? The reaction time for the experimental group was considerably slower. This finding suggests that word is a priority stimulus over color. So, the meaning of the texts caused interference in identifying the colors of the texts. "Read first, color second!" seems to be the brain's default setting.

Let's talk about the design example for interference by discordance. Do you know that once there was "a traffic light with a red arrow," as in Fig. 7.10? Normally, traffic lights are easy-peasy—red says "stop," green says "go." But an arrow? That's the universal sign for "this way, please." Mix them together, and you've got a "red arrow," a real head-scratcher. It's like getting an invitation to a party that says, "Come over! But actually, don't." This red arrow light originally meant "no turning on the red

[23] De Visscher and Noël (2016).

[24] Stroop (1935).

Fig. 7.10 Traffic light causing interference by discordance (created by DALL.E & Jeongmin Lee, 2023, Author's Collection)

arrow," but drivers were confused. Thus, an additional sign saying "no turn on red" had to be added (Fig. 7.10 right). Thankfully, this problem has been noticed, and we don't see this confusing traffic light anymore. As we can see in this instance, designers need to think like detectives, sniffing out any potential confusion or misunderstanding in their work. This is especially true when their designs pertain to safety.

So, here we are, completing our journey into the concept of the cognitive miser! We found that we are limited but efficient creatures. As humans, we've got our fair share of limitations, and juggling attention isn't our strongest suit. But on the flip side, we also exhibit remarkable ingenuity in optimizing our finite capacities. So, our brain makes these executive decisions on where to invest its resources, often choosing the path of least resistance to conserve energy. It's this unique blend of limitation and ingenuity that drives us to become smart and efficient cognitive misers. Therefore, it's clear that our brains have been doing a spectacular job of keeping us afloat in a sea of information while navigating the complexities of our daily lives. Let us celebrate the brilliance of our astute minds!

References

Corcoran, K., & Mussweiler, T. (2010). The cognitive miser's perspective: Social comparison as a heuristic in self-judgements. *European Review of Social Psychology, 21*(1), 78–113.

De Visscher, A., & Noël, M. P. (2016). Similarity interference in learning and retrieving arithmetic facts. *Progress in Brain Research, 227*, 131–158.

Do, A. M., Rupert, A. V., & Wolford, G. (2008). Evaluations of pleasurable experiences: The peak-end rule. *Psychonomic Bulletin & Review, 15*, 96–98.

Fiske, S. T., & Taylor, S. E. (1991). *Social cognition*. Mcgraw-Hill Book Company.

Fiske, S. T., & Taylor, S. E. (2020). Social cognition evolves: Illustrations from our work on intergroup bias and on healthy adaptation. *Psicothema, 32*(3), 291–297.

Glanzer, M., & Cunitz, A. R. (1966). Two storage mechanisms in free recall. *Journal of Verbal Learning and Verbal Behavior, 5*(4), 351–360.

Lidwell, W., Holden, K., & Butler, J. (2010). *Universal principles of design: 125 ways to enhance usability, influence perception, increase appeal, make better design decisions, and teach through design*. Rockport Publishers.

Miller, G. A. (1956). The magical number seven, plus or minus two: Some limits on our capacity for processing information. *Psychological Review, 63*(2), 81–97.

Shiv, B., & Fedorikhin, A. (1999). Heart and mind in conflict: The interplay of affect and cognition in consumer decision making. *Journal of Consumer Reserch, 26*(3), 278–292.

Simons, D. J., & Chabris, C. F. (1999). Gorillas in our midst: Sustained inattentional blindness for dynamic events. *Perception, 28*(9), 1059–1074.

Stroop, J. R. (1935). Studies of interference in serial verbal reactions. *Journal of Experimental Psychology, 18*(6), 643.

Tversky, A., & Kahneman, D. (1974). Judgment under uncertainty: Heuristics and biases. *Science, 185*(4157), 1124–1131.

Wilke, J., McInnes, F., Jack, M. A., & Littlewood, P. (2007). Hidden menu options in automated human-computer telephone dialogues: Dissonance in the user's mental model. *Behaviour & Information Technology, 26*(6), 517–534.

Zajonc, R. B. (2001). Mere exposure: A gateway to the subliminal. *Current Directions in Psychological Science, 10*, 224–228.

Chapter 8
Logic of Illogic: Bounded Rationality

Ever noticed how the number "9" seems to have cornered the market on price tags? There's $19.99, $49.99, and don't even get me started on the ever-popular $99.99. "It's not a hundred. It's ninety-something!" (Fig. 8.1).

Retailers do this trick to make things seem lighter on our wallets than they actually are. Even when we're totally aware that $49.99 is just a penny shy of $50, we often find ourselves gloating over a seeming bargain for a neat $40 something, telling others, "Hey, I just picked up this thing for 40 bucks!" This odd phenomenon is known as the left-digit effect, a psychological quirk retailers apply to their advantage.[1]

Our quirky behavior doesn't stop at pricing. Picture this: we've just bought a snazzy new laptop. Then, what do we do next? We play detective, of course, scouring the internet to compare our brand-new purchase to other laptops we didn't buy or, at least, to compare the prices of the same laptop from other retailers. Even though it doesn't make much sense (after all, you can't return an unboxed laptop), we still do it for now because we are anxious about whether we made the best choice. This seemingly illogical action, often causing us distress and potential regret, has a name, "post-purchase dissonance."[2] It's a self-generated mental hangover.

Last but not least, let's talk about those snap judgments we all make—the ones based on first impressions. For example, when a speaker looks trustworthy in the outer appearance, we're ready to buy whatever that person is selling. It's amazing how a well-ironed suit or a firm handshake can sometimes tip the scales in someone's favor. That's the power of first impressions.

The list for these kinds of irrational judgments can be endless. So, here's to our idiosyncrasies, these shared human foibles, making the world of consumerism a bit more labyrinthine. Don't criticize yourself too much, though. We're all human, and these quirks are just part of the package called "life."

---

[1] Thomas and Morwitz (2005).

[2] Shani and Zeelenberg (2007).

© The Author(s), under exclusive license to Springer Nature Singapore Pte Ltd. 2024

J. Lee et al., *The Psychology Behind Design*,
https://doi.org/10.1007/978-981-97-3426-9_8

Fig. 8.1 9-ending pricing (created by Jeongmin Lee, 2023, Author's Collection)

The grand dame of economics, utility maximization theory, assumes that humans are consistently rational and always go for the highest net benefit. However, we all know that our judgments often veer away from this model, and the above examples throw light on this fact. So, let's cut to the chase. Our day-to-day decisions cannot all be made in a "Sherlock Holmes" mode, guided by logic and precision. In other words, our judgments can be skewed by a concept known as "bounded rationality," a fancy academic term for "Hey, nobody's perfect!" Human rationality, for all its splendor, has its boundaries. For instance, think about those perplexing prompts: "If you understand English, press 1. If you do not understand English, press 2."[3] Sometimes, we don't even know what the problem is, and honestly, that's just us being human.

This realization is the core of behavioral decision theory. It proposed that our decision-making abilities might not be as prim and rational as utility maximization theory likes to assume. Why? It's because our talent for information processing seems somewhat modest. It is more "good effort" than "gold star." Echoing this sentiment, Dan Ariely's book, "Predictably Irrational," demonstrated that our cognitive slip-ups aren't just frequent but also repetitive and predictable.[4] This consistent irrationality hints that a hidden psychological principle is pulling the strings behind the scenes.

Because of this bounded rationality, we often go for the "good enough" option, instead of striving for the "absolute best," in most of our daily decision-making scenarios. "Satisficing," it's called—a linguistic blending of "satisfy" and "suffice."[5] For example, how would you pick a beer out of myriad brands available at a supermarket? Assessing each one's taste, color, alcohol, and price would be infeasible. So, we typically go for the beer that makes us say, "Yeah, that'll do." Thus, the mantra, "Good enough is the new perfect."

When you come down to it, we might compare rational judgment and bounded rationality as if they were members of a band. Each has a role to play there. Rational judgment is the bassist, steady and dependable, taking the lead when we have time

---

[3] On August 7, 2023, extracted and revised from https://www.readersdigest.ca/culture/70-funniest-jokes-readers-digest/.

[4] Ariely and Jones (2008).

[5] Simon (1955).

and important decisions to make. Bounded rationality, on the other hand, is the drummer, setting the tempo for quick decisions, the kind we need to make every day.

Before finishing this episode, let me put a bit of a spoiler for the following section—an interesting study conducted in a European supermarket.[6] When the store becomes crowded, what tempo of music would best assuage customer dissatisfaction resulting from overcrowding? Fast or slow? You might logically lean toward the gentle sway of slow-tempo music because it might soothe irritated shoppers. However, the study's finding surprisingly indicated that fast-tempo music proved more effective. Why, you wonder? Let me not spill all the beans here. Stay tuned to discover why this seemingly topsy-turvy result actually makes perfect sense with the cognitive bias caused by bounded rationality!

Owl of Minerva Behind the Scene

This chapter introduces you to an intriguing concept, *bounded rationality*, and some of the cognitive biases it brews. In Chap. 7, we dealt with the concept of cognitive miser, which is caused by the fact that humans have limited mental resources. While the previous chapter focused more on our brain's efficient allocation of limited cognitive energy, this chapter will focus more on the irrational aspect of our cognition brought about by human limitations.

Our story begins with Herbert A. Simon (Nobel laureate of 1978), who first introduced the concept of "bounded rationality,"[7] opening the gateway to behavioral decision theory. Afterward, in 1979, Daniel Kahneman (Nobel laureate of 2002) and Amos Tversky published their groundbreaking paper on prospect theory, which stirred the pot in the decision-making domain. And another entrant, Richard Thaler (Nobel laureate of 2017), came up with a concept called "mental accounting," adding another jewel to behavioral decision theory. With these heavyweight contributors, behavioral decision theory strutted onto the academic scene with panache. So now, let's start with those two intriguing human biases—prospect theory and mental accounting.

When Logic Flops: Prospect Theory

Kahneman and Tversky brought us the renowned *prospect theory*, which grapples with how people make decisions when faced with risk.[8] You might be familiar with the "utility maximization theory," the classical economic concept which assumes that decision-makers have access to all relevant information and rationally choose an action to maximize their utility under resource constraints. According to this theory,

[6] Knoeferle et al. (2017).

[7] Simon (1955).

[8] Kahneman and Tversky (1979).

people always make perfectly logical choices and pick the option with the highest absolute value. That is, it imagines us as flawless, logic-wielding computers. It's a bit off the mark, right?

On the other hand, prospect theory ushers us into a much-needed reality check and into the real-world messiness of how people actually think and decide. Imagine, in an ideal "Spock-approved," perfectly logical universe, answering a new mom's question, "Is it a boy or a girl?" with a mere "Yes."[9] That would be a perfectly logical answer. But in our wonderfully irrational world, flawless logic can sometimes make us feel very awkward. That's precisely what behavioral decision theory delves into: how we quirky humans muddle through decisions in this illogic-filled real world.

We want to highlight two concepts—loss aversion and reference point. *Loss aversion* is the idea that people are much more afraid of losses than they are excited about gains. Suppose you happen upon a $100 bill. That causes a mini-happy moment, right? But what if later, that same $100 bill suddenly vanishes from your wallet? The sour taste of that loss would make your earlier happiness seem flat. Look at Fig. 8.2, a famous prospect theory curve. The slide is steeper on the side of losses. The pain of loss overshadows the pleasure of gain, even though the actual amount of the gain and loss are identical, both $100. This is what loss aversion is all about. So, for example, if the genie grants you one wish, but with the condition that your enemy will get two times more, what will be your choice? Opting for 120/80 blood pressure, perhaps?[10] It's to avoid the enemy's gain, which will feel like our personal double whammy. Life's quirky that way, isn't it?

Now, let's put the spotlight on another key concept—the *reference point*. To illustrate a common example, please refer to the promotional material in Fig. 8.3. Promotional materials highlighting discounts invariably showcase the original price. It is because the original price serves as a benchmark, that is, a reference point, making the discounted price appear significantly more attractive.

Similarly, when making decisions, people don't think in absolute terms. Instead, they make decisions based on a certain reference point, which acts like a personal "starting line" (a personal zero point). For instance, if you're sitting on a stash of $1000, and along comes a windfall of $400, you'll feel good because you're better off compared to your starting line of $1000. But if you had $2000 and then lost $400, you would feel bad, even though you still have more money than in the first case.

Therefore, here's the interesting bit. The reference point isn't one-size-fits-all. It shifts based on each person's situation. That's why it is called a "personal" zero point. Let's apply it to a daily emotional experience. The fortune cookie message saying, "You will soon be reunited with a good friend," usually feels like an emotional gain. Still, it can become the misfortune cookie if you've just come back from a dear friend's funeral.[11] It's all about what your emotion's reference point is at the moment.

---

[9] On August 7, 2023, extracted and revised from https://upjoke.com/logic-jokes.

[10] On August 7, 2023, extracted and revised from https://upjoke.com/enemy-jokes.

[11] On August 8, 2023, extracted and revised from https://www.readersdigest.ca/culture/70-funniest-jokes-readers-digest/.

Fig. 8.2 Prospect theory curve (created by Jeongmin Lee, 2023, Author's Collection)

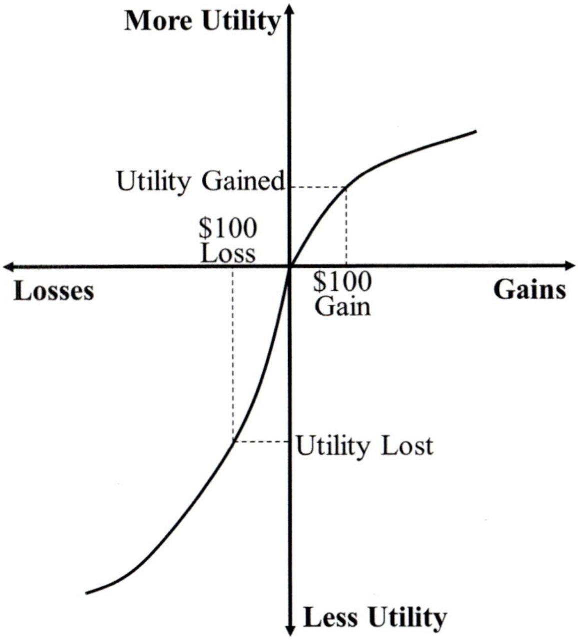

Fig. 8.3 IKEA's promotional material highlighting discount (created by Jeongmin Lee, 2024, Author's Collection)

So, according to prospect theory, we're not just calculators tallying up numbers to determine the final outcome. Instead, we're intricate, emotional beings who react to our "perceived" gains and losses, which are largely swayed by the dynamic duo of loss aversion and reference point.

Dividing Dollars: Mental Accounting

Next on the stage, we have *mental accounting* by Richard Thaler.[12] Essentially, this is our mind's version of homegrown bank accounts: we tend to divvy up our money into different "accounts" in our mind, like an "education fund," "grocery fund," "entertainment fund," or a "travel fund." In other words, we don't always consider our money as one big pool, free to reach in for any good reason. Instead, we're more like librarians, categorizing our money into distinct sections, treating each section with its own set of rules.

Let's consider a real-life example. Right after the COVID-19 pandemic, international travel didn't just bounce back. It did a full-on pole vault, leading to issues of over-tourism in Europe. This raises the question: why did so many people travel abroad at once even though the world was in a global economic downturn and travel expenses were higher than usual? First off, it can be attributed to "revenge consumption" syndrome, a trend where individuals indulged in activities they had abstained from during three years of the pandemic. And secondly? Too much savings have accumulated in the "mental account" for overseas travel, which they couldn't spend during the pandemic. So, people unconsciously thought they had enough money to splurge. That's the effect of mental accounting.

Another intriguing assertion of mental accounting that designers and marketers can't afford to ignore is the concept of *integrating losses and segregating gains*. It is a nifty application of loss aversion from prospect theory. This catchy concept suggests that humans treat gains and losses in different accounts in their heads, and thinking of gains separately adds more positive utility, while lumping together losses results in less negative utility.

To make it clearer, let's revisit the prospect theory curve in Fig. 8.2. Imagine getting a $100 gift, and you feel a happiness level of, let's say 10 units. The graph shows that the first $50 gives you 7 units of happiness, and the second $50 gives you only 3 units, making it a total of 10 units of happiness. This is what happens if the $100 gift is lumped together. However, suppose you're given two separate $50 gifts, one on Monday and another on Wednesday. In that case, your total happiness quota is 14 units (7 + 7), not 10, because these two gifts are treated as two separate instances of $50 each. We seem to enjoy a slow drip of happiness over time more than a one-time splash.

---

[12] Thaler (1985, 1999).

Let's talk about the downer side of things. Suppose you're hit with a $100 loss, and your sadness scale shoots to grim −20 units. Again, the first $50 loss will give you −14 units, and the second $50 will give you −6 units if lumped together. However, if they are treated as two separate losses, then the total sadness scale would be −28 units (−14 and −14), not −20. At the end of the day, we're still talking about a total loss of $100, but it stings more because it smacked you twice, adding an extra layer of "ouch." So, losses hurt less if we lose it all at once instead of little by little.

None of these makes sense in the cut-and-dry world of classical economics. $100 is $100, no matter how you gain or lose it. But because of the psychological quirks of humans, our feelings and behaviors can be affected by "how" the money is gained or lost.

Now, here is a good design example applying this psychological phenomenon. IKEA has cleverly woven it into the very fabric of its store design. Graphic materials explaining psychological gains such as member benefits, 365-day return service, and lower prices are separated and placed in various spots throughout the store (gains dispersed separately). On the other hand, those that can be felt as psychological loss are grouped together, waiting for you at the self-serve zone, located at the end of the IKEA journey (losses lumped together). These include reminders about why self-assembly is necessary, why there are not many guide staff in the store, why consumers need to take their own delivery, etc. So, IKEA gives a masterclass about how the human brain interacts with potential gains and losses.

As we can see in mental accounting and its fascinating psychological twists, we're not just rational, number-crunching machines. Far from it! Our brains diligently sort dollars into mental jars labeled for various spending purposes and nudge us to spend the money based on this whimsical ledger, not just our bank balance. Therefore, real-world economics isn't just dollars and cents; it's a rollercoaster of the curious, delightfully irrational human psyche.

Ever-powerful First Impression: Anchoring Bias

Let's turn our attention to another quirky side of bounded rationality—the ever-powerful "first impression." We humans tend to put more importance on the first information we encounter, a trait that is convenient but occasionally leads to irrational judgments.

The first stop on this aspect is the mental heavyweight champion known as the *anchoring bias*. This bias prompts us to place an excessive emphasis on the first piece of information we receive about a particular subject, often inhibiting us from appraising it objectively.

Imagine our mind as a ship floating on a sea of information. The first bit of information we receive becomes an anchor thrown into the water. Now, just as a ship is limited by the length of the anchor chain, our understanding of any further information is tethered and influenced by this first anchor of knowledge. So, even if we aspire to cruise the ocean of knowledge, we often find ourselves sailing in circles around this anchor of the first information.

Two behavioral economists, Tversky and Kahneman, brilliantly illustrated this effect through an insightful experiment.[13] Participants were first asked to spin a roulette wheel and take note of the outcome. Then, the subjects were asked whether there were more or fewer countries in Africa than the number they received. Those who got a 10 on the roulette wheel guessed around 25 countries, while those who scored 65 estimated 45 countries. Even though the initial outcome was purely random, this had an effect on the final guess! This result demonstrates the potency of the initial information in setting an "anchor" and swaying our judgments.

The second stop regarding the powerful effect of the first information is the *9-ending effect* and the *left-digit effect*. These are cognitive biases regarding the perception of prices, which can be interpreted under the anchoring bias. Consumers perceive prices ending in the numeral 9 (such as $49.99 or $99.99) as considerably lower than their round figure equivalents (like $50 or $100) despite the actual difference being a mere cent. That's the "9-ending effect." It generates the illusion of a more attractive deal. You may think, "We can't be fooled that easily." Nonetheless, the research conducted by Schindler and Kibarian proved that sales escalated by approximately 8% when the retailer used the catalog with 9-ending prices (e.g., $39.99) compared to the catalog with all prices ending in double zeroes (e.g., $40.00).[14]

This 9-ending effect is intricately linked to the "left-digit effect"[15]: humans tend to fixate on the leftmost digit (the first digit) and often overlook the rest when interpreting numerical values. So, when we come across a price like $199.99, we instinctively feel it's more in the "one-hundred-and-something" category than knocking on the door of $200. It's as if our brain has developed a special fondness for the first digit, sidelining the ones that follow. Now, if you can connect the dots, you might see how this bias can be linked to the anchoring bias: the initial impression set by the first digit tends to become an anchor and dictate the overall perception of the entire price.

Marketers and retailers have been in on this secret for ages and are not shy about using it. Anyway, bargaining, in essence, is making customers buy things they didn't know they wanted, at prices they can't resist.[16] Thanks to our brain's knack for this optical illusion regarding price perception, marketers can create a little more illusion of a better bargain. So, if you see a price like $199.99 and think, "Wow, what a deal!" take a moment and consider your brain's quirky tunnel vision at work.

---

[13] Tversky and Kahneman (1974).

[14] Schindler and Kibarian (1996).

[15] Thomas and Morwitz (2005).

[16] On August 8, 2023, extracted and revised from https://upjoke.com/bargain-jokes.

Fig. 8.4 Apple Fifth Avenue store, 2006, New York, USA (Marco Rubino/Shutterstock)

This anchoring bias finds a way into all corners of our lives, affecting our financial decisions or shaping our perceptions of people—you name it! Although, at times, the anchor may be spot-on, the over-reliance on this fragmentary information can often lead us down the path of irrational decision-making.

But there can be a twist in the tale. Awareness of this bias can also be our secret weapon, allowing us to play the game rather than be played by it. Consider, for instance, the charmingly named "sandwich method of criticism": when you deliver a critique, you'd better start and end with compliments, sandwiching the critique in the middle. Clever, right? The initial praise sets an anchor of a positive tone, making any following criticism seem more digestible and less likely to ruffle feathers, with no resentment or defensiveness. It's the perfect example of the wise saying, "It's not what you say but how you say it." Here, we see that even human foibles can be dressed up and marched out as strengths when cleverly employed.

Now, let's talk about the design principle related to the effect of the first impression. Ever thought about why you judged a book by its cover or why a brand store's display window is so captivating? The simple answer lies in the effect of the *entry point*.[17] It is a part of the design where the customer's attention is first captured and, thus, creates the anchoring bias. The first impression given by the entry point acts as the tour guide for our entire experience that follows. For example, imagine visiting a brand's flagship store. The façade is your entry point. If it's engaging, you're in for a treat, feeling the tone of being a VIP. Take a peek at Fig. 8.4, the Apple Fifth Avenue in New York, a masterclass example of how first impressions can usher the customers into the store and orchestrate the whole symphony of their experiences.

[17] Lidwell et al. (2010).

Fig. 8.5 Incheon International Airport, South Korea (photographed by Jeongmin Lee, 2023, Author's Collection)

Another important example of an entry point is the destination airport. When traveling to a foreign country, the first impression of that country is formed at the airport. Namely, the airport is like the appetizer to a grand feast. An impression of a clean, efficient, and beautiful airport can forge an anchoring effect for the whole trip, especially when the immigration officers are friendly! So, it is very important for countries to invest in the facilities and service quality of their airports. For instance, the Incheon Airport (Fig. 8.5) has performed this role well for South Korea and has been given numerous awards as the best-managed airport in the world.

So, what can we take away from our dive into the anchoring bias? Simply put, first impressions are like superglue for our brains. Whether it's fair or not, our minds love to latch onto that initial bit of info. But here's the kicker: once we know about this mental sticky tape, we can use it to our advantage. In the world of design, this means crafting entry points that captivate and anchor positively. Let's remember that our brains might love first impressions, but we're the ones in charge of them.

Other Cognitive Situations Forging Irrational Behaviors

Moving forward, let's delve into more cognitive situations that cause a burden or misunderstanding in our brains and, as a result, hinder us from making rational judgments and behaviors.

First on the list is the *choice overload effect*.[18] Picture this: you're standing in the supermarket aisle, staring at a sea of toothpaste brands, or maybe you're online, scrolling through hundreds of shoe options. There's way too much of it. This is where we're hit with the *choice overload* situation.

Why does this situation happen? As consumers, we want to make the perfect choice, getting the most bang for our buck. In addition, we also want to relish the freedom to choose that comes with a wide array of alternatives. However, there can be

[18] Chernev et al. (2015).

a tug-of-war between these two wishes because when we are overwhelmed by a wide array of options, we often end up making less-than-stellar choices, and dissatisfaction follows. This is none other than the "choice overload effect." Maybe having as many options as possible isn't such a luxury after all. Remember when TV only had three nationwide channels? Now, we have over 200 channels, and there's still nothing on.[19] Turns out, we might be a bit choice-choked rather than choice-blessed.

Because of the choice overload effect, the decision process of choosing the *satisficing* option also comes into play. This concept, coined by Herbert A. Simon, is not about securing the best choice; it's more about grabbing the first acceptable option and running with it. Namely, it is the choice that is good enough to get the job done. This kind of decision behavior can be adopted with the choice of everyday little items.

Satisficing choice happens because when we're lost in a jungle of choice overload, our brains tend to take some shortcuts. That is, as explained in Chap. 7, our brain uses heuristic processing in this situation. For example, you might pick the most popular brand because, well, a lot of people can't be wrong. Or, you go for the item with the lowest price tag—after all, who doesn't love a good bargain? They may not be the best possible option, but it is nonetheless "good enough." So, here's a comforting reminder: it's okay not to aim for perfection with every little decision. Sometimes, "good enough" is another form of being perfect.

Let's turn the spotlight from consumers to marketers. Believe it or not, they're caught in the same pickle with choice overload. Various strategies have been adopted to tackle this issue. One such strategy is providing limited alternatives, as exemplified by the wholesale corporation, Costco. Instead of offering a confusing maze of options, they put forth a curated selection of goods.

Another strategy to lessen the negative effect of choice overload is simplifying consumers' decision-making process, thus minimizing their efforts to shop. As an example, we have Stitch Fix, the online fashion trailblazer. Its design service provides a personal stylist who curates a tailored selection of fashion items based on the customer's preference, style, size, and budget (Fig. 8.6). For a $20 styling fee per Fix order (the price as of Jan 2024), the customer receives a personalized box (or a "fix," as they call it) containing five carefully chosen pieces. And the best part? If something doesn't tickle your fancy, you can return it without extra charges.

Choice overload in consumerism is a peculiarly modern phenomenon. It is like a buffet with too many food options—delightful to gaze upon but perhaps a tad overwhelming to indulge all. Yet, no worries, for businesses, especially those in retailing, are ever so thoughtfully offering diet plans for this burdensome luxury. In fact, curation would be welcomed in any category where there is choice overload.

The second cognitive situation forging irrational behaviors is the much-feared *post-purchase dissonance*. It also happens because of the peculiar plight of modern consumers—so many shiny goodies, so little time to choose just one. Consumers,

[19] On August 8, 2023, suggested by ChatGPT-4.

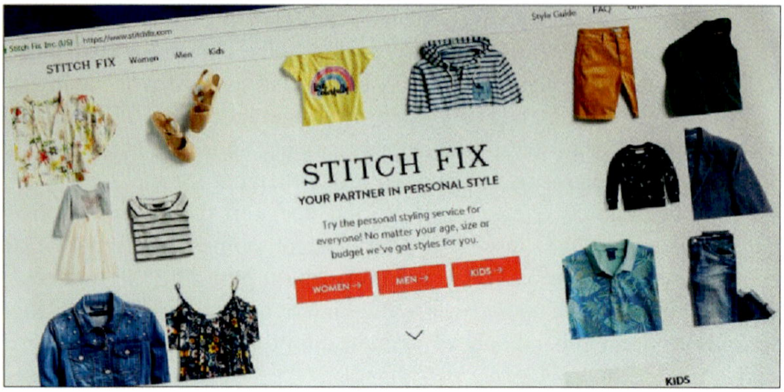

Fig. 8.6 Stitch Fix (sjscreens/Alamy Stock Photo)

when presented with an array of options, should select one alternative over others. Consequently, this selection often triggers doubts about their decision—"Did I really make the best choice, or is this just another silver medal in my shopping Olympics?" This psychological discomfort is "post-purchase dissonance."[20]

Unlike the situations where customers perform "satisficing" decision-making with heuristic processing, there are some situations when they use systematic processing, and these situations can cause post-purchase dissonance. Marketers and designers need to know the conditions that can prompt it and devise ways to lessen it. It usually happens when the purchase carries a heavy price tag, when the transaction is difficult to undo, or when an important decision is made by oneself.

Let's up the ante and think about buying a car, an acquisition that typically carries significant weight. Because the purchase is expensive, important, and difficult to undo, you invest time, emotion, and effort. But despite careful consideration and agonizing decision-making, you still can't shake off that little voice questioning whether you've made the optimal choice, the voice causing "post-purchase dissonance." It often compels consumers to invest extra effort into seeking further information about the product they have already purchased, which is quite an irrational behavior, often landing us in the swamp of unnecessary remorse.

Not only for customers but also for businesses, post-purchase dissonance is less than desirable. So, marketers devise some nifty ways to smooth over it. One common strategy is the comforting blanket of return and warranty policies. For example, Hyundai Motor Company achieved great success in the US market by offering a 10-year warranty, underscored by various advertising designs with the slogan, "America's best warranty" (Fig. 8.7).

Then, there's another approach of offering professional guidance so customers don't feel like navigating the shopping maze alone and making important decisions by themselves. Well-prepared staff in Apple stores exemplify this approach, ready and willing to dispel any clouds of confusion in the tech wonderland. And let's not

[20] Shani and Zeelenberg (2007).

Fig. 8.7 Hyundai Motors: America's best warranty ad (Patti McConville/Alamy Stock Photo)

forget still another strategy, "reinforcement advertising," which reaffirms the merits of the chosen product, thus assuaging any lingering doubts in the consumer's mind. It's intended to pat you on the back and tell you what a good job you've done with your choice. For instance, this could be a well-designed flyer tucked into the product packaging, highlighting why your purchase was a superstar choice.

Third on the list of cognitive situations that forge irrational behaviors is the enthralling *misattribution of arousal*. This idea addresses how individuals can often misinterpret the cause of heightened physical stimulation.

Imagine you're working out, your heart is racing, and your pulse is quickening—you're in a state of physiological arousal. Now, you run into someone during this heart-pounding moment. Your brain, not always the best at detective work, might connect your aroused state not to the workout but to this unsuspecting individual. With this wayward misattribution, your perception of that person can be twisted, and behaviors tweaked.

Ingenious research proves this effect.[21] An experiment was conducted on two different bridges—one on the towering suspension bridge and another on the low and safe one. Our unsuspecting males, aged between 18 and 35, were crossing these bridges when halfway across, they ran into a female assistant conducting a survey.

---

[21] Dutton and Aron (1974).

But here's where the actual experiment begins. After they finished the survey, she gave them her number, saying they could ring her if they wanted to know more about the experiment.

The result was thrilling. The rate of the suspension bridge-crossers who called her was significantly higher compared to the safe bridge-crosser. Why? Males from the suspension bridge unconsciously interpreted their physical conditions, like sweaty hands or a faster heartbeat, as their feeling of attraction to the female assistant. It is now called the *suspension bridge effect*.

Then, here's a nifty tip for a successful date, straight from the playbook of this theory—if you want to make someone feel attracted to you, swap the candle-lit dinner at a cozy restaurant for a thrill-packed amusement park or an adrenaline-filled sports event. Really! The pulse-pounding excitement and stimulated body conditions followed by those exhilarating activities might get misread as a romantic attraction for you!

Now, let's shuffle back to the earlier episode of this chapter, where we had the supermarket-music experiment and the counterintuitive result. When the store is in the optimal level of congestion (not too crowded, not too empty), slow-tempo music typically drives the highest sales, gently coaxing customers to stay longer and fill up their carts. But when the store is brimming with shoppers, the slow tunes aren't cutting it anymore. Instead, fast-tempo music was found to be more effective in boosting sales.[22]

The misattribution of arousal theory can make this brain-boggling result perfect sense. In a crowded environment, customers might experience physiological arousal, such as elevated heart rates and heightened irritability. In the midst of this arousal which might make them leave the store early, if there's fast-tempo music thumping in the background, their brain could misplace the blame and think, "Hey, this quickening heartbeat, this rush of adrenaline, it's the music, not this horde of shoppers around me." Oddly enough, this mental mix-up lessens their negative attitudes toward the crowded store. Surprising, yet somehow recognizable result, isn't it?

So, regarding environmental design, the pearl of wisdom hiding in this quirky finding is pretty nifty: when faced with a less-than-ideal situation that can't be swiftly dealt with, why not add a dash of misdirection? Introduce some environmental elements that customers can "blame" for their discomfort. It can be a win–win strategy anyway, providing a psychological buffer for customers' discomfort, thus maintaining a positive experience despite less-than-ideal conditions.

More Design Insights Added to the Scene

Before we end our journey into the concept of bounded rationality, let's explore one more vital cognitive weakness of mortal humans—*cognitive errors*. Here's the humbling truth: "To err is human." No matter how many times we double-check,

[22] Knoeferle et al. (2017).

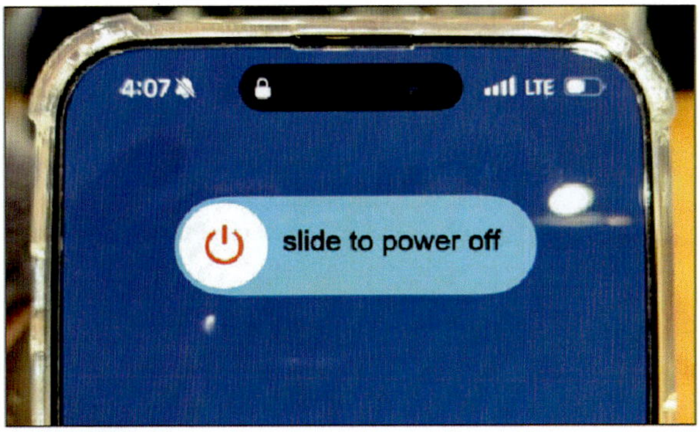

Fig. 8.8 iPhone's power off (photographed by Jeongmin Lee, 2023, Author's Collection)

triple-check, or quadruple-check, we're bound to slip up sometimes. That is an inherent cognitive trait of human beings. Thus, while the *cognitive error theory* might not be directly related to the concept of bounded rationality, it still provides further insights into it.

Designers must bear this human limitation in mind, and with this fact, it is the designer's responsibility to anticipate potential errors in their designs and devise countermeasures—that is, *error-proofing strategies*. Designers need to play the role of a gentle parent, always expecting a bit of clumsiness from their users and cushioning their falls.

In the design world, this approach has a feel-good name—*forgiveness*. This design principle implies that a good design doesn't scold us for our inevitable human errors. Instead, it either prevents them or aids us in cleaning up the mess. These are called the error-prevention and error-recovery strategies, respectively. *Error-prevention strategies* avert user mistakes before they occur, whereas *error-recovery strategies* restore an errored situation back to its original state.

Let's look into some examples of the error-prevention strategy. Think of our handy smartphone. To prevent accidental shutdown, smartphones are designed to follow a two-step process—first, a long press on the power button, then a swipe on the screen (Fig. 8.8). A child-proof medicine bottle is another classic example. You must push and turn simultaneously—a complex process that keeps the medicine away from tiny, curious hands.

Let's check applications of the error-recovery strategy, too, which works like an eraser, always ready to rub out your mistakes.[23] Once, there was a time when we trashed an important file on our computer, only to gasp when we realized our mistake. No more those panic moments with the Recycle Bin feature in Windows or Mac. It's like having a mini-time machine on your computer! IKEA stores also utilize this strategy with their 365-day return policy. You see its promo materials everywhere you turn in the store (Fig. 8.9). This design element acts like a friendly shop assistant

[23] On July 6, 2023, suggested by ChatGPT-4.

Fig. 8.9 IKEA: 365 days return policy promo design (photographed by Jeongmin Lee, 2020, Author's Collection)

whispering, "Don't worry, if you change your mind, we've got you covered." This tactic reassures customers, prompting them to fill up their carts without a second thought.

All these error-proofing strategies bring confidence to users, who can then interact with a design without fearing irreversible errors. It's a hidden force that can transform potentially stressful experiences into smooth, user-friendly encounters.

There you have it! We've journeyed the whimsical paths of "bounded rationality," influencing our decision-making process. The cognitive biases we've examined thus far can sometimes run counter to rational, objective judgments and behaviors. Even our own physiological responses can lead us astray. However, remember the sandwich method of criticism discussed earlier? We can turn these human frailties into useful tools. The more we learn about these biases, the better we can harness their power, turning them into our allies. So, as we wrap up our exploration, let's keep it in mind: knowledge truly is power. And using that knowledge wisely? That's pure wisdom. Therefore, while our cognitive processes might be complex and sometimes comical, understanding them can help us become savvy consumers and discerning decision-makers. Now, that's a happy ending, don't you think?

References

Ariely, D., & Jones, S. (2008). *Predictably irrational.* HarperCollins.

Chernev, A., Böckenholt, U., & Goodman, J. (2015). Choice overload: A conceptual review and meta-analysis. *Journal of Consumer Psychology, 25*(2), 333–358.

Dutton, D. G., & Aron, A. P. (1974). Some evidence for heightened sexual attraction under conditions of high anxiety. *Journal of Personality and Social Psychology, 30*(4), 510–517.

Kahneman, D., & Tversky, A. (1979). Prospect theory: An analysis of decision under risk. *Econometrica, 47*(4), 263–291.

Knoeferle, K. M., Paus, V. C., & Vossen, A. (2017). An upbeat crowd: Fast in-store music alleviates negative effects of high social density on customers' spending. *Journal of Retailing, 93*(4), 541–549.

Lidwell, W., Holden, K., & Butler, J. (2010). *Universal principles of design: 125 ways to enhance usability, influence perception, increase appeal, make better design decisions, and teach through design.* Rockport Publishers.

Schindler, R. M., & Kibarian, T. M. (1996). Increased consumer sales response though use of 99-ending prices. *Journal of Retailing, 72*(2), 187–199.

Shani, Y., & Zeelenberg, M. (2007). When and why do we want to know? How experienced regret promotes post-decision information search. *Journal of Behavioral Decision Making, 20*(3), 207–222.

Simon, H. (1955). A behavioral model of rational choice. *Quarterly Journal of Economics, 69*(1), 99–118.

Thaler, R. (1985). Mental accounting and consumer choice. *Marketing Science, 4*(3), 199–214.

Thaler, R. (1999). Mental accounting matters. *Journal of Behavioral Decision Making, 12*(3), 183–206.

Thomas, M., & Morwitz, V. (2005). Penny wise and pound foolish: The left-digit effect in price cognition. *Journal of Consumer Research, 32*(1), 54–64.

Tversky, A., & Kahneman, D. (1974). Judgment under uncertainty: Heuristics and biases. *Science, 185*(4157), 1124–1131.

Chapter 9
Eyes and Brain See Things Differently: Optical Illusions

Ever heard the saying, "Seeing is believing"? But what if seeing is also deceiving? As explained in the previous chapters, humans have limited cognitive energy and are constrained by bounded rationality. This cognitive limitation affects not only our decision-making processes but also how we perceive what's right in front of our eyes.

When it comes to what we see, we humans aren't quite the cold, logical processors. Rather than precisely processing visual information as our eyes receive it, our brains interpret and, at times, distort it. In other words, instead of acting like flawless cameras capturing a scene exactly as it appears, our brains are more like opinionated painters with their own interpretations, adding a dab of context here, a brushstroke of memory there, and occasionally producing something closer to abstract art rather than a realistic one. In short, the eyes and brain can see the same visual stimuli in remarkably different ways.

Let's illustrate this with a tangible example. Take a peek at the Nintendo Switch logo in Fig. 9.1. The two halves of the logo remind us of two detachable controllers of the Nintendo Switch console. At first glance, it looks like those two parts are the same in size. But the white part is actually a touch slimmer. It is to correct the optical illusion where a bright-colored shape appears slightly larger than a dark-colored one. So, to keep things in visual balance for human eyes, the white part has a subtle trim. If it were the same size as its darker (red) counterpart, it might appear larger. Check it with Fig. 9.2, which shows the logo design without optical correction. It's a little bit of design magic, making sure both halves of the logo appear equal to our all-too-easily tricked eyes. This sophisticated alteration is practiced in the professional design world to achieve the desired visual effect, ensuring that what we see feels just right.

The abovementioned phenomenon is a good example of an "optical illusion." This term refers to a perceptual anomaly where we see things differently from their actual nature. What's behind this visual shenanigan? The optical illusion occurs because our brains aren't just passive spectators. They're more like dynamic filmmakers: they direct, edit, and sometimes even rewrite the script. That is, to make sense of what we

© The Author(s), under exclusive license to Springer Nature Singapore Pte Ltd. 2024

J. Lee et al., *The Psychology Behind Design*,
https://doi.org/10.1007/978-981-97-3426-9_9

Fig. 9.1 Nintendo Switch logo (photographed by Jeongmin Lee, 2023, Author's Collection)

Fig. 9.2 Nintendo Switch logo without optical correction (created by Jeongmin Lee, 2023, Author's Collection)

see and to construct a coherent understanding from it, our brains constantly analyze and interpret visual information. To do this effectively, it relies on prior knowledge, context, and various other cues. However, this intricate process can sometimes result in misinterpretations, giving rise to optical illusions.

Do you know what the real kicker is? These optical illusions persist even when we are consciously aware that our perception is wrong. We cannot correct them. So, let's consider that optical illusions are more like plot twists in the storytelling of what we see—surprising, entertaining, and persistently part of our tale, even when we're wise to their tricks.

When the term "optical illusion" was mentioned above, many of you might have immediately thought of your experiences with the "trick eye museum," like the one in Fig. 9.3. Here, two-dimensional walls showcase a three-dimensional illusion using the "trompe l'oeil" technique, a French term translating to "deceive the eye."

Fig. 9.3 Trick Eye Museum, Busan, South Korea (photographed by Jeongmin Lee, 2022, Author's Collection)

Trompe l'oeil is a skillful artistic technique that creates hyper-realistic imagery in 3D style—no need for special glasses. That is, they craft paintings so convincing that you might reach out to snatch an apple or try to step into a painted room. This technique has been frequently employed in murals, paintings, interior designs, and even in advertising campaigns (as in Fig. 9.4) to captivate and deceive the observer's eye.

To highlight the charm of trompe l'oeil, let's turn the pages back to a legendary artistic duel between two ancient painters, Zeuxis and Parrhasius. Zeuxis, they say, painted grapes so convincingly vivid that birds fluttered down to peck at them. Not to be overshadowed, Parrhasius crafted a curtain that was so astonishingly lifelike that Zeuxis reached out to pull it back, expecting to reveal a hidden masterpiece behind it. In this ancient art-world showdown, Parrhasius wore the victor's laurel. This tale, as told by the Roman author Pliny the Elder in his "Natural History," might be a more delightful legend than rigid fact, but it's a captivating story nonetheless.[1]

Trompe l'oeil is not just a brush-wielding marvel but also a playful reminder of the core idea regarding optical illusions—seeing isn't quite the same as believing. And rest assured, trompe l'oeil is just the opening act in the grand performance of optical illusions that designers deftly weave into their creations. Ready to embark on

[1] Wade and Hughes (1999).

Fig. 9.4 Europcar ad (Robert vant Hoenderdaal/Alamy Stock Photo)

this illusion-filled expedition? Keep your eyes wide open! It promises to be a journey that twirls your perspective and teases your senses, having you do double-takes. You won't believe what you will see.

Owl of Minerva Behind the Scene

Optical illusions are diverse phenomena, spanning physical, physiological, and cognitive ones.[2] But here, we will focus on cognitive illusions because they are more intimately tied to design works.

In the world of cognitive illusions, there are four main types—fiction illusions, ambiguous illusions, impossible object illusions, and distorting illusions. Let's explore them one by one.

Fiction Illusions

Our first exploration of cognitive illusions introduces us to *fiction illusions*, also known as *illusory contours*.[3] Here, our brain perceives contours that are not present in the physical stimulus. For example, take a look at Fig. 9.5. Here, while there's no actual triangle drawn, people can perceive a white, upward-pointing triangle. Our brain, being the crafty artist it is, finishes the incomplete sides, thanks to the clever placement of the other shapes. That is, our brain tries to fill in missing information if necessary to create a coherent interpretation and, thus, a complete image.

---

[2] Gregory (1968).

[3] Zeki (1996).

Fig. 9.5 Fiction illusion: Kanizsa Triangle (created by Jeongmin Lee, 2023, Author's Collection)

Therefore, you can imagine the brain as Sherlock Holmes, piecing together clues to figure out the entire story—in the case of this illusion, to infer what the complete picture must be like and subsequently render the "solved" picture. With the Kanizsa triangle, it's as if the brain is saying, "Judging by these bits and pieces, there's definitely a triangle lurking here."

The design world adores this illusion, using it to craft engaging designs that invite viewers to fill in the gaps and see the complete picture. For example, the design in Fig. 9.6 presents only one person. Still, we can spot the presence of another ghostly person, sketched out by illusory contours.

The fascinating world of fiction illusions showcases our mind's remarkable ability to fill in blanks and create wholes from fragments. This clever trick of the mind is a testament to our brain's incredible interpretative powers. Whether in art or everyday life, these illusions remind us that sometimes, seeing is not just believing but also creating.

Ambiguous Illusions

Our second expedition of cognitive illusions introduces us to *ambiguous illusions*.[4] It happens when the image provides more than one possible interpretation. Look at the famous Rubin's vase in Fig. 9.7. You're going to say, "It's a vase… no, wait, it's two people staring at each other… hang on, it's a vase again!" Your brain may switch back and forth between these two equally competent players, much like a perceptual tug-of-war.

[4] Leopold et al. (2002).

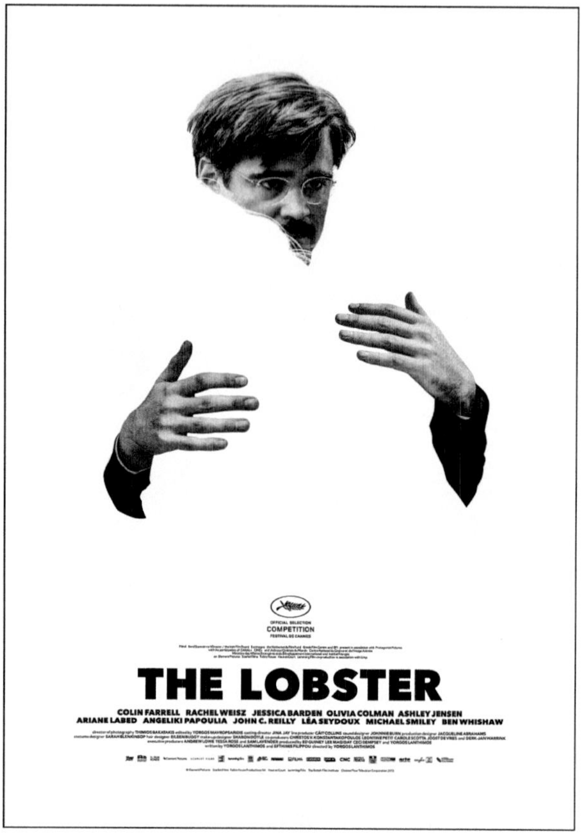

Fig. 9.6 "The Lobster" poster design (BFA/Alamy Stock Photo)

Fig. 9.7 Ambiguous illusion: Rubin's vase (created by Jeongmin Lee, 2023, Author's Collection)

Fig. 9.8 Pittsburgh Zoo and PPG Aquarium logo (Woodsnorth Photography/ Alamy Stock Photo)

What underlies this playful illusion? Again, it happens because our brain is like an over-eager detective, always on the hunt for clues to piece together so that it can deduce a coherent and meaningful narrative. But sometimes, the story has a plot twist, like the case of an ambiguous illusion. That is, the brain can't make up its mind between more than one equally plausible version.

Artists and designers have long been in on this secret. Check out the logo design in Fig. 9.8. It plays a prankish game with your eyes, switching between a big tree and two animals facing each other. As such, ambiguous illusion not only imbues the design with an eye-catching quality but also makes the viewer spend more time looking at it because dual interpretation may take time to process. In addition, such a design can be a talked-about design, as viewers might debate whether it depicts one thing or the other.

Like fiction illusions, ambiguous illusions illustrate that seeing is not a passive process but an active one: our brain vigorously interprets what we see. And in this waltz of active perception, sometimes our brains have two left feet. A real-life example? A beginner driver might think of a note on his car, saying "Parking fine," as a compliment.[5]

Impossible Object Illusions

Our third expedition of cognitive illusions introduces us to *impossible object illusions*, sometimes called *paradox illusions*.[6] These are the brain teasers that foster the perception of a three-dimensional object in two-dimensional images, even though

[5] On August 30, 2023, extracted and revised from https://www.readersdigest.ca/culture/70-funniest-jokes-readers-digest/.

[6] The Eye's Mind (2007), Mishra (2018).

Fig. 9.9 Left—Impossible staircase/Right—Impossible triangle (Left: Iryna Kuznetsova/Shutterstock) (Right: PumpedVisuals/Shutterstock)

such an object cannot exist in the real three-dimensional world. Take, for instance, the impossible staircase or the impossible triangle in Fig. 9.9. At a quick glance, they look normal, right? But stare a little longer, and you'll scratch your head. See the impossible staircase. Instead of leading upward or downward, it loops back to the beginning so that a person can climb it forever and never get any higher. They play tricks on our brains by manipulating elements of perspective, lighting, and shading, which we are accustomed to in the real world, and that's why they seem plausible at first.

This illusion makes its mark in design, too. Think of a video game that might incorporate an illogical layout to construct an enigmatic room. They're puzzling and intriguing and keep players hooked. Also, in advertising, designers employ impossible shapes to make their works memorable. For example, the advertisement design for the Pepsodent toothbrush cleverly shows a toothbrush going through a hole of an impossible triangle, with the tagline saying "REACHES IMPOSSIBLE PLACES." It's like telling the story of an adept toothbrush on a mission in your mouth and its quest to battle plaque in those hard-to-reach areas. Thus, it playfully delivers its sales pitch: "In a world full of ordinary toothbrushes, here's one that goes the extra mile, reaching the nooks and crannies that others merely dream of."

In one of LEGO's ad campaigns, "Tower, Waterfall, Belvedere," you're greeted by a 2D image of a LEGO model that, at first glance, looks like a charming medieval castle with multiple levels, towers, and staircases. But the star of the show is a central "impossible staircase." This ad suggests that with LEGO blocks, one can create not only realistic models but also fantastical structures that challenge the mind and perception. The tagline "Create the impossible" is a call to action for builders to create wonders that defy conventional boundaries. It's LEGO's way of saying, "In our world, the sky's the limit, and even the seemingly impossible is just another project waiting for your touch."

As you can see, the world of impossible object illusions is a playful challenge to our perceptions, teasing the brain with what seems plausible but is, in fact, a cleverly crafted impossibility. These illusions invite us to question our assumptions and look beyond the obvious. And isn't that a bit like life itself? Often, what we initially perceive isn't the full story. We are on a quest to explore, discover, and maybe even create a bit of the impossible in our everyday lives. So, if you encounter something that defies logic, remember that it might be an invitation to think outside the box!

Distorting Illusions I: Length Illusions

Our fourth expedition of cognitive illusions introduces us to *distorting illusions*, also called *geometrical-optical illusions*. It's about distortions of various visual elements. Given the vast array of illusions falling under this category, we will organize them into six sub-categories—length, size, depth, curvature, position, and motion illusions. Each of them has a surprising scenery for our expedition.

The first stop within the domain of "distorting illusions" brings us to *length illusions*. Here, you'll find lines look longer or shorter than they actually are. This distortion arises due to the influence of other elements within the image or the specific manner in which the object is presented.

Firstly, there is the *Muller-Lyer illusion*.[7] Glance over at the left image of Fig. 9.10. Two lines have equal length but don't seem equal (check it with the right image of Fig. 9.10). It's due to those arrowheads they wear. One is wearing the arrowheads pointing outwards, looking shorter, while the other sports inward arrowheads, looking longer.

Volkswagen's ad for the new Caddy Maxi played with this classic optical illusion. Two straight, equal-length lines (each looking like a road) are placed front and center, side by side (like the ones in Fig. 9.11). One line ends with circles positioned outside, while the other line ends with circles positioned inside, reminiscent of the arrowheads in Fig. 9.10. The result? The line on the left seems to have stretched itself a bit longer than the one on the right.

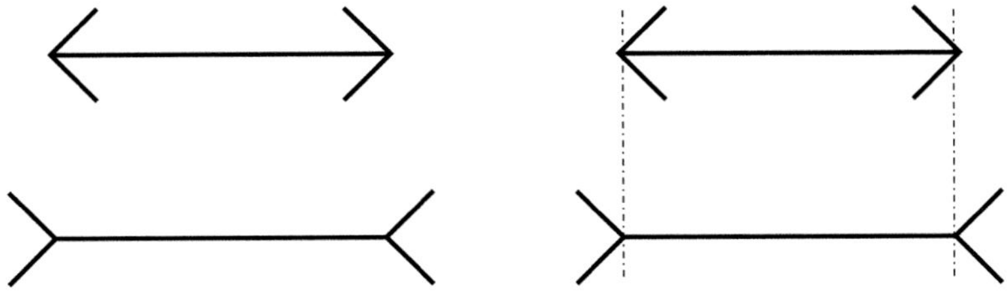

Fig. 9.10 Muller-Lyer illusion (created by Jeongmin Lee, 2023, Author's Collection)

[7] Tudusciuc and Nieder (2010).

Fig. 9.11 Road image with Muller-Lyer illusion (created by Jeongmin Lee, 2024, Author's Collection)

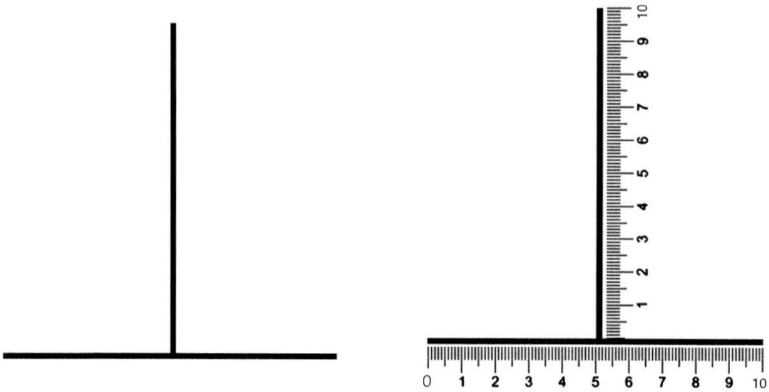

Fig. 9.12 Vertical-horizontal illusion (created by Jeongmin Lee, 2023, Author's Collection)

Volkswagen is implying here that driving the new Caddy Maxi is so comfy that it's like taking a delightful shortcut every time. It aligns with the tagline "The same distance feels shorter," hinting that the comfort and driving experience of the Caddy Maxi alters your perception of the journey's duration, much like the Müller-Lyer illusion alters your perception of line length. No need for long-winded explanations—the illusion does the talking.

Secondly, there is the *vertical-horizontal illusion*.[8] In the left image of Fig. 9.12, depicting two lines of identical length (check it with the right image), the vertical line seems to stretch taller than its horizontal twin.

Enter the realm of design, and we find a case-in-point—the Gateway Arch of St. Louis (Fig. 9.13). It has the same height and width, but you'd think it's stretching skyward more than sideward. Eye can believe it?[9] Check the right image. The ruler doesn't lie.

Designers, always the problem solvers, have their way around this illusion. When trying to make equal-looking height and width, they slightly reduce the height. Look at the McDonald's logo in Fig. 9.14. That "*M*" is subtly shorter in its height than its width, ensuring those golden arches look perfectly balanced. Check it with rulers in the right image.

---

[8] Künnapas (1955).

[9] On August 30, 2023, extracted and revised from https://punstoppable.com/illusion-puns.

Fig. 9.13 The Gateway Arch of St. Louis, USA (f11photo/Shutterstock)

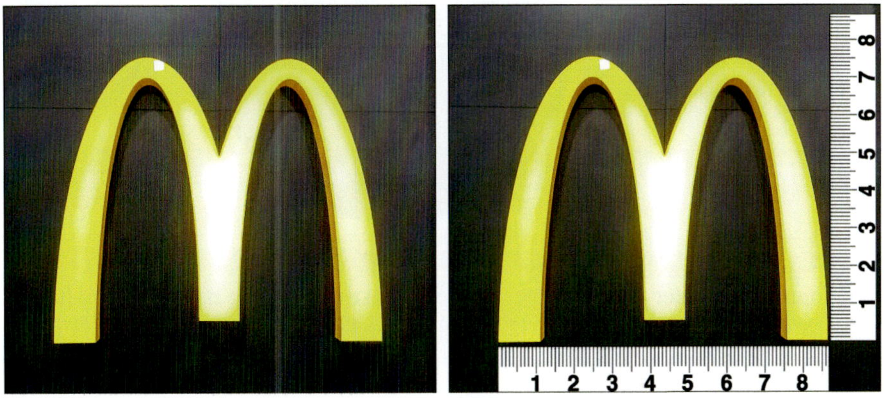

Fig. 9.14 McDonald's logo (photographed by Jeongmin Lee, 2024, Author's Collection)

Distorting Illusions II: Size Illusions

The second stop within the domain of distorting illusions brings us to *size illusions*. Here, an object appears larger or smaller than it actually is. Our brains, always trying to make sense of our surroundings, can get a little carried away with the contextual information, giving things a bit of a size makeover.

Firstly, there are the *Ebbinghaus illusion* and the *Delboeuf illusion,* which are pretty similar to each other. The Ebbinghaus illusion, depicted in Fig. 9.15, presents two identical circles in the center (gray circles). Yet, these gray circles appear to differ in size.[10] Think of it as the optical version of peer pressure. That is, when

[10] Roberts et al. (2005).

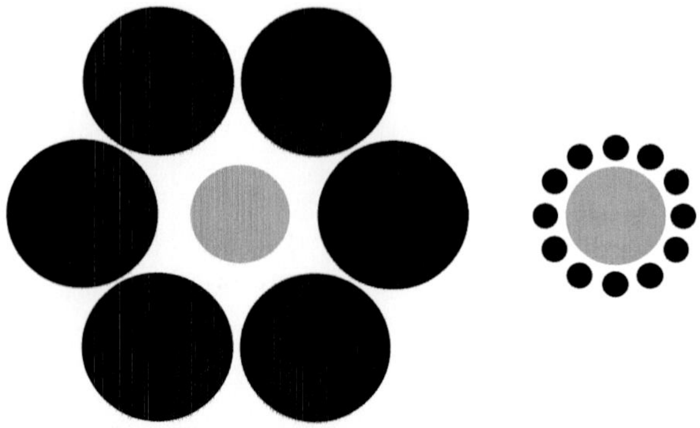

Fig. 9.15 Ebbinghaus illusion (created by Jeongmin Lee, 2023, Author's Collection)

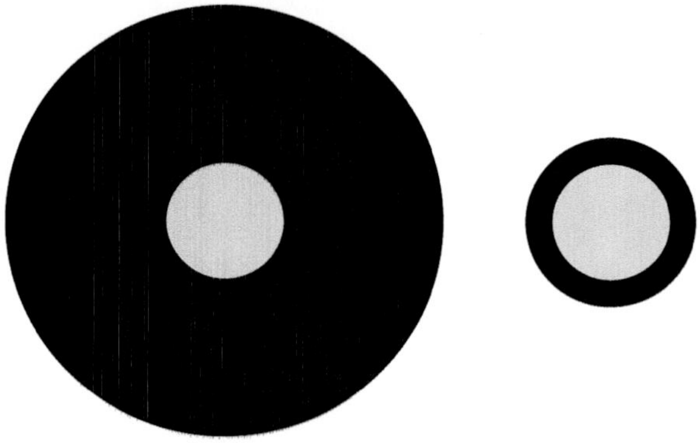

Fig. 9.16 Delboeuf illusion (created by Jeongmin Lee, 2023, Author's Collection)

its buddies are smaller (right image), it feels boastful, looking bigger than when its friends are larger and oppressive (left image). Social comparison and peer pressure seem unavoidable in human life, even in our perception.

Now, let's check the Delboeuf illusion,[11] showcased in Fig. 9.16. It's like the Ebbinghaus illusion's cousin. The central gray circle surrounded by a small black ring looks larger than the one surrounded by a large black ring, but they are the same size.

Bringing it to real life? Imagine hunting for the perfect sofa for your living room in a massive furniture store with a high ceiling. Amidst this expansive space, the sofa seems more politely sized than its actual size. Fast forward to getting it home, and surprise! Due to the smaller size of your living room space compared to the store space, the same sofa may seem considerably larger than you initially perceived. That's the magic of the context, playing tricks on your size gauging.

Volkswagen's ad design for the new Caddy Maxi utilized this illusion. The scene? There lies two petrol drops in the center, completely identical, each encased in a black ring (like the ones in Fig. 9.17). But here's the catch: on the left, the encircling black ring around the petrol drop is quite large, making the drop appear smaller, and

[11] Parrish et al. (2015).

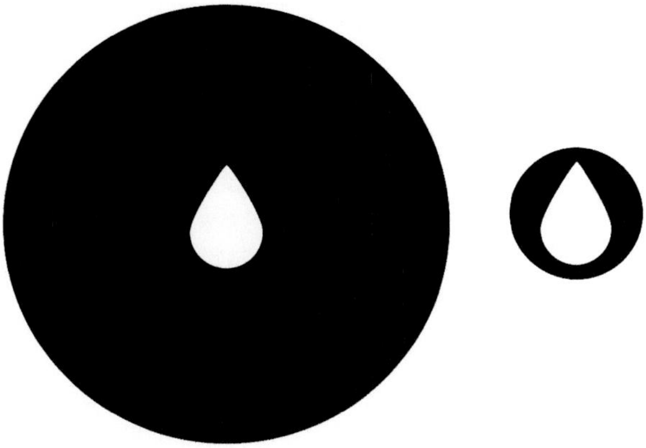

Fig. 9.17 Oil drop image with Delboeuf illusion (created by Jeongmin Lee, 2024, Author's Collection)

on the right, the encircling black ring is smaller, making the drop appear larger. With this, Volkswagen is whispering that in the world of the new Caddy Maxi, your fuel stretches further than you'd expect. Hence the tagline, "The same amount of fuel feels more." This ad suggests that just like the Delboeuf illusion plays tricks on size perception, the Caddy Maxi's impressive fuel economy makes your perception of fuel consumption do a double take.

Secondly, there is the *Ponzo illusion*.[12] Here, two identical objects, presented with distance cues, appear differing in size. It happens because of their perceived distance from us.

To illustrate, look at the left image of Fig. 9.18. The upper figure seems larger than the lower figure, but they are identical figures (see the right image with rulers). This effect happens because depth cues are added to the scene—in this case, the converging perspective lines of the road stretching out. Our brain, ever the storyteller, thinks the upper figure is further back and assumes he's taller since he occupies the same amount of visual space from afar.

The ad design in Fig. 9.19 also plays with similar converging perspective lines of the road. And we instantly perceive the faraway buildings as bigger than their actual size in the image. But check the right image of Fig. 9.19. Those seemingly gigantic buildings in the background are actually not so giant after all. They are much smaller than you thought they were at first glance.

Thirdly, there is the *moon illusion*.[13] Did you ever notice that the moon seems larger near the horizon than when positioned higher in the sky (Fig. 9.20)? But here's the fun part: it's all in our heads. The moon isn't changing its physical size, nor does it significantly change its distance from the Earth. You don't buy that? Take a picture of it near the horizon with a standard lens, and the camera will give you the real scoop. The moon appears much smaller in your photo than it does to your eyes because it records the moon's actual size rather than its perceived size.

[12] Prinzmetal et al. (2001).

[13] Kaufman and Kaufman (2000).

Fig. 9.18 Ponzo illusion (created by DALL.E, 2023, Author's Collection)

Fig. 9.19 Car ad (created by DALL.E, 2023, Author's Collection)

And to show we're not alone in this misperception, the design in Fig. 9.21 features the grand, horizon-hugging moon, just as our eyes like to see it.

The reason for this swing in size? When the moon is high in the sky without the company of trees, hills, or houses, our brain lacks contextual information to compare its size. Our brain goes, "Size comparison? No clue!" However, when the moon is near the horizon, our brain instinctively contrasts its size with neighboring objects on Earth. Our brain goes, "I see. Big moon. Tiny tree." Furthermore, our brain misgauges the distance of the moon. The moon on the horizon feels closer to us than the one high in the sky. So, really, it's not the moon. It's all about our brain playing the guessing game.

Fig. 9.20 Moon illusion (created by Imagine, 2023, Author's Collection)

Fig. 9.21 "ET" poster design (BFA/Alamy Stock Photo)

Fig. 9.22 The School of Athens (Fresco), Raffaello Santi, 16C, Apostolic Palace, Vatican City (Viacheslav Lopatin/Shutterstock)

Distorting Illusions III: Depth Illusions

The third stop within the domain of distorting illusions brings us to *depth illusions*.[14] Ever seen a two-dimensional painting and thought it had a deep space, like the one in Fig. 9.22? With clever manipulation of specific depth cues, you can make a flat surface take on a three-dimensional quality or cause the depth of three-dimensional space to feel deeper than it actually is.

There are certain visual cues that can trick our brain into seeing depth. Let's check what's in this toolkit. The top tools are "linear perspective," "atmospheric perspective," and "size gradient." The set has more tools, like texture gradient, overlapping, and shading, but let's keep our spotlight on the big three.

Linear perspective is the best magic trick for creating the illusion of deep space. Imagine standing on a straight road. The sides of the road appear to get closer together the farther away they are until it's just a teeny point on the horizon (Fig. 9.23). That point is called the "vanishing point." In the same way, by drawing lines converging at a vanishing point, a two-dimensional picture can don a three-dimensional feel. Check it with Fig. 9.22, Raffaello Santi's renowned painting "The School of Athens." You see those architectural lines? They converge at a vanishing point in the center of the painting. As a result, the painting seems to have a deep space.

[14] Shapter (1999).

Fig. 9.23 Linear perspective and Vanishing point (created by DALL.E, 2023, Author's Collection)

Atmospheric perspective is another way artists hint at the distance in their works. It is like the art world's version of a foggy memory. Much like distant memories get fuzzier, things are depicted as fuzzier and bluer as they get farther away. It mirrors our real-world experience of perceiving distant objects. Think of a mountain range. The nearby mountains are clear, but the distant ones appear hazier and slightly blueish due to particles in the air that scatter light. The depiction of this change in clarity and color gives a sense of depth to art. Let's check "The School of Athens" again (Fig. 9.22). Take a close look at the arches at the back. Their outlines progressively become hazier as they recede into the background.

The third tool for depth illusion is the *size gradient*. It's the method of depicting closer things as bigger and farther things as smaller. Again, it mirrors our real-world experience. For example, when perceiving people in the street, our brain interprets their size differences as the difference in distance. So, by drawing objects smaller as they recede into the background, you can create a sense of depth in art. Once more, let's check "The School of Athens" (Fig. 9.22). See how the arches and people shrink in size as they head farther away from our view.

These depth techniques are not confined to two-dimensional art. In the stage design of Fig. 9.24, designers applied these depth cues not to a two-dimensional surface but to a three-dimensional space. The pillars, walls, ceiling, and floor patterns are all designed to converge at a vanishing point in the background. Furthermore, the sizes

Fig. 9.24 Musical Doctor Zhivago (Robert Wallace/Wallace Media Network/Alamy Stock Photo)

of these elements are intentionally scaled down as they recede from the audience. For example, the second pillar is physically shorter than the first, and the third pillar is still shorter. Also, the sizes of floor tiles become physically smaller as they are farther away from the audience. The result? The illusion of a deeper stage space than it actually is.

Distorting Illusions IV: Curvature Illusions

The fourth stop within the domain of distorting illusions brings us to *curvature illusions*. Here, straight lines put on a curved appearance.

Firstly, there is the *Hering illusion*. See Fig. 9.25. Two horizontal lines, which are perfectly straight, seem to have a mild bend due to the direction of radiating lines in the background that can't help but interfere.[15]

In the curious case of Fig. 9.26, we stumble upon an unintentional effect of the Hering illusion. Designed to give off a vibe of motion and groove, the Sonos logo sports a series of radiating lines. But these same lines inadvertently invite the Hering illusion to the party. That is, the horizontal edges of this image seem to curve outward slightly.

Next up in our curvature illusion parade is the *curvature illusion of a long, straight line*.[16] Imagine you have a really long, impeccably straight stick. Now, if you look at

[15] Holt-Hansen (1961).

[16] Soyöz (2015).

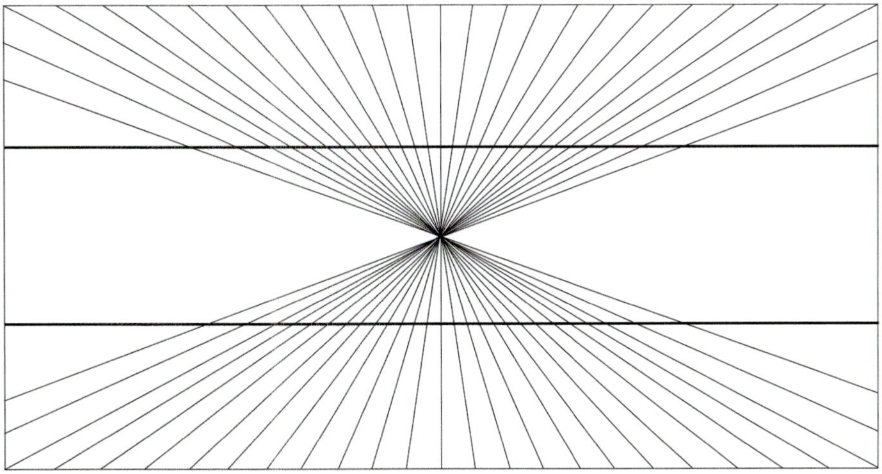

Fig. 9.25 Hering illusion (created by Jeongmin Lee, 2023, Author's Collection)

Fig. 9.26 Sonos logo, BMD (Bruce Mau Design)[17] (used with permission of Sonos Inc.)

it, you might start to wonder if your stick is feeling a bit droopy in the middle. Don't worry, it's not your stick; it's your brain playing visual tricks on you. That is, our brain expects long things to be weaker in the middle and projects this expectation onto our innocent stick, making us believe it's taking a slight bow.

[17] © 2024 Sonos, Inc. All rights reserved. Sonos* and the Sonos Amplification Logo are trademarks or registered trademarks of Sonos, Inc. *Reg. U.S. Pat. and TM Off.

This illusion isn't just a fun fact; it has real-world implications, especially in architecture, where long, straight lines are common. What's cool is that architects and designers are in on this secret.

The most famous case in point is the Parthenon, an ancient Greek marvel. We already talked about it in Chap. 1 (see Fig. 1.11). Let's briefly revisit it. Its architects, Ictinus and Callicrates, knew about this optical illusion and outsmarted it. For the columns, they employed a trick called "entasis." In plain English, the Parthenon's columns aren't perfectly straight. They've got a slight bulge in the middle. This subtle curve is a visual antidote to combat the illusion of saggy columns, making them look straight to human eyes. There's more. The Parthenon's stylobate and entablature aren't as flat as you'd expect. Instead, it has a gentle upward curve in the middle. So, when you take a step back and look at the whole structure in all its glory, it doesn't look like it's sagging under its own weight. Thus, the Parthenon is a shining example of how human perception can be beautifully manipulated for the better.

Distorting Illusions V: Position Illusions

The fifth stop within the domain of distorting illusions brings us to *position illusions*. It's like our brain's internal GPS gets a little disoriented, spotting objects slightly off their true spot. How come? Blame it on how these objects are presented and who they're hanging out with. Sometimes, sneaky visuals throw in a few curveballs, which interfere with the cues that our brain relies on to map out where things are.

Firstly, there is the *Poggendorf illusion*.[18] It's like watching a line play hide-and-seek: a continuous line appears misaligned after passing behind an obstructing shape. Peek at the left image in Fig. 9.27. Line C is partially obscured by a rectangle and makes us question, "Which line will it meet, A or B?" It looks like Line C is between Lines A and B. The answer? It meets Line B, as clarified in the right image.

This perceptual hide-and-seek is rather subtle than bewildering. Nonetheless, designers should take note of this illusion because it can mess with their work. For example, in the no-smoking sign of Fig. 9.28, a cigarette shape is overlaid with a shape symbolizing prohibition. With the Poggendorf illusion at play, the cigarette seems to re-emerge slightly off its original trail on the right side of the prohibition shape.

Secondly, there is the *Zollner illusion*.[19] Check out Fig. 9.29. Parallel lines appear slanted due to the orientation of short intersecting lines. It happens because our brain often makes assumptions based on contextual cues and, sometimes, gets swayed by them. Think about wearing glasses: it makes us look smarter, another optical illusion by contextual cues, experienced in everyday life!

Ever thought about jazzing up your wardrobe with a hooded T-shirt that's more than meets the eye, as in Fig. 9.30? It's a playful nudge to remember that appearances

---

[18] Day and Dickinson (1976).

[19] Prinzmetal et al. (2001).

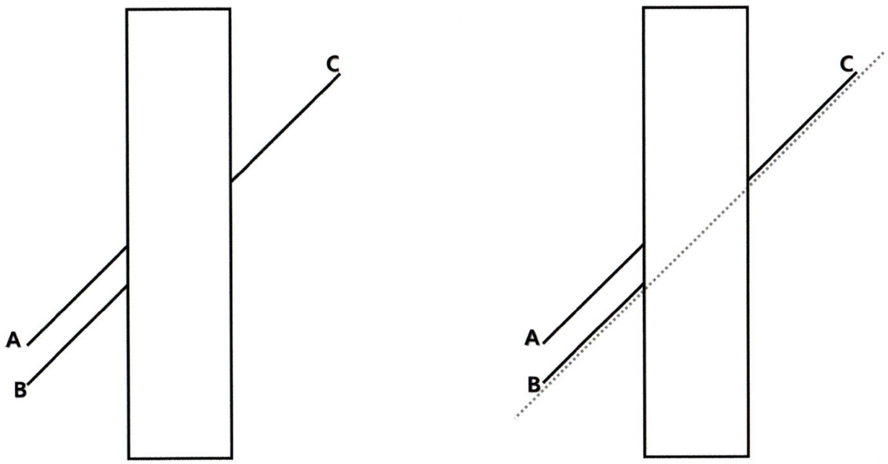

Fig. 9.27 Poggendorf illusion (created by Jeongmin Lee, 2023, Author's Collection)

Fig. 9.28 No-smoking sign (created by DALL.E, 2023, Author's Collection)

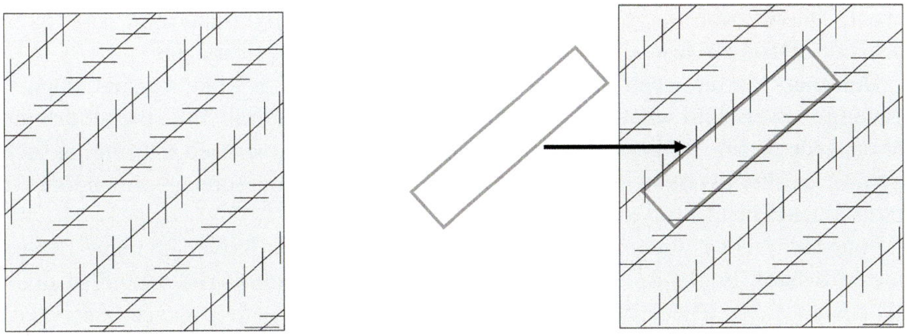

Fig. 9.29 Zollner illusion (created by Jeongmin Lee, 2023, Author's Collection)

Fig. 9.30 Hooded T-shirt with Zollner illusion pattern (created by DALL.E, 2023, Author's Collection)

can be deceiving, and wearing it is like carrying around a fun optical puzzle. This T-shirt is for those who enjoy a visual tease and don't mind being the center of attention, even if it's just for a double-take. It's a way of saying, "Hey, I'm the fun one!".

Thirdly, there is the *spiral illusion*, also called the *Fraser spiral illusion*, courtesy of British psychologist James Fraser.[20] Take a gander at the left image in Fig. 9.31. At a glance, it shows off as a spiral. But upon closer inspection, it's actually a bunch of concentric circles masquerading as a spiral. Check the right image for the big reveal. This illusion is typically achieved by alternating light and dark patterns to form concentric circles—circles that have a twisted cord appearance.

Designers tap into such tricks to keep our eyes hooked. It's like a visual magnet, drawing viewers into what appears to be a mesmerizing spiral. Take the ad design, for instance, in Fig. 9.32. Here, the Sony Bravia is being advertised as bringing such dynamic quality to colors that they seem to come alive on the screen—much like the spiral illusion brings life to a static image.

Fourthly, there is the *cafe wall illusion*.[21] This illusion derives its name from a cafe in Bristol, England. Here, Richard Gregory, the psychologist, stumbled upon this design quirk. Check out the left image in Fig. 9.33. At first glance, a series of black and white tiles separated by narrow horizontal lines seem slanted. However, the right image confirms they're straight and parallel.

[20] Fraser (1908).

[21] Gregory and Heard (1979).

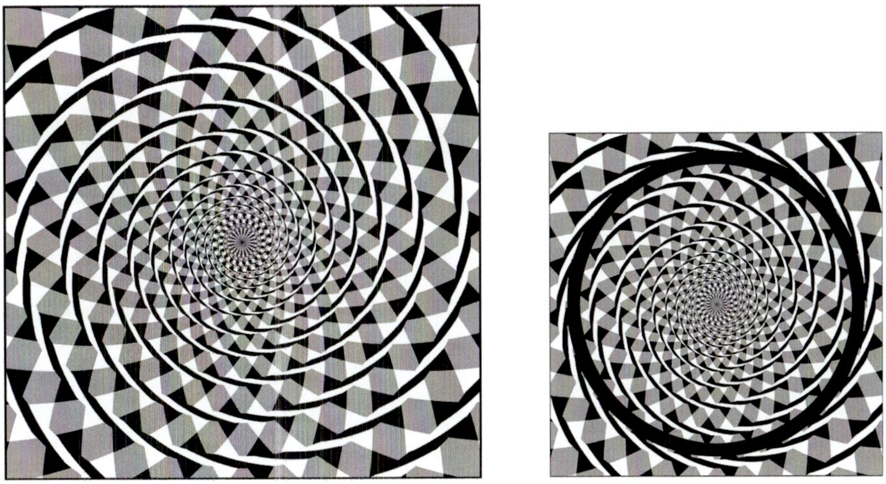

Fig. 9.31 Fraser spiral illusion (magr80/Shutterstock)

Fig. 9.32 Sony Bravia ad using Fraser spiral illusion (Creative Commons[22])

This illusion is attributed to the high contrast between the dark and light tiles, which can trigger an exaggerated response from retinal cells. The image with colors

[22] Image downloaded from https://www.flickr.com/photos/11304375@N07/2250423462/in/photostream/.

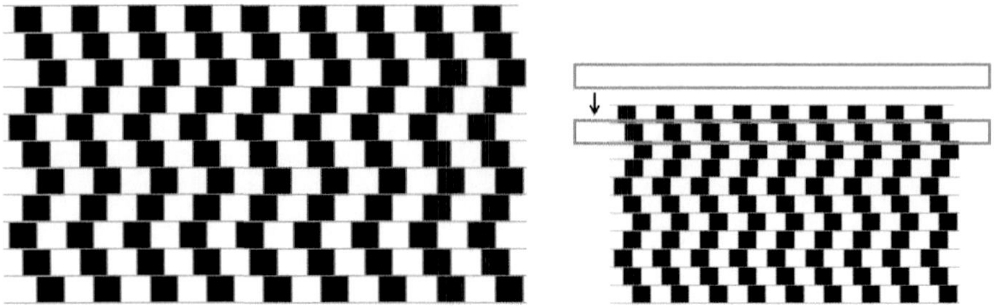

Fig. 9.33 Cafe wall illusion pattern (created by Jeongmin Lee, 2023, Author's Collection)

Fig. 9.34 Cafe wall illusion pattern with lower contrast (created by Jeongmin Lee, 2023, Author's Collection)

of lower contrast displays much less illusion (see Fig. 9.34). Thus, contrast polarities seem to be the determining factor.[23]

There was an aspirin ad inspired by this illusion. It presents a cafe wall illusion pattern with the challenging tagline, "Are the lines straight?" The message? It suggests that your headache can make reality feel a little unsettled, much like those crooked tiles. Therefore, the ad is saying, "Pop an aspirin, and watch as it straightens out your headache, much in the way you wish to straighten out those slanted lines."

Let's scale up the illusion game to architectural heights. See the imaginary building in Fig. 9.35. It's dressed up in the cafe wall illusion pattern, turning its walls into a warping wonder. It transforms the building into a large-scale interactive art piece, playfully challenging passersby to question what they see. It's like adding a dash of optical spice to the urban environment, making the cityscape a place to interact, wonder, and smile.

And it is not just imaginary. There is an actual architecture that has a facade with the cafe wall illusion pattern and, thus, playfully appears to be sloped—the Port 1010 Building in Melbourne, Australia (Ashton Raggatt McDougall, Baulderstone Hornibrook International Pty Ltd., 2006). But this design isn't just about aesthetics.

[23] Kitaoka et al. (2004).

Fig. 9.35 Building with cafe wall illusion (created by DALL.E, 2023, Author's Collection)

It also represents binary digital "bits" and includes two large blue circles that stand for zeros. It's a playful homage to the building's address, 1010, and its digital theme. This building has received architectural commendations and environmental awards for its innovative design and sustainability efforts.

Distorting Illusions VI: Motion Illusions

The sixth and final stop within the domain of distorting illusions brings us to *motion illusions*. Here, your brain is convinced that the static image is in a gentle motion. Again, it's a consequence of the complex visual interplay between our eyes and brain.

Fig. 9.36 Phi phenomenon: Download screen (created by DALL.E, 2023, Author's Collection)

Fig. 9.37 Current, Bridget Riley, 1964 (Nathaniel Noir/Alamy Stock Photo)

Firstly, there is the *phi phenomenon*.[24] Ever notice how some lights, when blinking in sequence, seem to move? We see it quite often on our computer screens (download screens like the one in Fig. 9.36). Also, remember those Christmas light decorations that seem to dance or move across the string? That's a classic example of the phi phenomenon. Our brains, always keen to find patterns, interpret this sequential flickering as a single light moving from one point to another. But, in reality, each bulb is firmly in place. Beyond decoration, the phi phenomenon also finds other useful applications in various contexts—from guiding us on roads to grabbing our attention in signage.

Secondly, there is the *illusion of visual vibration*. Here, patterns combine in a certain way that creates a sensation of vibrating or pulsating motion, even though it is static. If you're skeptical, cast your eyes over the Op Art painting in Fig. 9.37 and feel it yourself. Op Art, short for Optical Art, is an art form playing optical tricks on you with high contrast and precise arrangements of shapes and lines. The bigger the painting, the more the shimmering effect. It's intriguing to most but dizzying for some![25]

Let's hit the rewind button and revisit the logo of Sonos (an American audio products company) from earlier (see Fig. 9.26). It is an excellent example of using visual vibration. According to BMD's explanation, "Because the modern music experience is rich, dynamic, and diverse, the brand expression needed to reflect that."[26] So, what

[24] Britannica (accessed 2024).

[25] Oster (1965), Hencz (accessed 2023).

[26] Bruce Mau Design (accessed 2023).

Fig. 9.38 Sony Bravia ad using visual vibration illusion (Creative Commons[27])

did they do? They went for a design that's all about rhythm and movement, using repetitive lines that radiate out dynamically. It creates the illusion of visual vibration that generates the powerful feeling of sound waves pulsating out of speakers. It's like the logo is not only seen but almost heard, a piece of visual music.

Sony Bravia's ad design in Fig. 9.38 also utilizes a visual vibration effect. With a pattern that's so vibrant and full of life, it almost looks like it's moving, pulsating with energy. Along with the tagline "Colors become alive," it suggests that Bravia TV doesn't just display colors—it brings them to life. It works as a visual metaphor for the immersive viewing experience that this product can bring.

You might wonder why this happens. Our eyes, while brilliant, sometimes grapple with intense contrasts, like a stark black against white or a vibrant red beside the green. That is, when they are placed close together, our eyes have difficulty processing them smoothly. The outcome? Our eyes may keep trying to adjust and refocus, leading to the sensation of movement or vibration.

Thirdly, there is the *rotating snakes illusion*,[28] illustrated in Fig. 9.39. This one is quite the charmer, like a merry-go-round for your eyes. It's all very still, but your brain might be tricked into seeing them rotating as it attempts to process complex colors. This illusion is so mesmerizing and strong that it's hard to believe the image is not actually spinning.

---

[27] Image downloaded from https://www.flickr.com/photos/11304375@N07/2250423266/in/photostream/.

[28] Otero-Millan et al. (2012).

Fig. 9.39 Rotating snakes illusion (Ekaterina Koroleva/Red in Woman/Shutterstock)

One of Duracell's ads adopted the pattern of this illusion as background imagery, and in the center of this image lies a single Duracell battery, acting as a stable anchor amidst the dynamic swirl around it. It's as if a Duracell battery powers the turning motion of the ad itself. Thus, the background's constant motion is metaphorically linked to the energy and longevity that Duracell batteries are known for. After all, who wouldn't want a battery that keeps the world turning?

Fourthly, there is the *peripheral drift illusion*.[29] Have a side-eye look at Fig. 9.40, where the magic happens on the edges. When you're not looking directly at it, patterns on the side (which fall on the peripheral vision area outside the central focus) appear to shuffle around or "drift" fluidly. It tricks your brain into perceiving motion that isn't actually there. How does it happen? Our peripheral vision isn't as sharp as our central vision but is highly sensitive to movement and contrasts. Sometimes, the most interesting things happen just outside the spotlight.

Designers can use this illusion to sprinkle a dash of fun and a good dose of engagement into their works. They can also use it to deliver the message effectively. The A. A. (Alcoholics Anonymous) ad is a good example. In one of its ads, the whole ad is swimming in this illusion, conveying a message that as this illusion creates a sense of movement where there is none, alcohol can warp your perception of reality. And the message embedded in the center urges, "If this is common to you, look for A. A." The design cleverly symbolizes the confusion and lack of clarity that can be brought on by alcohol dependency—a creative approach to raising awareness about alcoholism.

[29] Faubert and Herbert (1999).

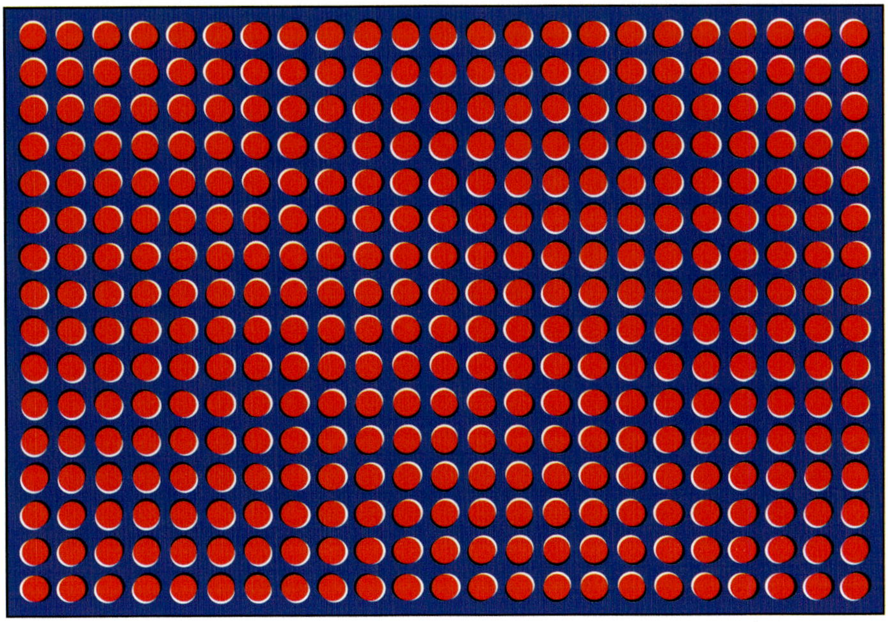

Fig. 9.40 Peripheral drift illusion (Peter Hermes Furian/Alamy Stock Photo)

Sony Bravia's ad in Fig. 9.41 is another example of using this illusion, which makes a static image feel lively. It is an intriguing way to draw attention and to communicate the TV's vibrant color quality.

Finally, we've put an end to our odyssey through optical illusions. However, I want to clarify that we ended this journey even though there are a lot more optical illusions that we couldn't discuss in this chapter. Some exploration to be done in the future, maybe.

If there's one thing we've learned from optical illusions in this chapter, it's that what we see isn't always a perfect reflection of reality. Instead, our brain often adds its own flair to what it sees. The funny thing is, as mentioned earlier, we can't correct our perceptions even when we are consciously aware that they are incorrect. Our brains still insist, "Trust me on this!" In addition, many designers, sensing an opportunity, harness these tricks to craft immersive design experiences for viewers. So, let's relax and enjoy our ever-creative brain's delightful ways of painting the world around us.

Fig. 9.41 Sony Bravia ad using peripheral drift illusion (Creative Commons[30])

References

Britannica. (accessed 2024). *Phi phenomenon.* Accessed January 25, 2024. https://www.britannica.com/topic/phi-phenomenon

Bruce Mau Design. (accessed 2023). *Sonos: Mix and remix—Music for the modern era.* Accessed November 20, 2023. https://www.brucemaudesign.com/work/sonos

Day, R. H., & Dickinson, R. G. (1976). The components of the Poggendorff illusion. *British Journal of Psychology, 67*(4), 537–552.

Faubert, J., & Herbert, A. M. (1999). The peripheral drift illusion: A motion illusion in the visual periphery. *Perception, 28*(5), 617–621.

Fraser, J. (1908). A new visual illusion of direction. *British Journal of Psychology, 2*(3), 307–320.

Gregory, R. L. (1968). Perceptual illusions and brain models. *Proceedings of the Royal Society of London. Series B, 171*, 279–296.

Gregory, R. L., & Heard, P. (1979). Border locking and the Café Wall illusion. *Perception, 8*(4), 365–380.

Hencz, A. (accessed 2023). Art movement: Op art—History and famous works. *Artland Magazine.* Accessed November 20, 2023. https://magazine.artland.com/art-movement-op-art/

Holt-Hansen, K. (1961). Hering's illusion. *British Journal of Psychology, 52*(4), 317–321.

Kaufman, L., & Kaufman, J. H. (2000). Explaining the moon illusion. *Proceedings of the National Academy of Sciences, 97*(1), 500–505.

Kitaoka, A., Pinna, B., & Brelstaff, G. (2004). Contrast polarities determine the direction of Café Wall tilts. *Perception, 33*(1), 11–20.

Künnapas, T. M. (1955). An analysis of the "vertical-horizontal illusion." *Journal of Experimental Psychology, 49*(2), 134–140.

Leopold, D. A., Wilke, M., Maier, A., & Logothetis, N. K. (2002). Stable perception of visually ambiguous patterns. *Nature Neuroscience, 5*(6), 605–609.

[30] Image downloaded from https://www.flickr.com/photos/11304375@N07/2249626279/in/photostream/.

Mishra, P. (2018, May 13). *New optical illusion: An oscillating visual paradox!* Accessed January 25, 2024. https://punyamishra.com/2018/05/13/new-optical-illusion-impossible-and-oscillating/
Oster, G. (1965). Optical art. *Applied Optics, 4*(11), 1359–1369.
Otero-Millan, J., Macknik, S. L., & Martinez-Conde, S. (2012). Microsaccades and blinks trigger illusory rotation in the "rotating snakes" illusion. *Journal of Neuroscience, 32*(17), 6043–6051.
Parrish, A. E., Brosnan, S. F., & Beran, M. J. (2015). Do you see what I see? A comparative investigation of the Delboeuf illusion in humans (*Homo sapiens*), rhesus monkeys (*Macaca mulatta*), and capuchin monkeys (*Cebus apella*). *Journal of Experimental Psychology: Animal Learning and Cognition, 41*(4), 395–405.
Prinzmetal, W., Shimamura, A. P., & Mikolinski, M. (2001). The Ponzo illusion and the perception of orientation. *Perception & Psychophysics, 63*(1), 99–114.
Roberts, B., Harris, M. G., & Yates, T. A. (2005). The roles of inducer size and distance in the Ebbinghaus illusion (Titchener circles). *Perception, 34*(7), 847–856.
Shapter, M. (1999). Perception of depth in photographs. *Journal of Audiovisual Media in Medicine, 22*(2), 71–74.
Soyöz, U. (2015). Optical measures: A design tool to attain truth or illusion? *Nexus Network Journal, 17*, 525–545.
The Eye's Mind. (2007). *Paradox illusions.* Accessed Jan 25, 2024. https://www.optical-illusion-pictures.com/paradox.html
Tudusciuc, O., & Nieder, A. (2010). Comparison of length judgments and the Müller-Lyer illusion in monkeys and humans. *Experimental Brain Research, 207*, 221–231.
Wade, N. J., & Hughes, P. (1999). Fooling the eyes: Trompe l'oeil and reverse perspective. *Perception, 28*(9), 1115–1119.
Zeki, S. (1996). Brain activity related to the perception of illusory contours. *NeuroImage, 3*(2), 104–108.

Chapter 10
Brain on Guard: Invisible Safety Toolkits for Survival

What do you think humans desire the most in their lives? Some might say it is the bond of relationships, while others might vouch for the accolades of accomplishment. Each person has different goals and desires in life. Yet, diving deeper, humans share one universal yearning, the strongest one—keeping the life lights on, that is, the desire for survival.

Enter Maslow's "hierarchy of needs" once more (see Fig. 4.1). Here, the building blocks of human existence are the "physiological needs" and "safety needs." It means that those boxes should be ticked before we begin to fulfill social and self-related needs. It's as if our brain knows a fundamental truth: only when we are alive can we seek other higher needs. Our brain whispers, "Safety first, then the good stuff!".

The fascinating bit? This survival need has etched psychological safeguards into our brains, an in-built safety protocol that evolved over time. There are psychological principles that humans have developed to protect themselves from threats to survival. Many automatic psychological responses that occur without conscious thought are likely sculpted by this evolutionary pressure.

Example? Let's talk about an automatic perceptual phenomenon that we experience every day. Ever notice how you don't hear your refrigerator humming until it suddenly stops? That's your ears giving the consistent noise a pass. But the moment it stops, it's like a dramatic pause in a symphony, making you wonder if you paid your electric bill. Do you remember when you dived into a cold swimming pool? Yikes! At first, it feels freezing, giving you a mini heart attack. But after a while, it doesn't seem so cold anymore. It's not the pool getting a heater but your skin adjusting to the sensation. And there is the mystery of the spicy food fanatic. The first time you tried that spicy dish, it felt like a volcano erupted in your mouth. But now, you're adding extra chili and wondering why it's not spicy enough.

© The Author(s), under exclusive license to Springer Nature Singapore Pte Ltd. 2024
J. Lee et al., *The Psychology Behind Design*,
https://doi.org/10.1007/978-981-97-3426-9_10

These commonplace experiences can be pinned on a perceptual phenomenon called "sensory adaptation."[1] Think of it as our senses playing the "been there, done that" game with a cool dimmer switch. When our senses are continuously exposed to a consistent stimulus, they start to lose their acuteness over time, causing us to perceive them with much-reduced intensity, if at all. But a change in the scene? They are back at full wattage, ready to savor every new sensation.

Curious about why our senses have this on–off switch? Let's explore sensory adaptation through the lens of survival. When we bump into something new, our senses go on high alert, acting like curious kids, all ears and eyes, because our brain has to determine whether it poses a threat to our survival or not. If, over time, we are still unharmed, our brain concludes that it is innocuous and that continuous alertness toward it is redundant. Why waste precious brain juice on something that's just a harmless background character? So, our brain reallocates its attention to conserve energy. A kind of cognitive miser phenomenon we talked about in Chap. 7.

Imagine journeying back in time, where you're an early human living in the vast wilderness. Here, each sound, movement, or scent could spell a potential danger or herald a meal. Your senses are your main tools for survival. Now, let's say you've set up camp beside a waterfall. Initially, the sound of rushing water dominates your auditory landscape. But suppose you stayed super tuned to that 24/7. You might miss other critical sounds—say, the rustling of a predator in the bushes or the approach of another human. That's where sensory adaptation steps in. It lets your ears put the background sound of the waterfall on mute and listen for new and potentially significant sounds.

Simply put, sensory adaptation is an evolutionary gift. It ensures that our senses don't get bogged down by unchanging and harmless stimuli. On the flip side of the coin, it allows us to remain alert and responsive to the changing scenes, not the monotonous reruns. Reflecting on modern urban life, ever wondered how we can live unfazed amidst all those honks and hustles of the city? As with our ancestors, our senses continue to adapt to our environment and know when to tune in and when to switch off, whether it's the dense jungle or the bustling streets of a metropolis.

Now, let me tell you about an exciting experiment that showcases human perception's astounding adaptability to various settings. George Stratton conducted an experiment using a pair of special glasses, which turned everything he saw upside down.[2] As you can imagine, at first, he was super disoriented. Simple tasks like walking around or grabbing objects were challenging. But here's where it gets wild. After several days of visual topsy-turvy, his brain started to adapt. The upside-down world began to feel normal. When he took the glasses off, his perception temporarily reverted, making the normal world feel disoriented until his brain readjusted. This experiment reveals that, given time, our brains can reconfigure themselves in surprising ways to adapt to altered realities.

---

[1] Nafe and Wagoner (1941).

[2] Stratton (1897a, 1897b).

But wait, this perceptual adaptability isn't our only psychological defense mechanism! Over the ages, human brains have developed many other cognitive tools to swiftly navigate and dodge the risks that can harm our survival. Modern life may differ vastly from our ancestral environments. For example, to modern people, the most heart-pounding moment that threatens our lives is when we realize we have left our phones at home.[3] However, our instincts still rock the old-school flair much more, and many of those ancient defense mechanisms are still deeply shaping our actions and choices up until now. So, let's dive deeper into innate psychological abilities to safeguard ourselves against potential threats, shall we? You will discover that, beneath our modern veneer, there is a hint of the Stone Age savvy—we are still profoundly primal at heart.

Owl of Minerva Behind the Scene

In this chapter, we will delve into the psychological realm closely tied to human survival, with a particular focus on the mental defense mechanisms associated with the desire for safety. Despite our departure from a wild environment brimming with tangible hazards, the need for safety remains a deeply ingrained desire within us. Our inner caveperson is still on the lookout for a cozy, saber-tooth-free cave!

So, what's the deal? It implies that even in the absence of actual threats, we can still experience feelings of safety or peril based solely on the visual cues in a design. That's why clever design gurus use certain psychological principles to craft designs that evoke a reassuring sense of security, saying, "All's well!".

Our exploration will navigate through three categories: firstly, the "preference for familiarity—our inherent inclination toward the known and the recognizable; secondly, the adept "ability to discern threats and safety signals"—our crucial capability to differentiate between danger and security; and thirdly, the "psychology of ensuring defensibility—our inherent mechanism to protect and defend ourselves.

So, let's start uncovering the secrets beneath each of these three facets. By doing so, we aim to shed light on how design can pull the strings of consumer behavior, fostering a sense of safety and well-being that guides our path through the urban jungle and beyond.

Safety Toolkit I: Familiarity

Let's kick off our journey by dipping our toes into the comforting waters of *familiarity*. Humans have an intrinsic preference for familiar things. Picture this: you are a prehistoric human, and your daily to-do list is basically a series of life-or-death decisions. In such times, familiarity is not just your buddy. It's your lifeline.

First off, familiar elements inherently signal safety. If you know a particular path, cave, or water source, this familiarity gives your brain reassuring pats on the back, saying, "Hey, I've been here before, and everything turned out okay." Contrastingly,

[3] On October 22, 2023, suggested by ChatGPT-4.

stepping into unknown territories is akin to opening a box of mysteries—it could be a surprise party or, less appealingly, a surprise predator. Also, familiarity equals efficiency, the original life hack. That is, familiar tasks are easier and quicker because you know the process. This efficiency can save valuable time and energy, which is vital for survival in a relentless environment.

In essence, familiarity acts as a soothing balm to stress. Imagine the toll of facing unseen dangers day in day out. Exhausting, right? But wrap yourself in the cozy cloak of the known, and voilà, anxiety takes a backseat. Back in the day of our ancestors, this comfy cloak wasn't just cozy; it was often the line between life and death. Zooming back to the present, while we might not face the same daily survival threats, our brains still find solace and security in the familiar. That's why we often prefer routines, stick with what we know, and sometimes give change the side-eye.

Let's dig a bit deeper into the psychological principles underscoring the inherent value of familiarity. First, we encounter the *mere exposure effect*.[4] We already discussed it in Chap. 1 with regard to the MAYA principle and in relation to the psychological equilibrium. Here, we will confer it more with respect to the psychology of familiarity.

The mere exposure effect is a psychological phenomenon where people tend to develop a preference for things merely because they are familiar with them. The more frequently we are exposed to a stimulus, the more we tend to like it. Ever experienced the growth of your feelings toward a song on the radio that initially didn't strike a chord? However, upon multiple hearings, you might catch yourself unconsciously humming along. Remember the hubbub when Instagram swapped its logo? Initial reactions were like a collective gasp at a surprise ingredient in a beloved recipe. But, give it time and numerous scrolls later, people not only accepted it but started liking it. Also, as we all know, our fridge is usually a gallery of kids' drawings, and the more we see it, the more it looks like Picasso. These examples illustrate the power of familiarity, significantly shaping our preferences, tastes, and decisions in everyday life.

The mere exposure effect plays a significant role in the arts and design world, too. Consider the advent of abstract art, for instance. Initially, it was met with lots of raised eyebrows and skeptical glances. However, as abstract art kept making the rounds, acceptance and appreciation followed suit. For example, today, the works of Piet Mondrian (e.g., Fig. 10.1), with their bold simplicity and utmost reductionist approach, are globally revered as iconic embodiments of the modernist movement, leaving his mark on everything from design to pop culture. But let's not forget, once upon a time, these were the artworks the general public scratched their heads over!

Then, there's the Guggenheim Museum in New York, a brainchild of the illustrious American architect Frank Lloyd Wright (Fig. 10.2). Forget the conventional museums with separate rooms or sections. This one threw the rulebook out the window, offering a spiral, open-view spectacle of art (Fig. 10.2, right). Inevitably, it was not exempt from initial criticism. Some even went as far as to describe it as an "inverted oatmeal

[4] Zajonc (2001).

Fig. 10.1 Piet Mondrian Exhibition posters (Lana Brow/Shutterstock)

Fig. 10.2 Solomon R. Guggenheim Museum, Frank Lloyd Wright, 1959, New York, USA (Left: Roy Harris/Shutterstock) (Right: Manuel Ochoa/Shutterstock)

dish" or a "giant toilet bowl." However, over the years, it has become a beloved symbol of visionary design in the Big Apple!

So, in a nutshell, the mere exposure effect in design is like a slow-brewed cup of tea. It might strike a peculiar note at first. Still, with a little time and familiarity, it might become the taste you never knew you loved!

The second psychological principle related to human inclination toward the familiar is the *top-down lighting bias*.[5] Picture yourself encircled by friends around a campfire, the atmosphere ripe for a ghost story. Then, you know the next drill: to amplify the spookiness, someone grabs a flashlight and illuminates their face from

[5] Lidwell et al. (2010).

Fig. 10.3 Effect of bottom-up lighting (Felix Mizioznikov/Shutterstock)

below, casting unsettling shadows and highlights that make the tale all the more spine-tingling (Fig. 10.3). But have you ever wondered why this simple shift in lighting sends a chill down your spine?

Welcome to the world of the "top-down lighting bias," the human brain's predisposition to expect objects to be lit from above. Since the dawn of our days, the primary light source, the sun, has always been casting its glow from up above. It's our oldest, most familiar light source, setting the rhythm of shadows and highlights we all know. Imagine, if our evolutionary journey had unfolded in a solar system blessed with multiple suns, our notions of light and shadow would be in a whole different universe. But here we are, creatures of one sun, finding comfort in the familiar top-down lighting as natural and ordinary. Flip the switch, light things from below, and suddenly, even the most familiar thing looks super unnatural. That's why the old flashlight-under-the-face trick never fails!

Delving into the art world, artists ingeniously leverage the top-down lighting bias to evoke specific emotions. The usual recipe? Light pours from above to make scenes look natural and familiar. On the other hand, a dash of light from below and a concoction of unease is served. Take a glance at Fig. 10.4. Here, to encapsulate the unnerving moment of beheading an enemy commander, a moment from the Book of Judith, Rubens positioned the light source (a candle) at the painting's lower part, thereby crafting an atmosphere tinged with the uncanny shadows of bottom-up lighting.

Similarly, designers harness this effect in various creative domains. For example, game designers use lighting to guide players. Areas illuminated from above might suggest safety or a path to follow, while unconventional lighting might signify potential danger or mystery. Filmmakers, too, manipulate lighting to craft atmospheres and tones. A sunny scene with top-down lighting can feel warm and welcoming, whereas dramatic scenes might employ unusual lighting to create surreal or ominous tension. Ever felt the shivers in a dimly lit basement scene with just a flickering glow from below in a thriller?

Fig. 10.4 Judith with the Head of Holofernes, Peter Paul Rubens, 17C (Artepics/ Alamy Stock Photo)

Third, there is the effect of *sensory adaptation*.[6] In the opening episode, we have touched upon its role in survival. Unchanging stimulus becomes the "familiar" stimulus, meaning it's safe, so our brain decides not to put unnecessary cognitive energy into it. For example, spritz on your favorite perfume in the morning, and by lunchtime, you might think it's vanished. But ask friends, and they'll assure you that you still smell divine. Your nose just got too familiar with it and decided to take a sensory nap.

Then, what implication does this phenomenon have for marketers and designers? Let's explore sensory adaptation through the lens of consumer psychology. Sensory adaptation is a bit of a double-edged sword. On the one hand, it has a positive effect on human survival, but on the other, it gives rise to what the ad world calls *advertising wear-out*: an ad campaign starts to lose its impact due to overexposure.[7] When audiences see an advertisement too often, they can become desensitized to the message, just like we become desensitized to unchanging sensory stimuli. It happens even with a very successful ad campaign.

Hence, in the world of advertising, it's a game of balance between consistency (which aids recall) and novelty (which captures attention). So, designers mix these ingredients and whip up various versions for one campaign. This approach ensures that each ad has consistent echoes but with a fresh twist so that consumers can snap out of their sensory snooze and zoom right back onto the refreshed ad. In this manner,

[6] Adibi et al. (2021), Nafe and Wagoner (1941).

[7] Craig et al. (1976).

Fig. 10.5 Absolut Perfection Campaign (Left and Right: Retro AdArchives/Alamy Stock Photo)

the dance between the known and the new continues, keeping the consumer engaged and the message alive.

The "Absolut Perfection" campaign by Absolut Vodka is a prime example of this strategy. It is known for its creative print ads showing the unique Absolut Vodka bottle shape in fun and imaginative ways. Each ad had the word "Absolut" and then tossed in a zesty word to match the scene (see Fig. 10.5). This campaign lasted over 25 years and made over 1500 ads. Still, people loved these ads so much that they always looked forward to the next one.

Sensory adaptation and advertising wear-out also explain our curious relationship with travel. Most days, we are surrounded by familiar conditions and routines—sipping the same coffee, walking the same streets, and nodding to the same neighbors. Comforting? Yes! But after a while, our daily environment might start to feel mundane or monotonous because sensory adaptation occurs, and even our favorite scenes can make us yawn. Thus, we grab the allure of travel, which exposes us to new environments, cultures, foods, and experiences. This unfamiliarity automatically makes us more bright-eyed and bushy-tailed with heightened senses. We are out of sensory adaptation. It's like our senses are given a jolt of espresso, and we feel refreshed.

Paradoxically, though, these challenges and unpredictabilities of travel also make us reappreciate the comforts of familiarity. There is always a sweet sigh of relief when we spot our familiar front door, saying, "There's no place like home." The stability and predictability become appealing again. Yet, the cycle continues: come the next vacation, we pack our bags with zest to hit the road again… unless we check our bank account and decide that we didn't get tired.[8]

[8] On October 20, 2023, extracted and revised from http://www.funny-jokes-quotes.com/daily-life-situations.html.

Thus, our journey through the realms of familiarity reveals a fascinating facet of human nature. The mere exposure effect, top-down lighting bias, and sensory adaptation collectively illuminate our deep-seated affinity for the known. Be it the comforting predictability of everyday routines or the strategic use of familiarity in art and advertising, our brains are wired to find solace in the familiar while cautiously embracing the novel. So, if you find yourself humming along to a once-irksome tune or eyeing the new with a hint of skepticism, remember, it's just your brain doing its age-old dance between comfort and curiosity. And hey, who knows, maybe the next unfamiliar turn could be your new favorite path!

Safety Toolkit II: Threat-spotting Ability

Now, let's pass through the realm of familiarity and move to the next survival realm—*threat-spotting ability*. The human brain has cultivated an alarm system, finely tuned and always on the lookout for dangers. That is, humans have psychological capabilities for discerning potential threats or safety cues, which increase the chances of survival.

Firstly, humans exhibit a distinct perceptual aptitude for *threat detection*, an in-built radar for spotting trouble.[9] We possess a perceptual mechanism finely tuned to identify threatening stimuli (such as images featuring predators, snakes, or spiders) more rapidly and efficiently than non-threatening ones (like those depicting flowers and trees). Threatening stimuli also retain our attention longer—it's hard to look away! Closely related to this ability is the *anger superiority effect*.[10] It refers to the perceptual phenomenon where angry faces are detected more quickly and accurately than happy or neutral faces. Angry faces grab our attention because they might hint at trouble. See Fig. 10.6. Which tiger keeps you hooked?

Fig. 10.6 Anger superiority effect (Left: MP Foto/Shutterstock) (Right: dangdumrong/Shutterstock)

[9] Lidwell et al. (2010).

[10] Hansen and Hansen (1988).

Fig. 10.7 Poison warning sign (Jongsuk/Shutterstock)

Both of these phenomena suggest that the human perceptual system is particularly sensitive to threat-related stimuli. In a nutshell, our brain, especially the spot called the *amygdala*, is like a secret agent, constantly scanning for danger, ready to hustle us into action—be it a swift flight or a fight to remember. So, when a frown catches your eye or a spider makes you jump, give a little nod to your inner guardian, working overtime to keep you safe.

In the design field, integrating this human knack for spotting potential threats holds considerable merit, especially when it comes to the design of safety signals and alerts. Designing those warning signs in a way our brains can't help but notice could markedly enhance their effectiveness. For instance, using symbols such as a lightning bolt for electricity or a skull to denote poison (Fig. 10.7) is akin to putting neon lights on a stop sign. Nonetheless, do you know what the best safety device is in today's road conditions? A rearview mirror with a police car in it.[11]

This designing wizardry is not just for dodging danger. It also shines bright in crafting designs that effectively command attention in places bursting with distractions. For instance, in action or survival video games, enemies might be highlighted with specific colors, move in certain patterns, or produce certain sounds, all in some threatening manner, ensuring the player's attention is firmly in grasp. Then, there is the battle of the supermarket shelves. Figure 10.8 illustrates a product package design that should compete with similar products on busy supermarket shelves. A design cue evocative of potential danger can be the visual magnet for the customer's eye amid a sea of options.

Crafty designers can play this threat card without actually scaring us. By abstracting threatening features, designers can activate our threat-detection mechanism without evoking the negative emotions typically associated with such stimuli. Consider the Chicago Bulls' logo design in Fig. 10.9. The aggressive facial expression of a fierce bull ensures that your attention is well caught. Yet, given its abstraction, it doesn't induce our fear response.

[11] On October 20, 2023, extracted and revised from https://jokojokes.com/safety-jokes.html#google_vignette.

Fig. 10.8 Monster Energy (photographed by Jeongmin Lee, 2023, Author's Collection)

Fig. 10.9 Chicago Bulls logo (Peter Kováč/Alamy Stock Photo)

This ancient threat-detection skill that kept us safe for millennia can sometimes get a bit overenthusiastic in today's world. A loud noise? It could be a book hitting the floor, but our brains might go into overdrive, thinking, "Red Alert!" Nonetheless, better safe than sorry, as they say. Our brains tend to overreact to a non-threat rather than to underreact to a real one. After all, erring on the side of caution never goes out of style.

Secondly, human perception sensitively detects an *imbalance*.[12] Our eyes are naturally drawn to areas of imbalance because they stand out in contrast to our innate desire for order and stability. Imagine a picture frame hanging on the wall of your living room. Even if it's just slightly crooked, your eyes can spot it right away. This visual imbalance gives you an unexplainable psychological itch, compelling you to rectify the tilt promptly. Similarly, how about seeing a crooked tie?

So, our brain has this in-built wonkiness detector, and there's a good reason for it. Historically, an off-kilter environment could spell "TROUBLE." A leaning tree or a lopsided rock could mean it's about to fall. Thus, human adeptness at detecting imbalance has deep survival roots. Fast forward to today, and while we're mostly safe from threats of wildlife, this old-school alert system still kicks in. Sure, a tilted artwork doesn't mean danger, but your brain is saying, "Hey, something's off here. Do the safety check and fix it, will you?".

This innate sense of balance doesn't just keep us safe. It also plays a fundamental role in our appreciation of aesthetics: the human eye instinctively finds designs with *visual balance* more aesthetically appealing compared to those that are unbalanced, as they typically convey a sense of harmony, stability, and order.[13] Let's check more about this world of visual balance, where both symmetry and asymmetry wear their own unique coolness.

Symmetrical balance (or *formal balance*) occurs when elements on either side of a central line mirror each other. It's common in art and architecture, especially with those trying to express authority. Iconic structures such as the Parthenon in Greece and Saint Peter's Basilica in the Vatican exemplify this form of balance. The Bahai Temple in Fig. 10.10 is another example. Every element on the left gives a polite nod to its twin on the right—a design echoing an air of sturdy, dependable calm.

On the other hand, with *asymmetrical balance* (also known as *informal balance*), different elements have equal visual weight, but they don't mirror each other. Different? Yes! Chaotic? Not at all! It's a well-coordinated composition of dissimilar objects. Take DDP in Fig. 10.11, for instance, where unequal shapes and forms still hold an intriguing visual balance. This type of balance can yield compositions that are often more engaging. So, in the colorful canvas of design, whether it's the predictable charm of symmetry or the spirited allure of asymmetry, balance always strikes a pose.

On the other hand, artists and designers also use a *visual imbalance* when creating works intended to evoke feelings of arbitrariness, chance, chaos, and detachment.[14] Consequently, it serves as a tool for symbolic representation of conflict or dynamic movement, making the viewer feel unsettled, curious, or more engaged. Take an advertisement, for instance. You'd expect the star product to be center stage. But what if it's tucked away in a corner with a vast empty space next to it? It piques curiosity and draws attention to the product. Similarly, movie directors frequently play this game to evoke specific emotions or presage forthcoming events. A character

---

[12] Pentak and Lauer (2016).

[13] McManus (2005).

[14] McManus (2005).

Fig. 10.10 Bahai Temple (Lotus Temple), Fariborz Sahba, 1986, New Delhi, India (photographed by Jeongmin Lee, 2011, Author's Collection)

Fig. 10.11 DDP (Dongdaemun Design Plaza), Zaha Hadid, Seoul, South Korea (Stock for you/ Shutterstock)

pushed to the edge of the frame with a sea of emptiness beside them? You're left with an itch of, "What's about to happen?" or "Why so lonely?".

The NordLB Headquarters in Fig. 10.12 is an architectural example of applying visual imbalance. The honeycomb structures are elevated, leaving space underneath. It creates an illusion that the building is hovering above the ground, thereby instilling a sense of dynamic tension and intrigue that compels a second glance. Far from projecting a static and immovable presence, the building emanates vivacity and energy.

Fig. 10.12 NordLB Headquarters, Behnisch & Partner, 2002, Hannover, Germany (Christian Mueller/Shutterstock)

Simply put, humans unconsciously prefer visual balance and its comforting embrace, but sometimes, there are intentional and impactful reasons for introducing visual imbalance. Nonetheless, buildings like NordLB Headquarters must make some people uneasy. So, it's better to be used cautiously. When done right, it can enrich the narrative, engage the viewer, and magnify emotional depth. Thus, whether it's the steady beat of balance or the jazzy rhythms of imbalance, both have their spotlight moments in the design world.

Thirdly, *contour bias* is another intriguing aspect in discussing the human ability to recognize threats and safety signals. We, humans, have a visual-aesthetic preference for objects with smooth, curvy outlines over those with spiky, jagged edges. Think of it as our visual preference for marshmallows over cacti. Smooth contours are perceived as more appealing, pleasant, and often more approachable than angular ones. However, there's a peculiar twist. Despite our preference for smoother shapes, our eyes can't help but be drawn to those edgy, pointy forms. It's those forms that captivate our attention and ignite curiosity.

A study by Moshe Bar and Maital Neta proved this.[15] They presented participants with pairs of objects that were similar in general appearance and meaning but differed in the curvature of their contours (e.g., a circular clock vs. a square clock). This included real objects like watches and sofas, as well as English characters and meaningless patterns. When asked to rate their preferences, participants significantly preferred curved objects over sharp-angled ones. Additionally, when observing participants' brain activity through fMRI (Functional Magnetic Resonance

[15] Bar and Neta (2006).

Fig. 10.13 Contour bias: Left—Smartphone app icons/Right—Disney characters, Disneyland, LA, USA (photographed by Jeongmin Lee, 2024 (left) and 1997 (right), Author's Collection)

Imaging), the sharper the object's edges, the more the amygdala became activated.[16] The amygdala is a part of the brain thought to have evolved to detect potential threats. Talk about the brain having a pointy object radar!

Why, you ask? The roots of the contour bias can be evolutionary. In wildlife, soft curves would have usually come off as safe. Think of juicy berries and smooth stones. Conversely, historical learning would have taught humans the potential dangers associated with sharp objects, be they thorns, fangs, or that unpleasantly pointy rock you stepped on. As a result, such objects automatically trigger our deep-seated fears and defenses. So, even today, our brain navigates this world guided by ancient memories, where round means cozy, and pointy equals "proceed with caution." There can be an exception to this cautious behavior, though—reflexive reaction! Imagine you have an adored cactus in your home, which you have grown for a long time. Then, imagine you dropped it today. Bad news... Worse news? Most probably, and reflexively, I bet you caught it!.[17]

This interplay between aesthetic preference and survival instinct offers a glimpse into how design elements can tap into deep-seated human desires, potentially influencing consumer behavior. Want something more appealing and inviting? Go round. That's why website buttons, icons, and those tempting clickable elements love a good curve, and that's also no wonder why most of the characters in Disneyland are rendered in exaggerated round shapes (Fig. 10.13). It's not just a trend—it's psychology. Those rounded corners are like a design version of a warm hug, exuding a "Come, let's be pals!" vibe. So, if you aim for a friendly and likable first impression, curvy contours are your wingman.

---

[16] Bar and Neta (2007).

[17] On October 23, 2023, extracted and revised from https://upjoke.com/cactus-jokes.

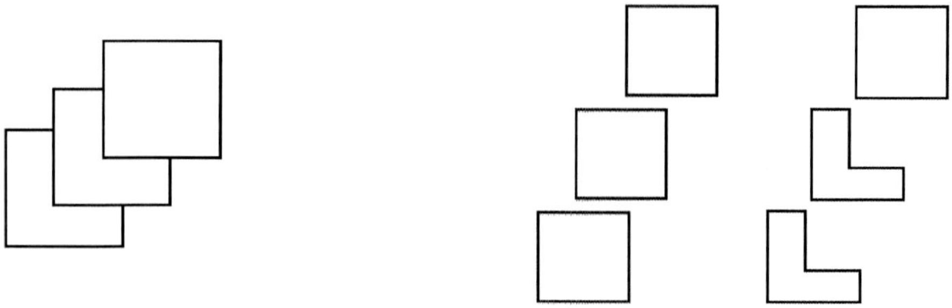

Fig. 10.14 Law of Prägnanz (created by Jeongmin Lee, 2023, Author's Collection)

However, it's not that angular designs are left gathering dust in the design toolkit. Just because curvy shapes are preferred over sharp ones, it doesn't mean that angular designs get the short end of the stick. Sharp-edged objects excel in capturing users' attention, awakening their senses, and activating cognitive functions. They poke our brains by making us sense potential threats, keeping us on our toes. So, if the goal of a design is to grab attention and provoke thoughtful engagement, going edgy and pointy might be the way to go (see the Monster Energy package design in Fig. 10.8).

Fourthly, let's turn our attention to another significant human knack for discerning safety in visual information, embodied by the *law of Prägnanz*.[18] It is one of the foundational principles in *Gestalt psychology*, a school of thought that focuses on how we organize visual information. The German word "Prägnanz" can be translated as "pithiness" or "good figure."

The law of Prägnanz refers to the tendency of human perception to interpret ambiguous or complex images as simple, orderly, and cohesive rather than convoluted and incomplete. It's like our brains have this built-in filter that goes, "Whoa, too complicated! Let's simplify that." Take the left image in Fig. 10.14, for instance. I bet most people would see three overlapping squares. But do you know another interpretation is also possible? One square flanked by two L-shaped figures on its sides (Fig. 10.14, right). Who would think of that option at first glance?

You want another example from real-life experiences? Think about the commonplace act of cloud-gazing. We often identify shapes in the clouds. A dragon here, a teddy bear there. It's not your wild imagination. It's your brain played by the law of Prägnanz, turning cloud chaos into simpler and recognizable shapes.

But why do our brains pull this penchant for simplicity? It happens because simpler patterns demand less cognitive exertion to process, and historically, a tidier, less chaotic environment often meant fewer surprises (and dangers). Imagine spotting a lion in a jungle vs. a wide-open meadow. Simpler scenes meant quicker reactions. In essence, complexity and disorder in our surroundings can pose survival risks,

[18] Van Geert and Wagemans (2023), Lidwell et al. (2010).

Fig. 10.15 Unilever logo (Tawab Daumi/Shutterstock)

propelling us to seek a semblance of order even in complex settings.[19] So, let's tip our hat to ancient instinct again. Our ancestors liked their views as clear and uncomplicated. Even in the modern day, Henry David Thoreau famously said, "Simplify, simplify." It would have been simpler to say it once, though.[20]

In the design world, the law of Prägnanz underscores the importance of order and clarity in effective communication. Here's the thing. If a design is too straightforward and simple, it is easier for consumers to grasp but runs the risk of being boring. But, make it too intricate, and you risk folks scratching their heads. Skillful designers, therefore, know the sweet spot. They often interweave complexity with a pinch of order and simplicity. The Unilever logo in Fig. 10.15 exemplifies this approach. This design offers a delightful mix of diverse elements that form the "U"—each piece unique, none identical. Yet, consumers first recognize it as a single "U." So, while your brain says, "Hey, that's a U!" your heart goes, "But look at all those fun details!" It's playful yet organized.

Judging from our exploration into the brain's threat-spotting ability, it's clear that our ancient instincts are still hard at work as vigilant guardians. Our brains are always on high alert, scanning for potential dangers and helping us navigate the world safely. But it's not all about dodging danger. These innate abilities also play a pivotal role in our appreciation of beauty and design. So, let's appreciate our brain's marvelous abilities. They're not just remnants of our survival past but are actively shaping our present, influencing everything from our safety to our aesthetic sensibilities. It's a dance with instinct, aesthetics, and psychology.

[19] Buss (2005).

[20] On October 23, 2023, extracted and revised from https://upjoke.com/simplify-jokes.

Safety Toolkit III: Ensuring Defensibility

Let's explore the third survival realm—the psychology of *ensuring defensibility*. It means the psychological line of defense humans build to protect themselves from possible threats, and this defense mechanism is more real than you think!

First and foremost, the psychological *personal space* is a very important concept in building this line of defense.[21] Ever felt like you're moving around with an invisible bubble around you? Humans come with this protective bubble, a zone of comfort we call "personal space" (Fig. 10.16, left). Inside this personal territory, we feel comfortable and safe. This is our unspoken "no trespassing" zone, where only a select few can enter. If someone, especially a stranger, crashes this bubble without an invite, our inner alarms go off, evoking feelings of discomfort (Fig. 10.16, right).

Why does this zone matter? Personal space acts like an emotional airbag, buffering us from unexpected social bumps. It helps us feel safe, respected, and in control. Breakage of our personal space by others prompts defensive reactions such as stepping back or avoiding eye contact to get our space back. Therefore, acknowledging and respecting other's personal space is a fundamental facet of social interaction. For example, when waiting in line, people often keep a certain distance from the person in front of them. Similarly, in communal spaces such as waiting rooms or public transportation, a common practice is to leave an empty seat between oneself and a stranger if possible. You're not being anti-social. It's us all subtly saying, "I respect your bubble, and here's mine." The real anti-social is the one who would say, "Call me anti-social… Just don't call me".[22]

Interestingly, this bubble isn't one-size-fits-all. The size varies depending on where we are, who we are with, and what we are doing. For instance, you'd probably let a close friend or family member stand closer to you than a stranger (Fig. 10.17). Cultural norms play a role, too. Some societies embrace closer contact, while other cultures often favor more distance. It also depends on the environmental context.

Fig. 10.16 Personal space (created by Jeongmin Lee, 2023, Author's Collection)

[21] Hall (1990).

[22] On October 23, 2023, extracted and revised from https://upjoke.com/antisocial-jokes.

Fig. 10.17 Classification of Personal space (created by Jeongmin Lee, 2023, Author's Collection)

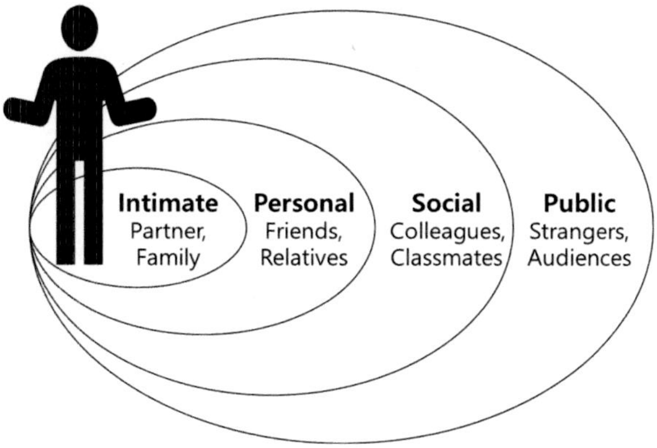

In crowded places, like a packed train, our bubble shrinks out of necessity. Moreover, some people naturally prefer larger personal space due to personality, past experiences, or other reasons. Bottom line? Personal space—it's real, it's fluid, and respecting it means social harmony.

When architects and designers get this concept of invisible frontiers, they're not just building spaces; they're crafting the feeling of safety and comfort in design, especially in places where human interaction is frequent. For example, when designing public spaces, designers can create clear, physical boundaries for temporary personal space. Consider those trendy open offices, originally conceived to foster collaboration yet often criticized for lacking personal space. They end up feeling a tad exposed. The fix? A movable screen here, a plant there to create a sense of boundary. Just like that, you've got a movable fort of solitude. In this regard, let's take a moment to appreciate the furniture design in Fig. 10.18, the understated hero for open-office diplomacy. It is a thoughtful piece of furniture that carves out a little haven of personal space amidst the daily buzz without building walls. That is, it balances openness with privacy, offering a retreat without isolation.

The design in Fig. 10.19 shows another example that ensures temporary personal space in public places. Beach clubs like this one often feature private cabanas or daybeds with their own shade, which serve as personal sanctuaries, allowing guests to relax without being disturbed. It's like giving customers a small "me-time" corner amidst the communal fun. So, if you feel oddly at ease in an open space, know that someone thought about your invisible bubble and made sure it had room to breathe.

Secondly, let's pull back the curtain on the *prospect-refuge theory*.[23] It is about how humans might be hardwired to seek out environments where they can easily see others (prospect) while remaining unseen (refuge). It's like having our cake and eating it too. Those spaces evoke feelings of safety, comfort, and appeal. Think about why treehouses are the ultimate childhood dream or why a balcony feels so ritzy. It's

[23] Dosen and Ostwald (2013).

Fig. 10.18 Woowa Brothers office, Seoul, South Korea (photographed by Jeongmin Lee, 2023, Author's Collection)

Fig. 10.19 Saadiyat Beach Club, Abu Dhabi, UAE (Beatrice Preve/ventdusud/Shutterstock)

all about that panoramic view of the surroundings (prospect) paired with the comfort of a secure, private nook (refuge). From an evolutionary perspective, this preference makes sense. If you can see potential problems from afar, you have more time to react. If you're hidden, you're less likely to be attacked.

Real-life examples? This theory explains why many people are willing to pay premium prices for homes that offer a panoramic view of the surroundings while ensuring privacy. Moreover, have you ever noticed how people often prefer comfy corner restaurant seats beside the window? This positioning allows diners the dual advantage of observing the outside view and the room while enjoying the security of a protective barrier.

This theory can be a guiding principle in designing spaces and experiences that balance our itch to watch the world and our craving for a snug corner. For example, in residential architecture, large windows or balconies facing beautiful vistas can provide the prospect. Meanwhile, introducing blinds, curtains, or tinted windows can offer refuge by preventing outsiders from looking in. Furthermore, who doesn't adore those quiet, secluded nooks or cozy reading corners? Outdoors, patios and gazebos can be placed at a place offering a panoramic view of a garden, but with the bonus of some shade and seclusion.

Now, consider the Treehotel in Fig. 10.20, a design example that applies the prospect-refuge theory in an unexpected way. Nestled among lush forests, this hotel offers unique treehouse rooms that are individually designed by various architects, ensuring each unit has its own distinct aesthetic and concept (Mirrorcube, Bird's Nest, The Cabin, The UFO, and so forth). Large windows, outdoor decks, and the elevated position among the trees invite guests into a one-of-a-kind observational experience of the forest. Each room also offers refuge, crafting a feeling of sanctuary amidst the foliage. Inside, it's spacious and modern—a serene tree-hugger's paradise with a hint of luxury.

Now, let's wrap up our journey. In the opening episode, it's been said that beneath our modern veneer, we humans are still profoundly primal at heart. So, the underlying beat of this chapter has been our deep-seated instincts to stay safe. Each psychological principle explored in this chapter underscores the profound impact of our innate desires for safety on design and consumer behavior. Whether it's the contours of objects or the spatial configurations we inhabit, the echoes of our survival history continue to shape our likes and dislikes. Therefore, for designers and marketers, this isn't just academic talk. It is about crafting experiences, products, and spaces

Fig. 10.20 Treehotel, 2010, Harads, Sweden (Kedardome/Shutterstock)

that resonate with the very core of human nature—creating a world that is not only aesthetically pleasing but also deeply attuned to our primal desires. Smartly weaving in these principles, designs can ultimately enrich human experiences and interactions.

References

Adibi, M., Zoccolan, D., & Clifford, C. W. (2021). Sensory adaptation. *Frontiers in Systems Neuroscience, 15*, 809000. https://doi.org/10.3389/fnsys.2021.809000

Bar, M., & Neta, M. (2006). Humans prefer curved visual objects. *Psychological Science, 17*(8), 645–648.

Bar, M., & Neta, M. (2007). Visual elements of subjective preference modulate amygdala activation. *Neuropsychologia, 45*(10), 2191–2200.

Buss, D. M. (Ed.). (2005). *The handbook of evolutionary psychology*. Wiley.

Craig, C. S., Sternthal, B., & Leavitt, C. (1976). Advertising wearout: An experimental analysis. *Journal of Marketing Research, 13*(4), 365–372.

Dosen, A. S., & Ostwald, M. J. (2013). Prospect and refuge theory: Constructing a critical definition for architecture and design. *The International Journal of Design in Society, 6*(1), 9–23.

Hall, E. T. (1990). *The hidden dimension* (pp. 113–130). Anchor Books.

Hansen, C. H., & Hansen, R. D. (1988). Finding the face in the crowd: An anger superiority effect. *Journal of Personality and Social Psychology, 54*(6), 917–924.

Lidwell, W., Holden, K., & Butler, J. (2010). *Universal principles of design: 125 ways to enhance usability, influence perception, increase appeal, make better design decisions, and teach through design*. Rockport Publishers.

McManus, I. C. (2005). Symmetry and asymmetry in aesthetics and the arts. *European Review, 13*(S2), 157–180.

Nafe, J. P., & Wagoner, K. S. (1941). The nature of sensory adaptation. *The Journal of General Psychology, 25*(2), 295–321.

Pentak, S., & Lauer, D. A. (2016). *Design basics* (9th ed.) (pp. 86–109). Cengage Learning.

Stratton, G. M. (1897a). Vision without inversion of the retinal image. *Psychological Review, 4*(4), 341–360.

Stratton, G. M. (1897b). Vision without inversion of the retinal image. *Psychological Review, 4*(5), 463–481.

Van Geert, E., & Wagemans, J. (2023). Prägnanz in visual perception. *Psychonomic Bulletin & Review*, 1–27.

Zajonc, R. B. (2001). Mere exposure: A gateway to the subliminal. *Current Directions in Psychological Science, 10*(6), 224–228.

Chapter 11
The Mystique of Insufficiency Spell

Within the mesmerizing expanse of Yellowstone Park, an air of excitement and anticipation pervaded as crowds gathered, eager to catch a fleeting glimpse of the elusive animal.

"Have you seen it? Can you believe it?" they exclaimed, their voices charged with enthusiasm as they reached out to share the moment with friends and family.

"It appeared but hid again. I have been waiting here for 3 h and finally saw it! I can't wait to tell all my friends about this," exclaimed a teenage boy, his face alight with triumph. You might wonder what this majestic creature that commands such attention is. A lion, perhaps, or a tiger? Maybe a mighty grizzly bear? Nay… Here, the crowd's collective gaze is fixed on something unexpectedly ordinary—a wolf. Yes, a simple, furry wolf.

Why do people so desperately want to catch a glimpse of a wolf? Wolves, once locally extirpated from Yellowstone, have been successfully reintroduced. However, wolves have never been a crowd favorite at zoos. Besides, wolves were the public enemy number one in fables and folklore. And yet, within the boundaries of Yellowstone, they are revered as superstars. What could explain this paradox?

When posed with this question, that teenage boy perfectly summed it up: "Do you have any idea how hard it is to spot a wolf in Yellowstone?" While we can easily bump into the presence of other wild animals there, wolves don't like to be encountered by humans, so they tend to hide in the deep forest. However, sometimes, they come to the edge of the forest, providing a fleeting opportunity for onlookers to witness their enigmatic beauty. And when that moment comes, it's not just a sighting; it's an exciting story of the chase, a badge of honor, a "you-had-to-be-there" kind of thing. So, people are just dying to see this elusive creature, waiting for hours, armed with high-performance binoculars and huge telescopic lenses, all for the slim chance of a sighting.

Indeed, Yellowstone offers a myriad of incredible opportunities to observe the majestic beauty of nature. The real spectacle, though? For me, it was watching the behaviors of the humans themselves and the activation of the psychological theory

© The Author(s), under exclusive license to Springer Nature Singapore Pte Ltd. 2024

J. Lee et al., *The Psychology Behind Design*,
https://doi.org/10.1007/978-981-97-3426-9_11

working in real life—the "scarcity effect." We're drawn to what we can't always have. Therefore, even a wolf can be idolized if it's rare.

Have you ever pondered why diamonds, basically just blinged-up carbon, make us go weak in the knees? It's their price tag, sure, but why so pricey? Simple—Mother Earth doesn't do diamond giveaways. It's rare and, thus, sought after. Drawing inspiration from the biblical text of Revelation, let us entertain the thought of inhabiting a dazzling city not unlike the new, divine Jerusalem descending from heaven. Jasper walls, golden streets, buildings bedazzled with jewels, and gates of pure pearls. Sounds heavenly, right? But what if it were real in this world? The allure? Surely gone. The wow factor would fade. Those gems will be regarded no different than common rocks, and the gold would seem as mundane as paved asphalt. The result? The sight of this city will not give us daily delectations anymore. In this perspective, don't you think our problems are like diamonds? We might inflate their value because they do not happen quite often and because we do not appreciate enough daily gems around us.

It tells us something intriguing: our idea of "precious" is less about the item itself and more about how much of it is around. Should we find ourselves on a planet where granite is extremely rare, we will surely put it on the wedding ring, adding the best symbolic meaning to it. So, this insight flips our typical understanding of "insufficiency" from something negative to a sort of magic spell that boosts value. It's not just having less; it's a powerful impetus that makes us desire something more.

In the world of "insufficiency," there's another special place for the things that are "less than perfect." An anecdote from the late sixteenth century Japan brings this concept to life. Takeno Joo, the tea ceremony master, once tasked his student, Sen Rikyu (who later became a very famous tea master, Sen no Rikyu), with preparing the garden. Rikyu meticulously cleaned and arranged the garden to perfection. However, after that, he began to shake the cherry tree so that the petals and leaves would fall naturally onto the yard.[1] In this story, we can understand his aesthetic philosophy. It seems that he was saying, "Too perfect is a mistake. Nature is not perfect, and we should embrace its imperfections."

While this aesthetic celebrating naturalness and imperfection is often referred to as the Japanese concept of "Wabi-Sabi,"[2] its core principles resonate with broader East Asian cultures, each with their unique interpretations, influenced by Buddhism, Taoism, and Confucianism. For instance, traditional Korean ceramics, such as Buncheong ware (e.g., Fig. 11.1), feature irregular shapes, textures, and glazes, embracing imperfections and the natural qualities of the clay.[3] They look like they've got stories to tell, the tales about being real, uneven, and genuinely themselves. Fast forward to today, and this appreciation for the imperfect has gone global. We're all realizing that it's okay if the bookshelf is a bit wonky or if the garden isn't exactly botanical garden material. It celebrates the beauty in the everyday wear and tear and the personality in the not-so-polished.

---

[1] Lidwell et al. (2010), Handa (2013).

[2] Crowley and Crowley (2005).

[3] Kim et al. (2013).

Fig. 11.1 Grayish-blue-powdered celadon, National Museum of Korea, Seoul, South Korea (Johnathan21/Shutterstock)

Why is this not-quite-perfect so appealing to the human mind? Those imperfect pieces leave room for our imagination to fill in the gaps, offering an invitation for personal interpretations. Thus, engaging with them becomes a dialogue, an interactive experience. Furthermore, this affinity for imperfection taps into our very humanity: whether it's a thing or a human, perfection might make us feel awe, but imperfection makes us feel a sense of kinship, stirring feelings of affection, empathy, and compassion.

Thus, we have begun to unveil the mystery of human attraction to something insufficient. The tales of the elusive wolf and the wisdom of a tea master set the stage for a deeper exploration into how this insufficiency spell influences our preferences, values, and definitions of beauty. Now, let us delve further into the captivating realms of the rare and the beautifully imperfect, shall we?

Owl of Minerva Behind the Scene

In this chapter, we will look into how something rare or a bit imperfect can actually make us like it even more. So, get ready to learn about the cool ways that these objects play a big role in shaping the landscape of design and consumer behavior.

Now or Never: Irresistible Pull of Scarcity

Let's start our investigation with the compelling magnetism of scarcity, a force with an unparalleled ability to sway consumer preferences. The *scarcity effect* is a psychological phenomenon where people find things more attractive and valuable when they believe those things are rare or in short supply. It influences our purchasing decisions, making us more eager to buy the product.[4]

So, how do the marketing gurus pull off this scarcity magic? Two main spells: one is limiting physical availability (*the scarcity of quantity*), and the other is narrowing opportunities or time (*the scarcity of opportunities*).

The first, "limiting physical availability," is a well-established strategy. Consider "limited edition" goodies. These items create a sense of urgency and exclusivity that makes people line up for hours, compelling them to purchase even at a premium price. Nike's Air Jordan sneakers stand as a quintessential example. Since 1985, Nike has been releasing these beauties in dribs and drabs, and guess what? We can't get enough. Thus comes a consumer frenzy, resulting in swift sell-outs and subsequent reselling at exponentially higher prices. The combination of their rarity and the Michael Jordan touch has made these sneakers a cultural phenomenon.[5]

The second trick is the ticking clock. "Narrowing opportunities or time" is another potent tool in the marketer's arsenal. When stores have signs saying "Everything Must Go!" or "Closing Down Sale," people rush to buy things they never knew they needed. And online? You might see those little pop-ups saying, "3 left in stock" or "20 people are eyeing this right now." They nudge us toward a quick purchase. It's all about making us think, "I better grab it now, or I'll never!".

Now, let's explore how the scarcity effect comes to life in design. High-end and budget-friendly brands employ distinct design strategies, tailoring their approaches to their respective target audiences and brand images.

In the realm of luxury, brands try to craft an atmosphere of exclusivity. They not only produce items in limited quantities, occasionally offering them exclusively in specific locales, but also put fewer products on display in their stores. Take, for instance, the elegant spacing and minimal product display in the Gucci store, as showcased in Fig. 11.2. It's like a fashion gallery, where each piece whispers, "I'm unique, and so are you." This design approach makes you feel like you're part of an exclusive club, where rarity and prestige are the secret handshakes.

On the flip side, let's stroll down the aisles of budget-friendly stores. It's a different world here, where abundance reigns supreme, accentuating value for money. These stores frequently employ time-limited discounts to create a sense of urgency. It's also the illusion of scarcity, not in quantity but in time. "Act fast! Limited time offer!" they proclaim. And suddenly, you're on a treasure hunt, racing against the clock. Thus, whether it's the hushed elegance of a high-end boutique or the bustling energy of a bargain haven, the psychology of insufficiency is at play. It's a subtle whisper in your ear saying, "This might be your only chance."

[4] Gierl et al. (2008).

[5] Kardes et al. (2014).

Fig. 11.2 Gucci store, Rome, Italy (Alessia Pierdomenico/Shutterstock)

Here's another captivating case—the Diet Coke bottle getting a makeover from none other than Jean Paul Gaultier, an esteemed French fashion designer. This partnership gave rise to a series of limited edition bottles of Diet Coke (Fig. 11.3, left), mixing the fizzy world of soft drinks with the glamor of fashion runways. One of the bottle designs featured the Breton stripes, a signature pattern of Gaultier's sailor-inspired fashion pieces. Another bottle drew inspiration from his legendary Cone Bra, Madonna's bold fashion choice for her tour (Fig. 11.3, right). The bottles successfully earned collectible status. Why? They were limited editions, they had the Gaultier glamor, and they turned an everyday beverage into a trendy accessory. It was a toast to Diet Coke's fashionable persona.

Fig. 11.3 Left—Coca-Cola and Jean Paul Gaultier, 2012/Right—Madonna in Cone Bra, Jean Paul Gaultier, Blond Ambition World Tour 1990 (Left: cypopcolour/Shutterstock) (Right: PA Images/ Alamy Stock Photo)

In a nutshell, scarcity is a big deal when it comes to enhancing perceptions of value. It can turn the ordinary into the extraordinary and, thus, increase the desirability of the object. From limited edition releases to the strategic use of low stock indicators and countdown timers, scarcity is the behind-the-scenes maestro, pulling the strings to make us reach for our wallets faster. So, getting a grip on the scarcity playbook is indispensable for adding a sprinkle of "wow" to the products and customer experiences. That is, a buzz, a little drama, and a dash of "I need this now!".

Bare Elegance: Minimalism and Power of Less

Let's shift our attention to a different facet of rarity value—the world of "*Minimalism*." In contrast to the scarcity effect's influence on consumer behavior, the allure of insufficiency can also stem from the realization that we do not need an abundance of material possessions to be happy or fulfilled. This can be very enlightening because we are living in a world where overconsumption is encouraged by all sorts of marketing strategies (such as the scarcity effect), and, as a result, our closets are so full even the skeletons don't have space anymore.[6] Minimalism promotes the idea that true contentment can be discovered in a life of elegant simplicity and mindful choices. Therefore, it is not only a design philosophy but also a lifestyle choice, an active rarity given by ourselves, not by others.

A minimalist lifestyle is about making room for more of what really matters. Embracing less can indeed lead to more because this kind of simplification can result in reduced stress, increased productivity, and an enhanced sense of well-being. That is, a minimalist lifestyle means we're not just clearing out our closets but also decluttering our minds. This concept can be integrated into various aspects of daily life, including home design, personal belongings, and even digital spaces. It encourages us to make more thoughtful purchasing decisions. After all, in the world of insufficiency, the richest person is the one who needs the least.

In the realms of art and design, minimalism is all about peeling back the layers to the essentials, like simple shapes, a restrained color palette, and a lack of decorative elements.[7] Imagine it as your favorite white shirt—simple, elegant, and never out of style. The focus is on creating functional and aesthetically pleasing designs with the fewest elements possible. The design maxim "Less is more" (attributed to the architect Ludwig Mies van der Rohe) succinctly encapsulates the minimalist ethos.[8]

Take, for instance, the Arco Lamp and the interior design showcased in Fig. 11.4 (left). The design of the lamp, in particular, stands out as both functional and elegant, making it an iconic piece of modern design. Even in simplicity, we find richness and depth, and that's the power of minimalist aesthetics. To fully grasp it, compare this to the opulent Empire Room and its chandelier in Fig. 11.4 (right). It's like

[6] On December 7, 2023, suggested by ChatGPT-4.

[7] Macarthur (2002).

[8] Evans (2023), Meyer (2021).

Fig. 11.4 Left—Arco Floor Lamp, Achille and Pier Giacomo Castiglioni, 1962/Right—Palmer House Hilton Hotel (Empire Room), Chicago, USA (Left: Jodie Johnson/Shutterstock) (Right: photographed by Jeongmin Lee, 2016, Author's Collection)

a maximalist's dream where "More is more." Both have their charms, but they're worlds apart, like comparing a quiet cup of tea to a full-blown tea party.

More familiar design examples? Ever notice how some everyday designs just feel right? Apple serves as a stellar example of this design philosophy. Think of the iPhone. It has a sleek, simple design with very few buttons, and everything serves a purpose. Then, there is Google's homepage—just a logo, a search bar, and a few buttons. Simple, but it gets the job done beautifully.

While some might argue that the appeal of minimalism is innate, there is a strong case to be made that it is also a cultivated taste. It's like developing a taste for black coffee, an acquired preference shaped by our culture and times. In the Western world, the minimalist aesthetic traces its roots back to the early twentieth century, when the Modernist movement decided to cut the clutters of traditional forms in favor of simplicity and functionality as a response to the industrial age.[9] This shift left a profound impact on art, design, and architecture, laying the groundwork for the popularity of minimalism we witness today. However, in the Eastern world, it has a much longer history. Similar concepts of simplicity and focus on essentials have long existed in various forms across different cultures, particularly in Eastern Asian philosophies.

Fast forward to the contemporary day, the backlash against consumerism and overconsumption has further propelled a preference for minimalist aesthetics. People are increasingly seeking ways to simplify their lives and reduce their environmental footprint. Moreover, in today's fast-paced, chaotic world, there's a growing appeal for minimalism as a way to create a sense of calm and order in their lives—a visual sigh of relief in the midst of 24/7 hustle.

[9] Macarthur (2002).

Therefore, we can say that minimalistic aesthetics, while potentially appealing at an innate level, can also be seen as a cultured response, offering a visual and lifestyle alternative that is aligned with contemporary values and aspirations.

Silent Persuasion: Hidden Message of White Space

Next, related to the power of less, let's look into the psychological impact of "*white space in an ad*."[10] White space, often referred to as negative space, is the area that's left intentionally blank. You might wonder, "How does something as simple as "white space" influence our psyche?" It is linked to the influences of scarcity and minimalism that we've discussed above. Far from being just "empty," it holds a treasure trove of psychological implications. It's like the pause between musical notes that makes you lean in and listen more intently, thus making the melody more captivating. That is, it acts as a silent but potent communicator.

The research titled "How Nothing Became Something" reveals that white space in ads is synonymous with prestige and luxury in the consumer mind.[11] Luxury brands have understood this. Take Chanel or Louis Vuitton ads, for instance, in Fig. 11.5. These ads contain large empty spaces, yet they speak volumes. It's a sophisticated invitation to a world of elegance.

White space in ads can also play an important role when it comes to saving our brains from information overload. It is a significant consideration in today's rapid-paced digital environment, where attention spans are notably brief and where we are suffering from daily SPAMs (those who send them do not seem to know that S.P.A.M. is a "**S**eriously, **P**oor **A**dvertising **M**ethod!").[12] In situations like this, white space

Fig. 11.5 Left—Chanel ad/Right—Louis Vuitton ad (Left: Sorbis/Shutterstock) (Right: Faiz Zaki/Shutterstock)

[10] Mothersbaugh et al. (2020).

[11] Pracejus et al. (2006).

[12] On December 8, 2023, extracted and revised from https://www.writeraccess.com/blog/2020-07-humor-marketing-guide/.

Fig. 11.6 Chinese Song Dynasty painting (Wirestock Creators/Shutterstock)

is like a visual breather, helping us process and retain information better. Thus, it makes the overall design more digestible and appealing.

While white space can be a powerful tool, like any tool, it requires a bit of finesse. It's all about balance. Too much, and you risk a sense of emptiness and a lack of content. The art lies in striking that sweet spot where the design feels opportune, not deficient.

Now, let's take a little journey into the concept of white space in traditional Oriental paintings.[13] The strategic use of white space has been recognized as a unique element of traditional Oriental paintings compared to their Western counterparts. It carries the weight of philosophical and aesthetic values of Eastern Asian cultures. Consider, for example, the artwork depicted in Fig. 11.6. White space here embodies simplicity and contemplation. Moreover, in many Eastern philosophies, emptiness is seen as a state of potential. The white space in art mirrors this concept, inviting you to fill in the blanks with your own stories and imaginations. Feeling like a cloud of words? Well, isn't philosophy somehow the field where most of us finish knowing less than when we started?[14] But, somehow, isn't that the beauty of it?

So, white space in art and design, when wielded with care, is not just a background element; it is a silent but eloquent constituent. It's a reminder that sometimes, what's not there can be just as powerful as what is there. Thus, it can stand as a powerful testament to the principle that "less can, indeed, be more." Therefore, when an ad with a good amount of white space catches your eye, bear in mind that it is far from a result of designer apathy. It's a carefully crafted piece of psychological artistry, the harmonious collaboration of absence and presence. This kind of ad might remind you of the witty saying, "Progress is made by lazy people looking for an easier way to do things"[15] But let's also call to mind that sometimes "not doing something" is as

[13] Fan et al. (2019).

[14] On December 8, 2023, extracted and revised from https://upjoke.com/philosophy-jokes.

[15] On December 7, 2023, extracted and revised from HUMORTHATWORKS.COM.

difficult as "doing something." Do you need real-life examples for that? Diet, saving money, anger management, holding off unnecessary criticism, patience…

Unfinished Business: Appeals of Incompleteness

As we explore the intriguing path of insufficiency, let us turn our eyes to another aspect of it—the psychological effect of the incomplete and imperfect.

Firstly, there is the *law of closure* in the Gestalt theory.[16] Think of it as the mind's love for completing puzzles. It describes the innate perceptual tendency to fill in the gaps of visual stimulus and see things as whole and complete, even when some parts are conspicuously absent. That is, when closure is not immediately attainable in a given visual stimulus, it sets off a spark in our brains, igniting a quest to find the missing pieces. This effect is a goldmine for designers and marketers, as it can be harnessed to capture attention, to weave intrigue, and, thus, to drive consumer engagement. A little mystery can go a long way with customers.

Consider the WWF (World Wildlife Fund) logo design illustrated in Fig. 11.7. It's not a full-blown panda portrait but more like a panda teaser. However, our minds effortlessly fill in the gaps, recognizing the panda in its entirety. This masterful use of closure not only makes the logo memorable but also works as a symbolic nudge toward the bigger picture of wildlife conservation, suggesting that there's still work to be done to fill in the gaps in nature's canvas.

Moving on to the sports arena, we find the logo design of tennis legend Roger Federer (Fig. 11.8). It's an artistic serve of his initials "RF," with a few strokes deliberately left out. Yet, in the viewer's mind, the initials are perceived as a whole. It's a visual echo of his style on the court, too. The open shapes and fluid lines are like a homage to Federer's playing style, known for its effortless grace and fluidity.

Fig. 11.7 WWF (World Wildlife Fund) logo (Fajar Adinda Putra/Shutterstock)

[16] Todorovic (2008), Soegaard (2020).

Fig. 11.8 Roger Federer logo (photographed by Jeongmin Lee, 2023, Author's Collection)

A cognitive phenomenon closely related to the closure principle is the *Zeigarnik effect*.[17] Think of it as our brain's sticky note for unfinished business. That is, it's the human tendency to remember uncompleted or interrupted tasks better than completed tasks. It's like our mind's way of nudging us, "Hey, weren't you in the middle of something?".

The movie "Matrix" played this card beautifully for its series release. By leaving a story unfinished, the audience is left craving resolution, turning them into eager beavers waiting for the next installment. Similarly, in the advertising sector, a message can be deliberately left incomplete or open-ended to keep the product lingering in customers' minds. Think about a teaser ad for a new car that often shows only a glimpse of the car or a storyline of an ad that ends with a cliffhanger. This creates suspense and anticipation, making sure we're all ears and eyes for the big reveal.

The teaser advertisement for the film "Gone Girl" is a good example. This psychological thriller centers on the mysterious disappearance of Amy Dunne, which spawns a whirlwind of media attention and a police investigation that casts suspicion on her husband, Nick Dunne. Now, take a look at the movie's teaser poster in Fig. 11.9. The tagline teasingly stops at "You don't know what you've got 'til it's…" And just like that, it has us hooked, wondering about the rest.

These examples, which apply the law of closure and the Zeigarnik effect, illuminate how the mind's desire for the unseen and the incomplete can be harnessed to forge impactful visual impressions. We could see that using a dash of incompleteness is akin to starting a conversation and leaving it intriguingly open-ended. Sometimes, it is the space between the lines that tells the most compelling story.

[17] Seifert and Patalano (1991).

Fig. 11.9 "Gone Girl" teaser poster design, 2014 (BFA/Alamy Stock Photo)

Perfectly Imperfect: Wabi-Sabi Aesthetic

What about the beauty of imperfection itself, then? Ever thought that a bit of imperfection could be a whole lot of beautiful? While the law of closure and the Zeigarnik effect leverage the psychological impact caused by incompleteness, there's a distinct design ethos that celebrates imperfection itself—*Wabi-Sabi*.[18] It encompasses the wear and tear of time and nature just as it is. In the contemporary design landscape, this aesthetic reflects a shift away from the pursuit of perfection and toward an appreciation of authenticity and the beauty of flaws. There is also an emphasis on using sustainable materials and ethical manufacturing practices, aligning with the philosophy of living in harmony with nature.

It has found resonance in various design fields. For example, modern interiors often feature materials that age gracefully and develop character over time (e.g., Fig. 11.10). It's a storybook of years gone by. In these interiors, handcrafted items and furnishings are preferred, not "in spite of" but "for" their unique imperfections. They're telling their life stories through their textures and tones. The color palette tends to be subdued—calm, earthy, and soothing, inviting you to slow down. All these design elements create a serene environment that encourages a more contemplative appreciation of the world around us. They seem to teach us that, in this hectic world, the easiest way to get someone's attention is to sit down and look comfortable.[19]

Products, too, can be crafted to highlight the marks of their creation, such as visible seams, irregularities in texture, or variations in color (refer to Fig. 11.11). This

---

[18] Handa (2013).

[19] On December 8, 2023, extracted and revised from https://upjoke.com/attention-jokes.

Fig. 11.10 Interior design in Wabi-Sabi style (Ground Picture/Shutterstock)

approach extends into the digital realm, where graphic designs frequently incorporate hand-drawn elements, irregular shapes, and textured patterns, eschewing digital precision.

In all these design examples, the common thread is the celebration of the natural, the unrefined, and the genuine rather than overly polished and perfect. In short, this design trend reflects a broader cultural shift toward valuing sustainability, authenticity, and a slower, more mindful way of living. It's a call to find beauty in the mundane and embrace the imperfect as an integral part of life.

So, it's the end of our quest into the psychological impacts of insufficiency. As we close this chapter, we hope that you're taking with you a fresh perspective: the

Fig. 11.11 Ceramics in Wabi-Sabi style (Anna Kim/Shutterstock)

power of the rare, the unseen, and the imperfect play pivotal roles in augmenting the perceived value and aesthetic appeal of objects and experiences. When we understand this, we can foster a deeper appreciation for the world around us and create designs that resonate on a more profound level.

References

Crowley, J., & Crowley, S. (2005). Wabi Sabi Style. Gibbs Smith.

Evans, G. (2023, April 5). Minimalism—Understanding it in art and architecture. Accessed December 12, 2023. https://www.commercialarchitecturemagazine.com/minimalism/

Fan, Z., Zhang, K., & Zheng, X. S. (2019). Evaluation and analysis of white space in Wu Guanzhong's Chinese paintings. *Leonardo, 52*(2), 111–116.

Gierl, H., Plantsch, M., & Schweidler, J. (2008). Scarcity effects on sales volume in retail. *International Review of Retail, Distribution and Consumer Research, 18*(1), 45–61.

Handa, R. (2013). Sen no Rikyū and the Japanese way of tea: Ethics and aesthetics of the everyday. *Interiors, 4*(3), 229–247.

Kardes, F., Cronley, M., & Cline, T. (2014). *Consumer behavior* (2nd ed.). Cengage Learning.

Kim, H. J., Ro, H. S., & Kim, W. S. (2013). Analysis of Korea Buncheong ware by Bunjang (white slip) technique. *International Journal of Contents, 9*(2), 70–76.

Lidwell, W., Holden, K., & Butler, J. (2010). *Universal principles of design: 125 ways to enhance usability, influence perception, increase appeal, make better design decisions, and teach through design.* Rockport Publishers.

Macarthur, J. (2002). The look of the object: Minimalism in art and architecture, then and now. *Architectural Theory Review, 7*(1), 137–148.

Meyer, I. (2021, April 7. Updated 2023, September 27). Minimalist art—An exploration of the minimalism art movement. In *Art in Context.* Accessed December 12, 2023. https://artincontext.org/minimalistart/#:~:text=Minimalist%20Art%2C%20or%20Minimalism%20Art%2C,leaving%20out%20any%20unnecessary%20elements

Mothersbaugh, D. L., Hawkins, D. I., & Kleiser, S. B. (2020). *Consumer behavior: Building marketing strategy* (14th ed.). McGraw-Hill Education.

Pracejus, J. W., Olsen, G. D., & O'guinn, T. C. (2006). How nothing became something: White space, rhetoric, history, and meaning. *Journal of Consumer Research, 33*(1), 82–90.

Seifert, C. M., & Patalano, A. L. (1991). Memory for incomplete tasks: A re-examination of the Zeigarnik effect. In *Proceedings of the 13th annual conference of the Cognitive Science Society* (pp. 114–119).

Soegaard, M. (2020). The laws of figure/ground, prägnanz, closure, and common fate—Gestalt principles (Part 3). Accessed December 12, 2023. https://www.interaction-design.org/literature/article/the-laws-of-figure-ground-praegnanz-closure-and-common-fate-gestalt-principles-3#:~:text=The%20law%20of%20Closure%20refers,third%20in%20the%20Gestalt%20series

Todorovic, D. (2008). Gestalt principles. *Scholarpedia, 3*(12), 5345.

Chapter 12
Hedonic Alchemy of Fun and Pleasure

Why do we revel in things we don't really need? Is the quest for hedonic pleasure just an indulgent extra in our lives?

Let's consider the role of play. The act of play, be it through sports, games, or art, is a celebration of freedom and creativity. It allows us to experiment, to laugh, to fail, and to try again because it resides in the domain of the non-essential. Here, we find a space where the mind can wander and wonder and where the only pursuit is the joy of the moment.

Picture a scene: a bunch of serious adults huddled around a table. The air is thick with concentration and tension, yet it's punctuated with bursts of laughter and cheers. They are knee-deep in a board game. Now, pause for a moment to ask why these adults, years away from their playground era, are still drawn to such playful experiences.

It might be tempting to view this scenario as a simple escape, a break from the "real" tasks of life. Yet, if we delve deeper, we uncover more dynamics at play. It's amidst this enjoyment and playful banter that we find a sense of renewal, a reset button for our emotions, akin to the effect of a good sleep. So, fun and pleasure are not just frivolities; they're essential to our well-being.

What, then, are the implications of fun and pleasure in consumer psychology? When companies add them to their products or experiences, they're tapping into something called "hedonic value.“ Here's a brief on how fun and pleasure work in consumer behavior.

First, they make products more noticeable, thus grabbing our attention, like a splash of color in a greyscale world. Second, they evoke positive emotions, of course. These emotions often rub off on the brand, enhancing our desire to purchase it. Third, they foster brand loyalty. When the brand experience is enjoyable, customers are more likely to return for more. Lastly, they promote social sharing, which acts as free advertising for companies. For instance, if you find a funny filter on a photo app, you're likely to share that selfie on Instagram. In essence, by making the brand

© The Author(s), under exclusive license to Springer Nature Singapore Pte Ltd. 2024

J. Lee et al., *The Psychology Behind Design*,
https://doi.org/10.1007/978-981-97-3426-9_12

experience fun and pleasurable, companies not only boost sales but also weave a stronger bond with customers.

Let's dive a little deeper into this hedonic business. Beyond the surface, there's an unexpectedly profound aspect—the "flow," a higher level of fun and pleasure. It's the concept from "flow theory" by Mihaly Csikszentmihalyi.[1]

To illustrate this concept, let's sketch a character named Julian. Julian had an extraordinary talent. When painting, he would become so absorbed in his work that the world around him seemed to vanish. Hours passed like minutes as his brush effortlessly graced the canvas. In these moments, he felt a deep sense of joy and fulfillment. This magical experience that Julian relished is what Csikszentmihalyi defines as the flow. It is a state of blissful immersion in an activity where time distorts, self-consciousness fades, and one's presence is entirely in the moment.

As Julian's brush gained fame, bigger challenges came knocking. One day, he was asked to paint a mural in the city hall. The canvas? Huge. The pressure? Immense. He felt overwhelmed. Doubt and fear of failure replaced the usual joy of painting. The flow that once carried him had ebbed away.

Julian's story shows us that flow flourishes where one's skills are perfectly matched with the difficulty level of the task at hand. Also, unlike simple pleasures like savoring a sweet flavor or listening to a soothing melody, the flow involves complexity, challenge, and sometimes a bit of struggle. It's about the joy of overcoming, of stretching one's limits, and, in doing so, of discovering one's true potential.

Now, before we set sail into our journey of fun and pleasure, let's pause for a moment to consider the psychological effects of "humor," a sparkling gem in the treasure chest of fun and pleasure. Humor isn't just a nice-to-have in life's toolkit; it's more akin to a multi-purpose wrench, essential and versatile.

First, humor is the ultimate social glue. It's like a magic potion that, when sprinkled into conversations, creates social bonding because a shared giggle can build a sense of camaraderie and trust in relationships. It's often used to ease social tensions, too. For example, if someone calls you a nobody, just smile and say, "Nobody's perfect!"[2]

Second, laughter and humor can be effective ways to manage emotions. When stress or the blues hit, a dose of laughter can be more effective than a bubble bath. It often provides a release of tension and can help in coping with stress, anxiety, and sadness. Humor can offer a different perspective on challenging situations, making life's mountains seem more like molehills.

Third, humor produces cognitive benefits, too. It nudges creativity, sparks out-of-the-box thinking, and thus enhances problem-solving skills by enabling people to see situations in new and different ways. Research by Isen, Daubman, and Nowicki backed this up.[3] Participants in this study faced difficult problems that required creative thinking. In this experiment, people who watched a short comedy film or received a small gift before the task performed better than those who did not.

---

[1] Csikszentmihalyi (2014).

[2] On December 21, 2023, extracted and revised from https://jokojokes.com/perfection-jokes.html.

[3] Isen et al. (1987).

Fourth, laughter accompanying humor has been shown to have numerous health benefits. Even the wisdom of the proverb says, "Laughter is the best medicine." It can boost the immune system, relax muscles, improve blood flow, and increase the production of endorphins. This can contribute to an overall sense of well-being.

So there you have it. Fun and pleasure are a social catalyst, an emotional healer, a cognitive stimulant, and a health tonic. Therefore, let's move beyond the misconception that fun and pleasure are just frivolous extras; they're fundamental to human life! It is our mind's way of ensuring that we don't just survive but thrive. "At the end of the day, if I can say I had fun, it was a good day," a quote from Simone Biles.

Owl of Minerva Behind the Scene

Welcome to the funhouse of the mind! In this chapter, we will embark on a journey into the realm of fun and pleasure. We will uncover that fun and pleasure are serious business—vital ingredients in the recipe for our psychological well-being.

To navigate this journey, we'll first dissect the complex spectrum of human pleasure, particularly as it relates to design.

The Spectrum of Pleasure in Design

Patrick W. Jordan's model of pleasure offers a holistic view of pleasure in design.[4] It provides four categories—physio-pleasure, psycho-pleasure, socio-pleasure, and ideo-pleasure. Understanding these categories allows designers and marketers to create experiences that can appeal to users on multiple levels.

Physio-pleasure is related to the physical and sensory experiences derived from tangible interactions with designs. It includes tactile sensations, ergonomics, and the overall physical comfort experienced when interacting with a product. Imagine the soothing sensation of a massage chair working on tense muscles or the comforting warmth of a ceramic mug cradled in your hands on a chilly morning. These are the physical and sensory delights that make life plusher.

Psycho-pleasure is associated with the cognitive and emotional aspects of an individual's experience. It involves mental enjoyment, such as the satisfaction from solving a problem, the joy of understanding how something works, or the emotional pleasure derived from aesthetics and design. This type of pleasure is often linked to the usability, functionality, and overall emotional experience provided by a product. For instance, solving a challenging puzzle or the "eureka!" moment when your new gadget works just as it should bring psycho-pleasure.

Socio-pleasure pertains to the enjoyment and satisfaction gained from relationships and social interactions. Whether it's the shared laughter over a meal with friends or the camaraderie found in online gaming communities, a sense of belonging and social engagement enriches our experiences, making us feel like we're part of a

[4] Jordan (2000).

bigger, happier whole. In product design, this could relate to how a product facilitates social connectivity or enhances social status.

Ideo-pleasure is rooted in the satisfaction of the values and ideals of the user. It's the pride in supporting a noble cause or the inner peace from living your truth. Thus, it can be derived from products or services that align with an individual's self-image, personal values, or ideals. For example, using environmentally friendly products may give ideo-pleasure to someone who values sustainability.

Now, equipped with this multifaceted understanding of human pleasure, we will delve further into the psychological theories that underpin fun and pleasure.

Thrills Versus Chills: Arousal Theory

Arousal theory is one of the psychological principles that sheds light on how fun and pleasure play a role in shaping consumer behavior.[5] Arousal is a state of mental and physical readiness, characterized by alertness, engagement, and heightened sensory experiences, and feeling fun and pleasure means that our senses and brains are aroused.

Arousal theory explains how varying levels of arousal can influence a person's pursuit of fun and pleasure. It suggests that there is an *optimal arousal level*, a sweet spot where we perform and feel our best. Too little arousal might lead to boredom, while too much could result in overstimulation. As already mentioned in Chap. 1, it is especially called the *Yerkes-Dodson law*.

Actually, the "Yerkes-Dodson law" can be considered a part of the broader arousal theory in psychology. While "arousal theory" addresses the general impact of arousal on behavior and performance, the "Yerkes-Dodson law" offers a more detailed explanation of how this relationship functions across different levels of task complexity. It's an important concept within the wider framework of arousal theory, providing valuable insights into the dynamics of arousal and performance.

Furthermore, this "optimal arousal level" isn't one-size-fits-all: it varies from person to person. Take, for instance, the preferences for leisure activities. Some find their groove in heart-racing activities like skydiving, while others find it in the peaceful concentration of a golf game. Even for social interactions, different people want different levels of arousal. Introverts wish for a sitcom-like life: most of their social interaction occurs with the people they live with and lasts about 20 min a day.[6] But extroverts? They can interact with people for hours on end.

In the realms of marketing and design, arousal theory guides professionals to create experiences that resonate with their target audience. Consider the automobile industry as illustrated in Fig. 12.1. Among the well-heeled who have the means to purchase luxury cars, some are drawn to the high-octane appeal of a Lamborghini, while others prefer the refined elegance of a Rolls Royce. Similarly, advertisements

[5] Zuckerman et al. (1964).

[6] On December 21, 2023, extracted and revised from https://jokojokes.com/interaction-jokes.html.

Fig. 12.1 Left—Lamborghini Sián FKP 37/Right—Rolls Royce Phantom (Left: Mike Mareen/Shutterstock) (Right: Yurgentum/Shutterstock)

are tuned to this theory, too. A high-energy ad, with its loud music and rapid scene transitions, might resonate more with individuals thriving on high arousal levels, while an ad with soft music and a slower pace might appeal more to those having a lower arousal threshold.

In a nutshell, arousal theory provides insights into why people make specific choices for fun and pleasure, guided by their unique arousal needs. By understanding this, professionals in marketing and design can more effectively tap into the varied rhythms of customers' desire for excitement, thereby enhancing their ability to engage their audience.

Lost in the Moment: Flow Theory

Next, let's explore more for the *flow theory*, which was previously touched upon in the episode section. It describes a state of deep immersion in an activity, where a person is fully absorbed to the point that they lose track of time and are completely focused on the task at hand. This "flow" state is often associated with high levels of enjoyment and satisfaction.[7] It is especially important in shaping customer experiences that unfold with time (e.g., video game design, customer journey map design in flagship stores, etc.).

To understand flow more easily, picture yourself indulging in a beloved hobby, such as creating handmade crafts. Your skills are well-matched to the challenge that it imposes, and while it's demanding, it's not overly so. The hours melt away unnoticed as you're engrossed in the activity, and you're not distracted by thoughts of other tasks or worries. In this moment, you're so-called "in the zone," a perfect embodiment of the flow state.

Sports stars often talk about being in the zone during a nail-biting match. This is flow in action, where their abilities perfectly align with the challenge of the game, resulting in peak performance and exhilaration.[8] This isn't just limited to sports.

[7] Csikszentmihalyi (2014).

[8] Young and Pain (1999).

Even in the workplace, there are moments when someone is so engrossed in a challenging yet skill-appropriate project that even coffee breaks seem like unnecessary interruptions. Your colleague, who never experienced the flow, might sigh, saying, "Life is so much easier without challenges." But actually, without challenges, life would just be a series of tasks![9] The only problem is the balance between your skill and the difficulty level of that challenge. When the two meet at the right level, even a workstation can be transformed into a PlayStation.

In design, video games are a prime illustration of flow theory at work. These games are meticulously crafted to usher players into a flow state. They provide escalating challenges that are just right to keep players engaged without feeling overly difficult or too simple. Ever played "Tetris" or "Super Mario?" If you've ever looked up from these games and wondered where the day went, you've experienced the flow. "Time flies when you're having fun," as the saying goes.

Therefore, flow theory is essential in understanding how to design experiences that captivate and delight users. By creating the right balance between challenge and skill, fostering concentration, offering immediate feedback, and minimizing distractions, designers can effectively induce flow states. When done right, it provides a journey into a world of deep immersion, high pleasure, and great satisfaction.

Shared Smiles: Social Presence Theory

Fun and pleasure can be amplified by the company of other people. The *social presence theory* explains it and is related to socio-pleasure.[10] It's just a fancy term for "The more, the merrier." Even the word "T.E.A.M." can be the acronym for "Together Everyone Achieves More."[11]

Picture this: you walk into a cozy little shop, and immediately, the warmth of a friendly greeting washes over you. That's the social presence in action—the comforting sense that someone else is there. And it's not just for brick-and-mortar stores anymore. Given our current era, where various social media platforms connect people regardless of physical distance, the consideration of social presence has become more important than ever. That is, different mediums should still convey a sense of human connection on the other side of the screen, nudging that feeling of "Hey, you're not alone here."

Why does this matter for consumers? It's because the presence of other people just makes everything better. Therefore, social presence theory is a reminder that even in the digital age, the old human desire for connection and social interaction is alive and kicking. When we feel like we're in good company, we trust more, we share more, we enjoy more, and yep, we buy more.

---

[9] On December 21, 2023, suggested by ChatGPT-4.

[10] Cui et al. (2013).

[11] On December 21, 2023, extracted and revised from https://www.teampedia.net/wiki/Team_Building_and_Teamwork_Quotes.

Fig. 12.2 Brochure for Super Mario Bros. Wonder for Nintendo Switch (photographed by Jeongmin Lee, 2023, Author's Collection)

In design terms, this theory helps in crafting products or experiences that make users feel more connected. Consider multiplayer games, where camaraderie and a bit of friendly rivalry make everything more exciting. An example is Super Mario Bros. Wonder for the Nintendo Switch (Fig. 12.2), which allows up to four players to engage in both competitive and cooperative gameplay. It turns an ordinary gaming session into an uproarious gathering.

Fitness apps such as Fitbit or Strava also apply social elements to spur users into more physical activity. They employ points, badges, and leaderboards, transforming personal exercise into a competitive and rewarding game where users can share their achievements, challenge friends, earn accolades, and monitor progress. These aspects transform a solitary workout into a friendly sports league.

These examples illustrate how a sense of togetherness significantly boosts fun and pleasure. So, when you're designing the next big thing, remember that a sprinkle of social presence can be the secret spice that makes all the difference.[12] However, social presence is not always positive. In life, social presence can be the source of both fun and stress. For example, we call someone who makes difficult tasks look easy a professional, but what do you call someone who makes easy tasks look difficult? A coworker![13] It's two sides of the same coin.

A Feast for the Senses: Sensory Marketing

Now, let's turn our attention from the theories to the practical approaches that boost fun and pleasure in marketing and design.

---

[12] Kelleher et al. (2019).

[13] On December 21, 2023, extracted and revised from https://upjoke.com/professional-jokes.

First, let's dive into *sensory marketing* as it relates to physio-pleasure. This approach focuses on engaging the five senses (sight, sound, touch, taste, and smell) to foster a memorable bond between customer and brand.[14]

Here's how sensory marketing taps into each sense to enhance physio-pleasure.

- Sight: Visually appealing designs can create a sense of pleasure. Consider the sleek designs of Apple products or the iconic blue of a Tiffany & Co. box whose packaging alone evokes excitement and a sense of luxury.
- Sound: The right music can make shopping more enjoyable and entice people to linger more in a store. Starbucks, for example, enhances its coffee shop ambiance with soothing music, complementing the taste of the coffee.
- Touch: The tactile experience is also a very important element in arousing sensory pleasure. Consider the smooth interior of a luxury car or the tactile comfort of a Nike Dri-FIT shirt.
- Taste: Sampling in grocery stores is a direct form of sensory marketing. Once you taste something delightful, you're more likely to buy it. Lindt chocolate shops often offer samples to entice shoppers with their product's rich flavor.
- Smell: Scents can evoke memories and emotions. Real estate agents baking cookies during open houses to create a warm, welcoming atmosphere or Abercrombie & Fitch's signature store scent are strategic uses of olfactory marketing.

Lush Cosmetics offers a masterclass example for this sensory symphony. Its store designs are like sensory theme parks, highlighting the brand's focus on freshness and natural ingredients. First of all, Lush stores are visually stimulating, reminiscent of a vibrant farmers' market with an abundance of fresh produce (Fig. 12.3, left). Customers are also encouraged to touch, feel, and experience the products, from the fizz of bath bombs to the textures of soaps. Most stores even have a wash basin, encouraging customers to wash their hands with their soap. This tactile approach allows customers to experience a sense of discovery and playfulness. Furthermore, the stores' natural scents invite curiosity and draw in passersby, while the energetic music and the chatter of enthusiastic employees giving product demonstrations make the aural landscape lively and fun. Lastly, though Lush products are not edible, the brand incorporates a metaphorical "taste" through products resembling fruits or vegetables (Fig. 12.3, right) and occasionally offers edible treats during special events.

Then there are Zippo lighters, celebrated not only for their classic look but also for their distinctive sound—the "click" of the lighter opening and the "clunk" when it closes. This sound factor has been marketed so well that it has been identified with the brand, akin to the iconic sound of a Harley-Davidson engine.

The key to successful sensory marketing lies in subtlety and congruence. The sensory elements must complement each other and align well with the brand's message to create a holistic experience. When executed skillfully, sensory marketing can significantly enhance overall consumer satisfaction.

---

[14] Krishna (2012).

Fig. 12.3 Lush store, Seoul, South Korea (photographed by Jeongmin Lee, 2023, Author's Collection)

Once upon a Purchase: Storytelling Marketing

Another approach that boosts fun and pleasure is *storytelling marketing*. This approach is related to psycho-pleasure and infuses designs with an intriguing narrative. It enhances customers' engagement and satisfaction far better than the usual sales pitch.[15] That is, it's like opting for a thoughtfully crafted short story over a dry instruction manual.

Then, what gives storytelling its magnetic appeal? Stories have a unique ability to draw people in, allowing them to see themselves within the narrative, thus making the experience personal. Hence, consumers feel the product with a story speaks directly to them. In addition, stories stick better in our memories. A product with a story is more likely to be remembered and shared, increasing its impact on the consumer's life. Above all, stories are powerful emotion-evokers. When people feel emotionally connected, they find the experience more enjoyable. Consider the following situation, which shows the power of incorporating storytelling. There once was an engineer and a doctor, but they both loved the same woman. The doctor would give her a rose every day to show his love. The engineer would give her an apple every day. This confused her, so she asked, "What is this apple supposed to mean?" The engineer replied, "An apple a day keeps the doctor away."[16] Who do you think won her heart?

The "Tomb Raider" trilogy for the Sony PlayStation, particularly "Shadow of the Tomb Raider," exemplifies the storytelling effect in video game design (Fig. 12.4). It explores the origin story of Lara Croft, a legendary gaming character, transforming the game into an immersive experience of unraveling her story. It also intertwines the story of physical adventures with a deep, psychological journey. Set in Latin America, Lara's quest against the paramilitary group Trinity and her race to prevent a Mayan apocalypse are both thrilling and emotionally charged. Furthermore, it delves deeper into Lara's psyche, exploring themes of obsession and her inner struggle to reconcile her actions with their impact on the world.

[15] Woodside et al. (2008).

[16] On December 21, 2023, extracted and revised from https://upjoke.com/confused-jokes.

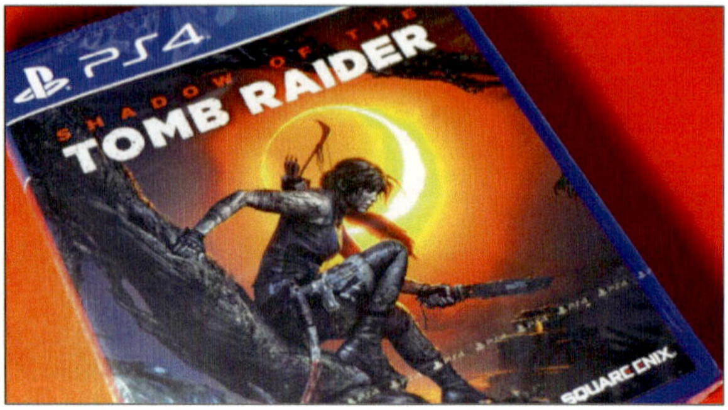

Fig. 12.4 Shadow of the Tomb Raider, 2018 (Stefano Chiacchiarini '74/ Shutterstock)

In the realm of advertising, the power of storytelling is equally evident. Consider Budweiser's "Puppy Love" ad, which narrated the heartwarming story of a puppy and a Clydesdale horse (the symbol of the brand). The ad's focus wasn't on the beer itself but on creating a narrative that tugs at heartstrings, thereby fostering a positive brand association. Then there is Apple's "The Crazy Ones" ad, part of the "Think Different" campaign. It used a montage of innovators and dreamers of history like Albert Einstein, Martin Luther King Jr., etc. The narrative celebrates those who see the world differently and, by association, aligns Apple with revolutionary thinking, implying, "You're not just buying a gadget. You're buying into a legacy of innovation."

These storytelling techniques in commercials turn ordinary products into memorable characters. They build an emotional connection and, thus, significantly amplify the ad's impact and appeal.

Chuckle with Design: Humor Appeal

The third approach that boosts fun and pleasure is the *humor appeal*, which incorporates humorous elements into designs. We dealt with it in Chap. 2 as a tactic of the emotional nudge, but let me talk more about it with regard to forming preferences through fun and pleasure.

Think about a design that not only serves its purpose but also cracks a smile on our faces. Just as a good joke can lighten the mood in a room, humorous design enhances the overall user experience. It happens because humor can make products seem more approachable. That is, these designs seem to wink at us, inviting us into a more playful relationship. Humor makes experiences more memorable, too. When a product makes us smile or laugh, we're more likely to remember it and share this experience with others. Think about Snapchat filters (Fig. 12.5). Why are they so popular? They transform our ordinary selfies into something hilarious and share-worthy, thus helping us form connections with others through shared laughter.

Now, let's travel to Italy, home to Alessi, a brand that knows how to mix humor with household items. Take the famous Juicy Salif Citrus Squeezer by Philippe Starck, for

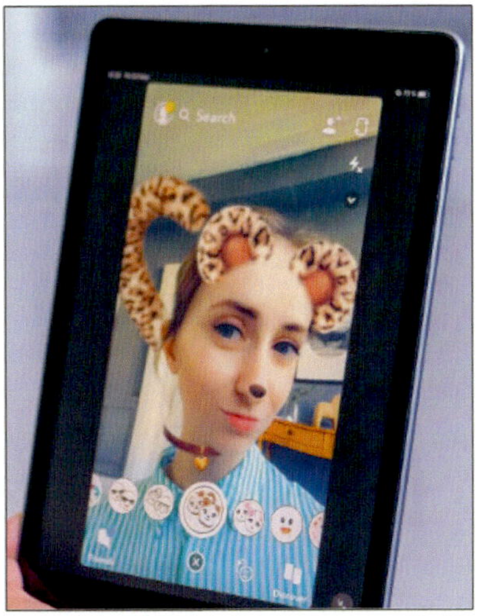

Fig. 12.5 Snapchat filter (Aleksey Popov/Alamy Stock Photo)

example (see Fig. 6.10, far right item). This juicer, looking like a spider, can act as a conversation starter and adds a playful twist to a mundane task. Every squeeze of lemon becomes a moment of fun. Alessi Cico egg cup (Fig. 12.6) is another example. It's a charming example of how humorous design can turn a routine breakfast into a whimsical experience. This little guy, with its big eyes and spoon in hand, seems to cheer you on as you start your day. Peeling off his hat to reveal your breakfast egg is like a mini performance. It's these small, humorous touches that transform routine mornings into something a tad more enchanting.

Ad world also uses touches of humor frequently. Remember Burger King's "Subservient Chicken" campaign? This interactive online campaign, where a man in a chicken suit performed actions based on user input, was quirky and unforgettable. Snickers' "You're Not You When You're Hungry" campaign featured celebrities hilariously out of character when hungry, who then returned to normal after eating a

Fig. 12.6 Alessi Cico egg cup, Stefano Giovannoni (dpa picture alliance archive/Alamy Stock Photo)

Snickers bar. And let's not forget Raid's cheeky ad, where Spiderman is shown dead because of the power of Raid's insecticide.

As seen with the above examples, incorporating humor into a design is about evoking emotion, creating moments of joy, and sparking connection. However, it should also be noted that humor can be subjective and culturally dependent. What is humorous in one culture may not be in another, and some humorous designs could be misinterpreted. Still, when used wisely, it's a powerful tool that can transform a simple daily task into something extraordinary.

Serious Side of Fun: Gamification

Next, let's explore the fourth approach to boost fun and pleasure—*gamification*. It is the method of incorporating game design elements into non-game contexts. The goal? To make an ordinary activity more fun, thereby encouraging specific behaviors.[17] It's like turning your to-do list into a treasure hunt, making life's routine a little more delightful.

Then, what are the important features of gamification that motivate us to act? A key component is the "reward system," a powerful tool for stimulating our brain's reward centers. By completing tasks and receiving rewards, our brain celebrates with a little release of dopamine, a neurotransmitter associated with pleasure and satisfaction. Additionally, gamification often incorporates short-term goals or challenges.[18] These bite-sized achievements align perfectly with our natural drive for accomplishment, offering quick, satisfying wins. These are the low-hanging fruit of our daily endeavors—small but enough to bring a smile. Another cornerstone of gamification is the "immediate feedback loop." Instant feedback in games, like scores or progress bars, tells us how well we are doing and can be very motivating.

Consider the case of Duolingo, the language learning app. It's a good case of gamification, which transforms the arduous task of learning a new language into an enjoyable, game-like experience. It leverages points, levels, and streaks to maintain user enthusiasm. In essence, gamification is about turning everyday tasks into small yet delightful adventures.

In 2009, Volkswagen decided to play a game—the famous Volkswagen "Fun Theory" initiative. It was not about horsepower or fuel efficiency but about injecting a dash of delight into our daily deeds. This project serves as an exemplary case of gamification, proving that a spoonful of fun can indeed change people's behaviors for the better.

One of the most famous interventions from the Fun Theory was the piano staircase in the Stockholm subway (similar to the one in Fig. 2.5). One day, commuters were met with a musical surprise—they found their regular staircase transformed into a piano keyboard. Each step on the stairs played a note, turning an ordinary walk into an

[17] Hamari et al. (2014), Marczewski (2013).

[18] Mouchabac et al. (2021).

impromptu melody. Suddenly, choosing stairs over escalators wasn't just a healthier option. It was fun! The result? More people chose to commute with a little stairway symphony. Equally amusing was the transformation of a public trash bin into "The World's Deepest Bin." Toss in your trash, and you'd hear the echoing sound of it falling for what seemed like an eternity. This funny twist on waste disposal turned a basic civic duty into a moment of mirth, nudging more folks to pitch in for a cleaner space.

Volkswagen's Fun Theory became a buzzing topic and sparked meaningful discussions about how playful elements could be woven into urban spaces and public systems. Especially in design circles, it became the go-to example, showing that a dash of creativity and a hint of fun could encourage positive changes in everyday behavior.

Thrill of Deviation: Deconstructivist Approach

Lastly, let's look into the *deconstructivist approach (deconstructivism)*[19] and the wild joy it brings through the pleasure of deviation. In design, the "pleasure of deviation" describes the thrill and satisfaction that arise when a design boldly defies conventions, turning the norms upside down. This may cause some people to frown, but for others, it can provide a vicarious satisfaction for deviance.

It works for several reasons. First, humans have an innate attraction to novelty, which captures our attention by standing out against the backdrop of the predictable. Second, it sparks curiosity. When we encounter something that doesn't immediately make sense, we are compelled to explore it, stimulating our intellectual quest. Third, the deviation from the norm often incorporates elements of surprise, a key component of delight. Fourth, it can trigger an emotional response, which may range from exhilaration to discomfort but is often memorable and impactful.

Deconstructivism best represents this kind of deviation in the design world. It breaks away from the conventional rules of harmony, unity, and balance, opting instead for fragmented, seemingly chaotic creations. From the deconstructivist perspective, even the "Oops!" in the fashion runways can be interpreted as just another word for "Avant-garde".[20]

The poster child for this delightful rebellion is Jean Paul Gaultier's iconic Cone Bra for Madonna's 1990 Blonde Ambition Tour (Figs. 12.7 and 11.3 right). Think about how revolutionary it must have been at that time—it was 1990! He took an intimate piece of clothing (a corset) and turned it into a bold fashion statement. It was like saying, "Hey, world, watch me turn lingerie into a loudspeaker for self-expression!" By doing that, he not only subverted fashion rules but also sparked discussions on sexuality, gender norms, and fashion itself. That is the power of deconstructivist design.

---

[19] Hoteit (2015).

[20] On December 21, 2023, suggested by ChatGPT-4.

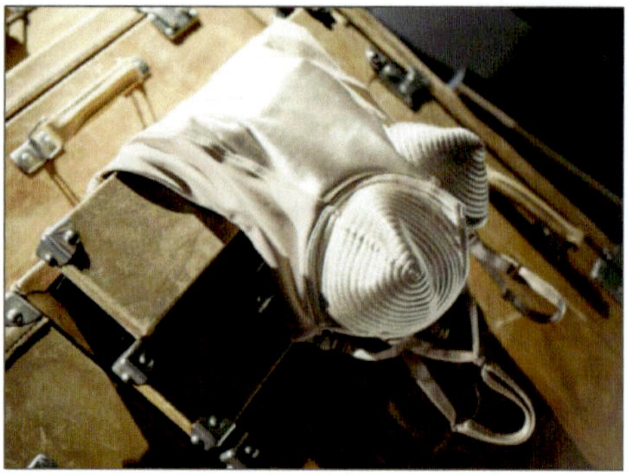

Fig. 12.7 Cone Bra, Jean Paul Gaultier, 1990 (NDTeam/Shutterstock)

Another excellent illustration is the Centre Pompidou in Paris (Fig. 12.8), a masterpiece that blends high-tech architecture with a deconstructivist touch. The building wears its insides on the outside. That is, by boldly displaying its structural and mechanical elements externally, it challenges traditional architectural aesthetics. The colorful pipes, transparent escalators, and exposed framework disrupt the convention, offering a playful contrast to the historical Parisian landscape. Let's pay tribute to the citizens of Paris who allowed this defiant maverick within the old-world scenery of Paris in 1977!

These examples highlight how designers can leverage the power of deviation to engage audiences. There is a certain charm in the unconventional, a hidden delight in the atypical. So, they celebrate the notion that straying from the norm can be a source of great pleasure, a secret way of getting vicarious satisfaction for deviant behaviors that entice us.

Fig. 12.8 Centre Pompidou (Centre National d'Art et de Culture Georges-Pompidou), Renzo Piano and Richard Rogers, 1977, Paris, France (Jorge Felix Costa/Shutterstock)

More Design Insights Added to the Scene

Before we end this chapter, let me talk more about the intriguing world of Lush stores and their metaphorical use of "taste." This whole concept is a little nod to the fascinating phenomenon of *synesthesia*, which is a wonderful mix-up of senses, making the world a slightly more colorful place.

Imagine your senses had a group chat and shared their experiences. That's synesthesia in a nutshell. It is a unique condition where the stimulation of one sense leads to experiences in another sense. For instance, if someone listens to a sad tune and suddenly feels their world is painted in shades of blue, it's the synesthesia between hearing and color vision.

Now, why does this happen? The brain science behind synesthesia is still a bit of a mystery. It is believed to involve the crossing of neural pathways.[21] This cross-activation could occur due to increased connectivity between sensory regions in the brain. However, it's also important to note that synesthesia is a subjective experience. In addition, some synesthetes report that their experiences add richness to their sensory world, while others might find the additional sensory input overwhelming or distracting.

Synesthesia, when it steps into the world of art and design, refers to the blending of sensory experiences to create immersive and innovative works. For example, Wassily Kandinsky, a renowned abstract painter, experienced synesthesia and often described his work in terms of music. His canvases are like visual symphonies, where each color and shape hits a note, creating a melody of emotions. The Sonos logo design in Fig. 9.26 is another example. It is designed to give off a vibe of motion and groove of the modern music experiences, and we can almost hear the rhythm of dynamic music. And let's not forget Lush's fruity and veggie-shaped products (peek at Fig. 12.3 again). They are an example of synesthesia between vision and taste and practically pop a burst of flavor in our mouth.

These examples show how synesthesia can jazz up art and design, turning ordinary experiences into sensory concerts and enhancing the engagement of users. By transcending traditional walls between the senses, these designs invite us to a more vibrant and engaging world.

Let's wrap up our journey through the psychology of fun and pleasure. I hope you now understand that hedonic values are a vital ingredient of our well-being, enriching the human experience with its vibrant hues and energy. They remind us that humans are not only survivors but also thrivers! In addition, as consumers, we gravitate toward experiences that promise this sense of fun and pleasure, often without conscious thought. Therefore, as this chapter closes, let's acknowledge that the pursuit of fun and pleasure is not a diversion from the serious business of life. It "is" serious business. So, laugh, and the world laughs with you!

---

[21] Ward (2013).

References

Csikszentmihalyi, M. (2014). Toward a psychology of optimal experience. In *Flow and the foundations of positive psychology: The collected works of Mihaly Csikszentmihalyi* (pp. 209–226). Springer.

Cui, G., Lockee, B., & Meng, C. (2013). Building modern online social presence: A review of social presence theory and its instructional design implications for future trends. *Education and Information Technologies, 18*, 661–685.

Hamari, J., Koivisto, J., & Sarsa, H. (2014). Does gamification work?—A literature review of empirical studies on gamification. In *Proceedings of the 47th Hawaii International Conference on System Sciences (HICSS)* (pp. 3025–3034).

Hoteit, A. (2015). Deconstructivism: Translation from philosophy to architecture. *Canadian Social Science, 11*(7), 117–129.

Isen, A. M., Daubman, K. A., & Nowicki, G. P. (1987). Positive affect facilitates creative problem solving. *Journal of Personality and Social Psychology, 52*(6), 1122–1131.

Jordan, P. W. (2000). *Designing pleasurable products: An introduction to the new human factors*. Taylor Francis.

Kelleher, C., Wilson, H. N., Macdonald, E. K., & Peppard, J. (2019). The score is not the music: Integrating experience and practice perspectives on value co-creation in collective consumption contexts. *Journal of Service Research, 22*(2), 120–138.

Krishna, A. (2012). An integrative review of sensory marketing: Engaging the senses to affect perception, judgment and behavior. *Journal of Consumer Psychology, 22*(3), 332–351.

Marczewski, A. (2013). *Gamification: A simple introduction*. Andrzej Marczewski.

Mouchabac, S., Maatoug, R., Conejero, I., Adrien, V., Bonnot, O., Millet, B., Ferreri, F., & Bourla, A. (2021). In search of digital dopamine: How apps can motivate depressed patients, a review and conceptual analysis. *Brain Sciences, 11*, 1454. https://doi.org/10.3390/brainsci11111454

Ward, J. (2013). Synesthesia. *Annual Review of Psychology, 64*, 49–75.

Woodside, A. G., Sood, S., & Miller, K. E. (2008). When consumers and brands talk: Storytelling theory and research in psychology and marketing. *Psychology & Marketing, 25*(2), 97–145.

Young, J. A., & Pain, M. D. (1999). The zone: Evidence of a universal phenomenon for athletes across sports. *Athletic Insight: The Online Journal of Sport Psychology, 1*(3), 21–30.

Zuckerman, M., Kolin, E. A., Price, L., & Zoob, I. (1964). Development of a sensation-seeking scale. *Journal of Consulting Psychology, 28*(6), 477–482.

Chapter 13
Hey, Faces Are Super Important! Pay Attention!

Have you ever come across your singular ability to spot faces in random, everyday objects, as in Fig. 13.1? You may have been delighted with your unusual imagination. Sorry, but it's not just you who enjoy this game. The sage said, "Remember, you are unique." Though, they conveniently leave out the punchline—"Just like everyone else."[1] The paradoxical riddle of wisdom! The propensity to spot faces in lifeless objects is clearly related to creative imagination—coincidentally shared by just about everybody. As it turns out, there's an innate reason behind this proficiency in finding faces. So, how about embarking on a little expedition to discover the importance of facial recognition in the human psyche?

In life's vast visual stimuli, the human face reigns as the VIP. Psychologists have uncovered that the human brain (especially the infant's brain) processes faces more quickly and with more attention.[2] It is as if we possess an inbuilt face detector. Why this obsession with faces, you wonder? It all boils down to the survival instinct (yes, again!). Recognizing faces and deciphering emotions from them are nifty skills that help us determine friends from foes, whether someone's ready to attack or cooperate.

How can we be sure it's instinct? Take a gander at newborn babies. To them, a human face isn't just a sight for sore eyes—it's their lifeline. Therefore, even before they learn a social smile, these little rascals offer a smile to anything resembling a human face. This pre-social grin is the built-in survival gadget that makes the parent squad hover nearby to react to them and always be at their beck and call.

Because faces bear such crucial importance in human minds, it's natural that people want to keep their facial images for themselves and posterity. However, this desire has an entertaining twist. As mentioned earlier in Chap. 6, human beings have both actual and ideal self-images. Who do you think we want to meet, and who do you think future generations should meet? You got it! The "tailored to perfection you," of course!

---

[1] On May 25, 2023, extracted and revised from https://www.actualized.org/forum/topic/1982-enlightenment-jokes-here/?page=3.

[2] Mondloch et al. (1999).

© The Author(s), under exclusive license to Springer Nature Singapore Pte Ltd. 2024

J. Lee et al., *The Psychology Behind Design*,
https://doi.org/10.1007/978-981-97-3426-9_13

Fig. 13.1 Human faces in inanimate objects: Left—Clouds/Right—Monumento a la Humanidad, Marcahuasi, Peru (Left: Artjazz/Shuttestock) (Right: Carlos Sala Fotografia/Shutterstock)

Then, let's imagine we visit a photo studio for a keepsake portrait. In an unfortunate circumstance, you might stumble upon a photographer who is a purist, flawlessly capturing all the good and the bad in you. Would you be a satisfied customer? You'd probably lament how that photo doesn't do you justice. Shouldn't photographers weigh the client's thoughts and emotions, for mercy's sake, even though they have the legal liberty to "shoot" us and "frame" us to their hearts' content?[3]

Now, let's flip the script. The photographer is a magical artisan casting spells with lens, lighting, and a good dose of Photoshop, tweaking a bit here, correcting a bit there until you look as if you've just stepped out of a fashion photoshoot. You would undoubtedly be over the moon, and no surprise if this studio becomes the hottest ticket in town. That's what we call a professional, at least in the realm of consumerism!

Back in the day, before we were graced with cameras, it was the skilled brushwork of artists that froze us in time. Naturally, the ones who excelled at the idealized immortalization were the go-to painters for the wealthy. However, there was a 17th-century maestro who didn't quite hit the jackpot in the portrait department despite being hailed as a great artist—Rembrandt van Rijn.

He's among the rare specimens people affectionately refer to by their first names (Michelangelo and Raffaello being other examples). Nonetheless, people couldn't accept his way of depicting themselves at that time. Why? In his paintings, together with his revolutionary method of using light, he showed a genius for looking deep into a person's soul and spilling it onto the canvas, not the idealized ones. Talk about a pure artistic soul, and he couldn't repress it for the sake of customers. As a result, he ran a studio where clients probably would have lamented how the images didn't do them justice, where there should have been a warning sign saying, "Soul split lighting ahead." So, even though Rembrandt was quite successful with his portraits in his earlier years, later in life, he faced financial difficulties due to personal expenditures, broader economic factors, and, of course, his artistic style.

[3] On May 25, 2023, extracted and revised from https://punstoppable.com/frame-puns.

Fig. 13.2 Self-portraits, Rembrandt van Rijn, 1634 (left) and 1669 (right) (Left: Wide Eye Pictures/Alamy Stock Photo) (Right: Mariano Garcia/Alamy Stock Photo)

Fig. 13.3 Car front designs: Left—MINI Cooper/Right—Jeep Wrangler Sahara (photographed by Jeongmin Lee, 2016 (left) and 2023 (right), Author's Collection)

Still, he left us many self-portraits (Fig. 13.2), in which you can observe what the "soul split lighting" means. From the exuberant confidence of his youthful self to the weathered visage of his later years stricken with poverty, he remained true to his purist nature. Take a close look at old Rembrandt's face, especially the eyes. Now that's dedication! The same reason that makes many masterful art films flop at the box office also held Rembrandt back in his day. Yet, if it were you, would you be brave enough to let him immortalize your image with his brutally honest brushstrokes? You'd better pose and consider it carefully!

Even though it's not the level of Rembrandt's knack, we, ordinary human beings, also have a decent talent for reading emotions in facial expressions. Furthermore, this aptitude extends far beyond human faces to reach unexpected objects. For example, check the car designs in Fig. 13.3. Can you spot the different facial expressions? These designs incorporate facial features, thus exuding friendliness or a hint of aggression.

Fig. 13.4 Mona Lisa, Leonardo da Vinci, 1503 (GL Archive/Alamy Stock Photo)

Let me explain more. Do you know how humans recognize emotions in the face? It's through observing the eyes and the mouth.[4] Another pop quiz to explain it better. Do you know the most iconic face in the world with a unique facial expression? Right, it's the Mona Lisa (Fig. 13.4). But have you ever wondered why this painting is hailed as humanity's best portrait? It's not just her "smile," as it is commonly known, but rather the elusive facial expression that the lady wears. Da Vinci found out that the essence of facial expression rested in the corners of the mouth and the eyes. He transferred this discovery onto Mona Lisa, intentionally smudging the edges around the corners of her mouth and eyes. And voilà! The cryptic smile of the Mona Lisa was born.[5] Her emotion alters at the whim of the beholder—joyous, miffed, or poker-faced.

Now, let's get back to car designs again. Not only the Mona Lisa but automobiles also wear emotions in their eyes and mouths. Therefore, in the car designs of Fig. 13.3, their emotional expressions hinge on the shapes of headlights (representing eyes) and the grille or bumper (representing mouth). Not only Da Vinci but also clever designers today know how to mobilize the human ability to recognize facial expressions. With this knowledge now, you'll never look at car designs the same way again!

Hence, here is the earlier statement revisited: the face is such an essential stimulus in human minds. So, if you catch yourself spotting faces in the unlikeliest places, remember it's not just your creative imagination at play. Your brain is reminding you, "Hey, faces are super important! Pay close attention!".

---

[4] Calvo et al. (2014).

[5] Bohrn et al. (2010).

Owl of Minerva Behind the Scene

In this chapter, we will make a journey into the psychology related to human faces. Our companion, Minerva's owl, will unfurl a handful of theories with an air of wisdom—anthropomorphic design, pleasure-arousal theory, baby-face bias, uncanny valley, and Face-ism.

Shall we start with human-like features in design?

Humanizing the Inanimate: Anthropomorphic Allure

First, we shall look into *design anthropomorphism*—a term that's quite a burden to pronounce. We briefly talked about it in Chap. 6 with the design example of Anna G. Corkscrew (Fig. 6.10). Here, let's explore it more deeply. In simple terms, it is a "personification of objects," doling out human-like features to otherwise inanimate things.

Humans are social animals, meaning we need other humans to survive. Therefore, we have a soft corner for things resembling human features, especially friendly ones. Moreover, we have an amazing aptness for seeing faces in all sorts of shapes and patterns whenever possible, so much so that we end up seeing a human face even on the moon. Thus, non-human objects imitating human characteristics have been created for thousands of years, and even today, anthropomorphism is used in various designs ranging from animations to products, automobiles, and even buildings. Designers eagerly use these human-ish forms because it is advantageous in eliciting consumers' affection. Seeing a little bit of themselves in these designs, people feel a sense of kinship and trust.

A study by Aggarwal and McGill[6] has proven this effect: anthropomorphic product designs are rated more positively than non-anthropomorphic designs. This research also highlights that the success of anthropomorphism in design requires a thoughtful approach to ensure that the human-like features in design are congruent with consumers' ideas of what constitutes human-like qualities.

Figure 13.5 introduces design examples mimicking human faces. On your left is the LG logo with a cheeky wink, and on your right is Thomas Train, an animated train with friendly facial features. Examples in Fig. 13.6 describe more than faces. They also mimic human body postures, from amusing characters of "Beauty and the Beast" all the way to Frank Gehry's quirky "Fred and Ginger."

Next, let's proceed to *brand personality*[7] and its anthropomorphic makeover, *brand character*. "Brand personality" refers to human characteristics attributed to a brand. That is, a brand character is shaped like a specific person so that its customers can go, "That's so me!".

[6] Aggarwal and McGill (2007).

[7] Aaker (1997).

Fig. 13.5 Anthropomorphic designs (faces): Left—LG logo/Right—Thomas the Tank Engine (Left: photographed by Jeongmin Lee, 2023, Author's Collection) (Right: Wangkun Jia/ Shutterstock)

Fig. 13.6 Anthropomorphic designs (body postures): Top—Beauty and the Beast / Bottom Left—Nationale-Nederlanden Building (Fred and Ginger, the Dancing House), Frank Gehry and Vlado Milunić, 1996, Prague, Czech Republic/Bottom Right—Waxwork of Fred Astaire and Ginger Rogers in Madame Tussauds, LA, USA (Top: Entertainment Pictures/Alamy Stock Photo) (Bottom Left: Lucag G/Shutterstock) (Bottom Right: photographed by Jeongmin Lee, 2016, Author's Collection)

In their pursuit of self-expression and self-esteem, today's consumers know it's more convenient to find a backup for their selves with the right choice of brand personality. After all, why put a Herculean effort searching for its support in the often-disappointing human companionship when one can pick it off the brand rack? Take, for instance, the domestic scenario where the wife asks her husband, "Do you prefer a beautiful woman or an intelligent woman?" The husband, quick on his feet, might deflect with, "None of them. You know I only love you!"[8] What a well-meaning disappointer! A good reason why brand personalities are thriving for self-support.

Research by Park and John has found that this tendency is especially true for consumers who think their personality is fixed and cannot be developed further by their own efforts.[9] Under the circumstances, these consumers desire to sprinkle a bit of fairy dust on their self-image: they want the chosen brand to convey its personable charm to themselves and others. Thus, this research shows that brand personality isn't just another pretty face of artful marketing. It's the behind-the-scenes influencer that subtly reshapes a customer's self-image.

Life, being the capricious creature it is, often leaves our self-batteries in need of a jumpstart. At such times, any endorsement of our uniqueness, any nod to our self-boosting, is seized upon. Even a credit card company reminder stating, "You have an outstanding balance," might be cheekily seen as a charming compliment.[10] Brand personalities can be a handy gadget in situations like this. I don't judge whether this kind of consumerism is good or bad. I mean to say it just is.

A popular design strategy for delivering brand personality is creating attractive "brand characters" in human-like forms (e.g., Fig. 13.7). This anthropomorphic makeover for brand personality isn't just window dressing. They make brand personality more palpable—the living and tangible envoy of the brand's attraction. In addition, because humans have a soft spot for anthropomorphic features, they can act as adorable handshakers that bring the brand's essential appeal into consumers' hearts.

Figure 13.7 shows some examples. In M&M's characters, each color represents a distinct personality—Red, the cynic; Yellow, the happy and gullible; and Brown, the bossy, etc. Then, there's the Michelin Man and Pillsbury Doughboy, which capitalize on the positive feelings of round forms and thereby deliver an innocent, trustworthy brand impression.

When we consider the anthropomorphic design examples we've seen above, it's evident that brands are selling not just products but also a narrative where we feel a sense of belonging and kinship. Therefore, design can be a profound reflection of the human need to connect, even with inanimate objects. So, when we chuckle at a character or feel a surge of affection for a brand, let's remember that it's a testament to our wonderfully human nature of seeing a bit of ourselves in the world around us.

---

[8] On May 26, 2023, extracted and revised from https://upjoke.com/prefer-jokes.

[9] Park and John (2010).

[10] On May 26, 2023, extracted and revised from https://upjoke.com/self-esteem-jokes.

Fig. 13.7 Left—M&M's characters/Center—Michelin Man/Right—Pillsbury Doughboy (Left: Borimat Praokaew/Shutterstock) (Center: photographed by Jeongmin Lee, 2024, Author's Collection) (Right: Keith Homan/Shutterstock)

Oxymoron of Friendly Fury: Pleasure-Arousal Mix

Our second journey regarding the psychology of human faces is into the *pleasure-arousal theory*.[11] It suggests that our emotional responses to an object, situation, or environment can be classified based on two dimensions of how much pleasure and arousal we feel. I should clarify one thing here with the term "pleasure." The word "pleasure" used here has a slightly different meaning from the "pleasure" discussed under the theme of "Fun and Pleasure" in Chap. 12. Specifically, "pleasure" in this chapter denotes a soothing sense, as opposed to arousal.

In the context of design psychology, this theory is used to understand how design elements can elicit these emotional responses. For instance, pastel-tone colors with soft, curvilinear forms could be the design equivalent of a feel-good movie (pleasure), while vibrant colors coupled with angular shapes might be more akin to a thrilling adventure movie (arousal). The combo of colors red, white, and blue is also a joyful trio symbolizing freedom, thus kindling pleasure. But… only until they are flashing behind you![12] Then, they suddenly become adrenaline-pumping arousal, a potential speeding ticket.

When we recognize a "face" in a design, it becomes easier to read which feeling is imparted. The perceived emotion can be friendliness giving us warm pleasure, or aggressiveness, which sparks arousal. It's no secret that humans are wired to chase pleasure, making it an essential determinant of overall liking for the design. The friendlier the design, the more pleasure we get.

But things are not that simple. Pleasure and arousal interact with each other, too. Research proved that arousal is a moderator, amplifying the positive effect of pleasure.[13] Simply put, it's like adding cold whipped cream (arousal) to your hot chocolate

---

[11] Russell (1980).

[12] On May 27, 2023, extracted and revised from https://upjoke.com/color-jokes.

[13] Landwehr et al. (2011).

Fig. 13.8 Pleasure-Arousal combined: Ferrari SF90 Stradale (Maurizio Ciabatti/Dan74/Shutterstock)

(pleasure). It just tastes better. So, consumers' liking can be maximized by this hot–cold combo, by a design that simultaneously elicits the pleasure of friendliness and the arousal of aggressiveness.

Let's get back to the earlier episode for a moment. You remember the Mona Lisa and car designs, where eyes and mouth played the leading roles in making facial expressions. Then, guess who plays a more important role. It's the "mouth!" When it comes to friendliness, the mouth is the belle of the ball, with eyes playing backup. So, to capture that toothpaste-ad smile, a product's mouth needs to be depicted with an upward curve. On the other hand, aggressiveness can be perceived equally in the product's "eyes" and "mouth."

Then, what if we want to stir up a cocktail of friendliness and aggressiveness in one design? In that case, because the mouth is already reserved for a friendly smile, it's up to the eyes to channel aggressiveness: they need to appear angry by being slanted. Take a look at the car design in Fig. 13.8. The eyes (headlights) glare with an aggressive slant, yet its mouth (grill) is slightly upturned. This is not New Beetle type of round-eyed friendliness, but a cheekier one, a mischief-meets-mirth version of a grin.

I concede that "aggressive-friendliness" sounds contradictory. But then again, we have a long list of such oxymorons—"only choice," "civil war," "definite possibility," "random order," "original copies," and so on.[14] Why not "aggressive-friendliness"? After all, who doesn't enjoy a little mischief with their mirth?

Baby-face Paradox

Our third exploration regarding the psychology of human faces is the *baby-face bias*.[15] It deals with the beguiling charm of cherubic countenance, those facial traits reminiscent of sweet, innocent babies—bulbous eyes, a roundish face, a stubby chin,

---

[14] On May 27, 2023, extracted and revised from https://upjoke.com/work-jokes.

[15] Borgi et al. (2014).

Fig. 13.9 Facial features: Left—Baby face/ Right—Mature face (Left: sajaa668/Shutterstock) (Right: Michael Jaszewski/ Shutterstock)

a dainty nose, and delicate skin. Why is it a bias? Interestingly, any adult endowed with such facial features is often considered more naive, harmless, and honest than those who do not, a pretty perplexing case of mistaken identity.

However, this visage carries its share of pros and cons. While baby faces might win the day when it comes to earning trust, they might fare badly in the cut-throat world of professionalism. Think of an advertisement featuring a baby-faced adult endorsing a new shampoo. Her wide-eyed innocence helps her approval resonate with authenticity. However, swap the shampoo commercial for a medical talk show, and this very charm can backfire because her facial features will make it difficult for the audience to take her professionalism seriously. By the way, do you know the difference between amateur and professional robbers? Both should have mature countenances, but an amateur says, "Give me all your money!" while a skilled, professional robber says, "Sign here, please."[16] An assistant with a touch of a baby face might accompany the latter.

Now, let's step into the world of design. The most important design elements forming baby-face bias are large saucer-like eyes and round faces (Fig. 13.9 left). However, if the goal is to channel an aura of professionalism and authority, designers must apply mature features like narrowed eyes and elongated, chiseled faces (Fig. 13.9 right).[17] Disney characters, Snow White and her nemesis, the Queen, illustrate this effect well (Fig. 13.10). Snow White, the beacon of innocence and kindness, was sketched with the doe-eyed baby face, while the Queen bore mature features.

Baby-face bias also manifests itself delightfully in the renderings of our beloved feline hero, "Puss in Boots." It was an affectionate spectacle when he sought to elicit innocence and tug at our heartstrings—he morphed his countenance to resemble a baby (Fig. 13.11). This clever stratagem, which originated from "Shrek," achieved such popularity that it found its way into the standalone film "Puss in Boots." Excellent job, amazing insights into human cognitive biases!

Product designs can also bring the tunes of these facial cues into play. Consider the kettles in Fig. 13.12. The design on the left, with its sterner lines, conveys a

---

[16] On May 27, 2023, extracted and revised from https://upjoke.com/professional-jokes.

[17] Masip et al. (2004).

Fig. 13.10 Disney characters in "Snow White and the Seven Dwarfs": Left—Snow White/ Right—The Queen (Left: Animeofficial/Shutterstock) (Right: Entertainment Pictures/Alamy Stock Photo)

Fig. 13.11 Puss in Boots (Left: Ching Yun Song/Shutterstock) (Right: Photo 12/Alamy Stock Photo)

serious, adult-like manner. The design on the right, with its roundish outlines, seems ready to burst into a playful baby giggle.

As we can see, while baby-face features might open doors to trust and endearment, they won't be helpful in settings demanding authority and professionalism. Therefore, designers should choose with a delicate sense, much like choosing the right outfit for the occasion. So, if you encounter a baby-faced design, remember it might be the result of the designer's clever application of human biases.

Fig. 13.12 Left—Alessi kettle, II Conico/ Right—Stainless steel stovetop kettle (Left: Elizabeth Whiting and Associates/Alamy Stock Photo) (Right: zbigniew jankowski/monticello/ Shutterstock)

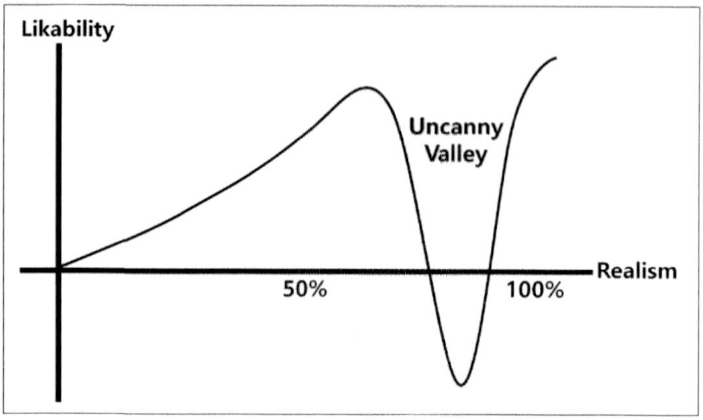

Fig. 13.13 Uncanny Valley graph (created by Jeongmin Lee, 2023, Author's Collection)

Dilemma of Almost Human: Uncanny Valley

The fourth stop in our itinerary for the psychology of human faces is the *uncanny valley*. It's about the relationship between realism and likability in rendering human forms. For a human form, people prefer either abstraction or hyper-realism. But the moment it goes into the tricky area where it looks almost human, but not quite exactly, it becomes unpleasant. This phenomenon was first observed by Mori Masahiro, who named it the "uncanny valley."[18] As an essential cause for the uncanny valley, the *dead eye syndrome* should be noted in particular. It happens when the eyes of characters lie stagnant, making them eerily lifeless.

The graph in Fig. 13.13 charts the journey into (and out of) this valley. On the left side, likability increases in proportion to realism. As you can see in Fig. 13.14 (The Simpsons, Little Mermaid, and The Incredibles), the relatively abstract depictions of human forms are greeted with cheers.

Then, when we tiptoe into the land of the uncanny valley, likability plunges abruptly. For example, in the animated film "Polar Express" (Fig. 13.15), the filmmakers aimed for a highly realistic depiction of human characters, but some audiences and critics felt that the characters, while technically impressive, fell into the uncanny valley. Mind you, the rest of this artwork is lauded for its impeccable quality.

Finally, as we emerge from this depth, with human renditions mirroring real humans hyper-closely, likability precipitously rises again, as in Fig. 13.16 (a wax figure of Bruce Willis).

Therefore, this eerie landscape of "uncanny valley" is a tightrope walk between realism and likability. You had better remember that straying too close to "almost human" can send shivers down our spines. So, if the design can't don the cape of hyper-realism, embracing a cloak of abstraction is advisable.

[18] MacDorman and Chattopadhyay (2016), Mori (1970).

Fig. 13.14 Abstract representations of human forms: Left—The Simpsons/Center—Little Mermaid/Right—The Incredibles (Left: cfg1978/Shutterstock) (Center: cfg1978/Shutterstock) (Right: Sarunyu L/Shutterstock)

Fig. 13.15 The Polar Express, Robert Zemeckis, 2004 (RGR Collection/Alamy Stock Photo)

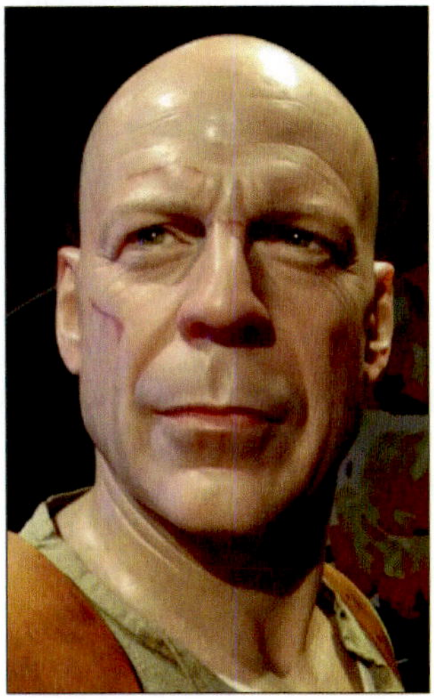

Fig. 13.16 Hyper-realistic representations of human forms: Waxwork of Bruce Willis in Madame Tussauds, LA, USA (photographed by Jeongmin Lee, 2016, Author's Collection)

Fig. 13.17 "Hope" poster for Barack Obama, Shepard Fairey, 2008 (Juli Hansen/ Shutterstock)

Discriminating Power of Facial Prominence

Let's visit the fifth and last spot in our journey looking for the psychology of human faces—the land of *face-ism*, also called *facial prominence*. Studies have shown that the degree of facial prominence in design can meddle with our perceptions of the person depicted.[19]. When our eyes scan a face-dominated portrait, our brain is more likely to focus on the person's intelligence or personality. However, when the body proportion increases, the focus somehow swims with the tide, stirring thoughts about the person's physical attributes. This phenomenon is called "face-ism" or "facial prominence," another cognitive bias regarding faces.

In the world of political campaigns, designers know this effect well, so politicians are often portrayed with high face-ism to convey authority and competence. Take, for instance, the illustrious "Hope" poster for the 2008 United States presidential election (Fig. 13.17). In its design, the focus is primarily on Obama's face, with a high face-ism index. This choice was to amplify a leader's personality, such as intelligence, determination, and thoughtfulness. And then there's that upward gaze, a visual symphony of optimism, vision, and looking toward the future, which aligns perfectly with his campaign's emphasis on hope and change. The poster was very successful. It became not only an iconic campaign tool but also a cultural phenomenon that found its echo in parodies and tributes.

In the chic world of magazine cover design, comparing TIME and GQ reveals interesting insights into how each publication uses face-ism to convey different

[19] Archer et al. (1983).

Fig. 13.18 Time cover designs (Left: Mirko Popadic/Popartic/Shutterstock) (Right: Elnur/Shutterstock)

messages and to appeal to their respective audiences. TIME tries to engage its audience through thought-provoking imagery that frequently relates to global issues, politics, or significant cultural events. To achieve this goal, its covers often feature close-up shots of individuals (not always, though) that scream importance and urgency (Fig. 13.18).

Meanwhile, GQ is less about the furrowed brows of world leaders and more about the elegant charm of what we'll loosely term "the good life." Thus, GQ covers often feature their subjects in full or half-body shots (not always, either) (Fig. 13.19). This lower "face-ism" index allows for showcasing more about lifestyle, fashion, and personal success stories.

For good measure, if you take a stroll through the glossy pages of other fashion-forward publications like Vogue, Cosmopolitan, or Bazaar, you'll also find them frequently adopting the lower face-ism index (Fig. 13.20). However, I should also acknowledge that this can vary between individual issues and editorial choices. As you can see in Figs. 13.18, 13.19 and 13.20, there are cover designs of GQ and Vogue, which adopted a high face-ism approach, and the TIME cover designs, which adopted a lower face-ism ratio.

The movie poster designs are another good example of utilizing face-ism. Did you notice that the poster designs for psychological thrillers often use a high face-ism index? Think of "Black Swan," "Joker," "The Others," or the classic "The Silence of the Lambs." Take "The Silence of the Lambs" poster in Fig. 13.21, for instance. Here, through two close-up faces, we can perceive the very souls of Clarice Starling (played by Jodie Foster) and Hannibal Lecter (played by Anthony Hopkins). That is, this emphasis on faces is to convey the intense psychological characteristics of the film. Foster's gaze is sharp, mirroring Clarice's fierce determination. Meanwhile, Hopkins' shadowed eyes make us perceive his dangerous and calculating personality. And let's not overlook the stark contrast between Foster's white face and the ominous red surrounding Hopkins, which adds additional visual tension. Therefore, by leveraging

Fig. 13.19 GQ cover designs (dennizn/Alamy Stock Photo)

Fig. 13.20 Vogue cover designs (Elnur/Shutterstock)

Fig. 13.21 "The Silence of the Lambs" poster design (Moviestore Collection Ltd/Alamy Stock Photo)

face-ism, this poster presents a psychological map, hinting at the film's dark and complex storyline.

In summary, "face-ism" is a powerful tool. It's not just about how you see others but also how others can see you. Therefore, it can provide intriguing insights when you create your own image, which is intended to appeal in a specific way. That's why professional networking sites often feature profile pictures with higher face-ism. It isn't just for showing off your best smile; it's your personal billboard, saying in a visual whisper, "Here I am, the epitome of professionalism and competence."

More Design Insights Added to the Scene

Before we end our journey into the psychology of human faces, I want to add a charming but ironic design case—a formidable yet baby-faced warrior in Japanese animation. To skillfully sidestep the dreaded "dead eye syndrome," Japanese animators came up with a lively eyeball technique. Take a look at Fig. 13.22.

The conspicuous eyes of these heroines are not even close to realistic renderings of actual eyes, but they certainly convey spirited impressions of human eyes. Nevertheless, to make this lively effect, they needed oversized eyes, and to suit these large eyes, they also needed roundish facial contours. As mentioned earlier, these two are the essential design elements in creating the baby-face effect. Consequently, this warrior against the evil forces ends up looking like an innocent, naive novice. This irony is no accidental by-product, though, but rather a calculated stroke to resonate with its intended audience, primarily children. So there you have it, the power of

Fig. 13.22 Sailor Moon (PictureLux/The Hollywood Archive/Alamy Stock Photo)

design techniques, skillfully exploiting biases, and gifting us a paradoxical heroine who battles evil with a dash of wide-eyed wonder.

Well, life is full of paradoxes anyway. Let me tell you about other ironies in our lives. The paradox of getting a job: you get a job so that you won't be homeless, but you're home a lot less when you get a job.[20] The dilemma of the word "abbreviation": why is it such a long word?[21] The amusing irony of the word "queue": just the alphabet q with a long line of silent letters following it.[22] Life's paradox, isn't it? Hence, a design with a bit of irony is rather beguiling than perplexing because we already live in a world like that.

And so, our journey through the fascinating world of human faces and their psychological impact on design concludes. We've seen how faces captivate us, from anthropomorphic designs to the thrilling blend of pleasure and arousal in design elements. We also navigated the baby-face bias's delicate balance between innocence and professionalism, tiptoed through the eerie uncanny valley, and appreciated the power of face-ism in conveying personality and authority. All these explorations reaffirm the profound connection we have with faces, whether in people, products, or art. It's a reminder of our innate tendency to seek human connection. Thus, as we part ways with these insights, remember if you see a face in an object or a design, it's not just your imagination; it's a deeply rooted aspect of our human experience.

References

Aaker, J. L. (1997). Dimensions of brand personality. *Journal of Marketing Research, 34*(3), 347–356.

[20] On May 28, 2023, extracted and revised from https://www.boredpanda.com/ironic-jokes/?utm_source=google&utm_medium=organic&utm_campaign=organic.

[21] On May 28, 2023, extracted and revised from https://upjoke.com/conscience-jokes.

[22] On May 28, 2023, extracted and revised from https://www.boredpanda.com/ironic-jokes/?utm_source=google&utm_medium=organic&utm_campaign=organic.

Aggarwal, P., & McGill, A. L. (2007). Is that car smiling at me? Schema congruity as a basis for evaluating anthropomorphized products. *Journal of Consumer Research, 34*(4), 468–479.
Archer, D., Iritani, B., Kimes, D. D., & Barrios, M. (1983). Face-ism: Five studies of sex differences in facial prominence. *Journal of Personality and Social Psychology, 45*(4), 725–735.
Bohrn, I., Carbon, C. C., & Hutzler, F. (2010). Mona Lisa's smile—Perception or deception? *Psychological Science, 21*(3), 378–380.
Borgi, M., Cogliati-Dezza, I., Brelsford, V., Meints, K., & Cirulli, F. (2014). Baby schema in human and animal faces induces cuteness perception and gaze allocation in children. *Frontiers in Psychology, 5*(411), 1–12.
Calvo, M. G., Fernández-Martín, A., & Nummenmaa, L. (2014). Facial expression recognition in peripheral versus central vision: Role of the eyes and the mouth. *Psychological Research Psychologische Forschung, 78*, 180–195.
Landwehr, J. R., McGill, A. L., & Herrmann, A. (2011). It's got the look: The effect of friendly and aggressive "facial" expressions on product liking and sales. *Journal of Marketing, 75*(3), 132–146.
MacDorman, K. F., & Chattopadhyay, D. (2016). Reducing consistency in human realism increases the uncanny valley effect: Increasing category uncertainty does not. *Cognition, 146*, 190–205.
Masip, J., Garrido, E., & Herrero, C. (2004). Facial appearance and impressions of 'credibility': The effects of facial babyishness and age on person perception. *International Journal of Psychology, 39*(4), 276–289.
Mondloch, C. J., Lewis, T. L., Budreau, D. R., Maurer, D., Dannemiller, J. L., Stephens, B. R., & Kleiner-Gathercoal, K. A. (1999). Face perception during early infancy. *Psychological Science, 10*(5), 419–422.
Mori, M. (1970). Bukimi no tani (the uncanny valley). *Energy, 7*, 33–35.
Park, J. K., & John, D. R. (2010). Got to get you into my life: Do brand personalities rub off on consumers? *Journal of Consumer Research, 37*(4), 655–669.
Russell, J. A. (1980). A circumplex model of affect. *Journal of Personality and Social Psychology, 39*(6), 1161.

Chapter 14
The Freudian Footprint: Psychoanalyzing the Objects We Created

Step into a world where every object more than meets the eye, speaking in the language of our deepest emotions and thoughts. In this world, many artists and designers' motto is, "If life gives you lemons, make art, not lemonade."[1] This enchanting world will tell you the story of how psychoanalysis, art, and design are old friends who love to chat over coffee.

Sigmund Freud, the father of psychoanalysis, saw art as a secret playground for the subconscious, a place where repressed desires and hidden fears can frolic in the open, disguised as artistic flair.[2] Thus, in his view, art can be a medium through which the subconscious mind communicates. Let's take an example. What's your take on the design of Fig. 14.1? Or, what thoughts or feelings arise?

There are many approaches that art historians use to interpret artworks—formal analysis, iconographic analysis, contextual analysis, biographical studies, stylistic analysis, semiotic analysis, and, yes, psychoanalytic analysis, to name a few.[3] When examining Autumn Intrusion in Fig. 14.1, you could also view it through various lenses, but let me try on the psychoanalytic one. Surprising? Well… It's not that uncommon. Critics often concoct interpretations that bewilder even the artists themselves. It's all part of the art world's charm, where not only the "freedom of creation" but also the "freedom of interpretation" are the essential features. So, here I am, your free-spirited critic, about to dive into Autumn Intrusion with a psychoanalytic lens.

> Here, abstract linear forms intertwine with the straightforward realism of a building, creating a visual contrast. The building's interior appears as a metaphor for the subconscious mind—a deep, mysterious place. Emerging from this depth are the fluid, curving forms, symbols of the subconscious desires constantly striving to break free, yet often held back by the Superego (here, represented by the building's solid, imposing structure). Together, they mirror the dynamic interplay between the id and the Superego, a tug-of-war of our innermost urges and societal restraints. The swirling lines, bursting with energy, seem to be even more

[1] On December 31, 2023, suggested by ChatGPT-4.

[2] Storr (2001).

[3] Ferrari (2011).

© The Author(s), under exclusive license to Springer Nature Singapore Pte Ltd. 2024
J. Lee et al., *The Psychology Behind Design*,
https://doi.org/10.1007/978-981-97-3426-9_14

Fig. 14.1 Autumn Intrusion (Harvey Nichols Department Store window), Heatherwick Studio, 1997, London, UK (Steve Speller/Alamy Stock Photo)

potent than the building itself and try to undermine the groundwork of the building from underneath, symbolizing the power of repressed emotions to rattle the framework of our carefully constructed identities.

This interpretation might be subjective but shows an example of the psychoanalytic approach to art and design. Psychoanalysis posits that art can be a means of catharsis, a pressure valve for the release of pent-up emotions. These repressed desires are like a software update. You can postpone it, but eventually, it's going to shut down everything for attention if we don't give them a way to release it softly.[4] Thus, a poignant photograph, a provocative sculpture, or an avant-garde building—each has the potential to showcase something deep inside.

The interpretation we just explored is a glimpse into how psychoanalytic concepts might "unconsciously" influence artists and designers. However, there's another side to this coin, where these ideas are "consciously" and "intentionally" stitched into their creations. "Surrealism" stands as a prime example. Deeply inspired by Freud, Surrealists dived deep into the unconscious, treating it like a treasure trove for unexplored creativity.

Freud's focus on dreams as portals to the unconscious resonated profoundly with the Surrealists. They translated this fascination into their art. Take Salvador Dali's "The Persistence of Memory" (Fig. 14.2), for instance—the epitome of this dreamy style.

The partnership between psychoanalysis and surrealism turned out to be one of the epic conversations between art and science in the twentieth century, and it's still sending ripples across the art and design world. The story of psychoanalysis and design, therefore, is an ongoing narrative. It reminds us that art and design aren't just about the things we create but also about the thoughts and feelings they stir up in us, an invisible but palpable heartbeat of our inner world.

[4] See Footnote 1.

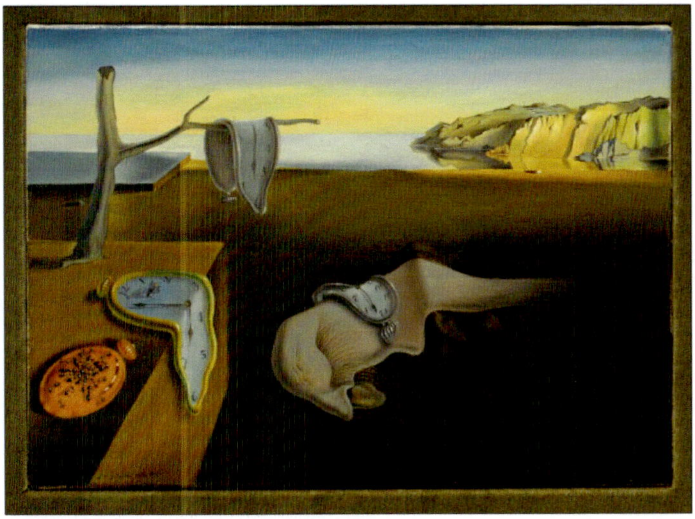

Fig. 14.2 The Persistence of Memory, Salvador Dali, 1931 (Martin Shields/Alamy Stock Photo)

So, let's admit these unconscious influences on our lives. Look around—the phone in your hand, the chair you're sitting on, the car you drive. Each may carry a hidden episode of your unconscious desires. The world around us is not just a physical landscape. It's a canvas rich with our psychological stories waiting to be read.

Owl of Minerva Behind the Scene
At last, we reached the final chapter of this book. Let me finish our long journey with the most famous psychological theory—"*Psychoanalysis by Sigmund Freud*." There are other aspects of psychoanalysis, like the theory by Carl Jung. Still, here, our focus is narrowed down to Freud's legacy and its imprint on art and design.

Now, let's unravel the key concepts of Freudian psychoanalysis[5] and its applications in the design world. But before we start our journey, let me clarify that all the psychoanalytic interpretations of design works in this chapter can be subjective and might even be speculative because of the characteristics of the psychoanalytic approach.

Iceberg Analogy: Mind Layers

At the heart of Freudian theory lies the notion of the human mind having three layers—the conscious, the preconscious, and the unconscious (sometimes referred to as the subconscious). It is often likened to an iceberg (Fig. 14.3).

---

[5] Freud (1921).

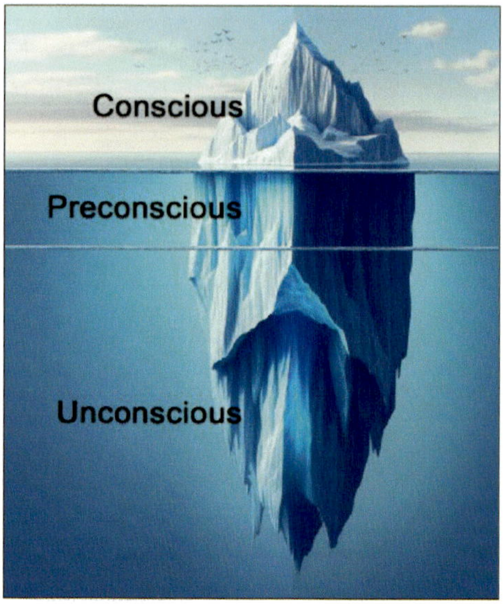

Fig. 14.3 Mind layers in Freud's psychoanalysis (created by DALL.E, 2023, Author's Collection)

The conscious is the tip of the iceberg that's showing off above the water. It's where all our current thoughts, feelings, and perceptions hang out—the stuff we're actively thinking about at any given moment. For instance, when you're weighing the pros and cons of a design, that's your conscious mind in the director's chair.

Just below the waterline lies *the preconscious*, holding information not presently in our awareness but readily accessible. In the design world, this could be like suddenly remembering the cozy feel of your old armchair while critiquing a new sofa design.

However, the vast expanse of the iceberg beneath the surface is *the unconscious*. This is the deep, dark basement of our minds, home to our deepest thoughts, feelings, and urges, which might be too distressing for our conscious minds to handle.

Understanding these mental layers can offer insight into those unexplainable likes and dislikes we have toward certain designs. For instance, the charm of retro designs might be a nod from the preconscious, where old memories are nudging our current choices. Or the reason some ergonomic designs just feel right might be linked to the unconscious, where organic, naturally soothing shapes sing in harmony with our deepest senses.

Trio of Human Psyche: Id, Superego, and Ego

In the fascinating theater of the human psyche, Freud introduces us to three main characters—the Id, the Superego, and the Ego (Fig. 14.4).[6]

[6] Lapsley and Stey (2011).

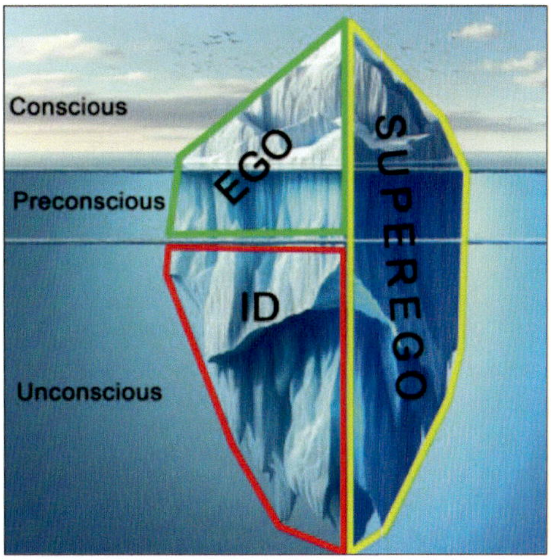

Fig. 14.4 Id, Superego, and Ego (created by DALL.E and Jeongmin Lee, 2023, Author's Collection)

Let's start with the *Id*, the instinctual, primitive character in our mental narrative, mostly lurking in the unconscious. It's all about pleasure and immediate satisfaction. That is, it seeks to satisfy basic urges, desires, and needs immediately and without concern for reality or morality. Think about freshly baked cookies—nature's way of appealing to the Id, saying, "forget about that salad."[7] In consumer behavior, think of it as the allure of "buy now, think later," the voice that urges you toward an impulsive purchase, favoring immediate joy over long-term consequences.

Moving on to the *Superego*, think of it as the dignified, moral-conscious sage of the group, instilled with values and ethics acquired from our parents and society. This character of our mind, straddling the conscious and unconscious realms, acts as our inner judge, leading to feelings of pride or guilt. In consumer behavior, it's like the voice that encourages us to choose eco-friendly products or steer clear of brands with questionable ethics. This noble superego is like Mr. and Ms. know-it-alls: they know everything but only don't know how annoying they are, especially to Id, and that's why we need the next character.

The *Ego*, the level-headed mediator of this ensemble, operates based on the reality principle and is mostly conscious or preconscious. It acts like a seasoned diplomat, balancing the whims of the Id with the Superego's moral compass and working to satisfy the Id's desires in ways that are realistic and socially acceptable. You know we can depend on the skillful diplomats' mediation because they are the ones who can even tell you to go to hell in such a way that you will look forward to the trip.[8] In the context of consumer behavior, the Ego is your savvy shopping advisor encouraging you to do your research before purchasing or to aim for lasting satisfaction rather than instant gratification.

---

[7] See Footnote 1.

[8] On December 31, 2023, extracted and revised from https://onelinefun.com/travel/.

Fig. 14.5 Dior Sauvage ad (John B Hewitt/Shutterstock)

The Freudian concepts of the Id, the Superego, and the Ego can open up intriguing avenues for design and marketing. Take, for instance, the Dior Sauvage. The very name "Sauvage" (in English, "savage") echoes the Id's primal nature, disregarding the refined and the civilized. In line with this, its advertising designs often feature rugged landscapes and a sense of untamed nature (e.g., Fig. 14.5). It strikes a chord with the deep-seated yearnings for freedom, the escape from societal constraints, and the untamed version of masculinity.

On the other hand, to appeal to the Superego, a company might highlight a brand's ethical attributes. Brands like Patagonia, with their commitment to environmental sustainability, are perfect examples. Their marketing efforts focus on sustainable material use, ethical manufacturing, and donations to environmental causes, striking a chord with those green-hearted consumers (e.g., Fig. 14.6).

Now, engaging the Ego requires a balanced approach. It often highlights the practicality and morality alongside its emotional and sensory qualities. IKEA exemplifies this approach. Its functional, affordable products are marketed with a focus on sustainability and responsible sourcing, appealing to the Superego. On the other hand, its store experience, from visually pleasing showrooms to the smell of Swedish meatballs in the cafeteria, caters to the Id's sensory desires. IKEA's founder once said that hungry customers do not want to shop. It means that they have to satisfy the Id's basic desire to sell more products. That's why IKEA stores are equipped with a restaurant, bistro, and cafe, located at the right spots in its expansive and time-consuming shopping environment.

As you can see, this insight into the psychoanalytic characters of the human psyche allows designers and marketers to fine-tune their strategies to resonate more with their target audience.

Fig. 14.6 Patagonia ad (used with permission of Patagonia)

Design with Flirtation: Libido's Artistry

In psychoanalytic theory, human personality and behaviors are seen as a dance choreographed by two dominant drives—the "libido (or the life instinct)" and the "thanatos (or the death drive)." The push and pull between these two forces create inner tension.[9]

The *libido (the life instinct)* is primarily associated with the preservation and perpetuation of life. It is basically the energy of the sexual drive but isn't just about steamy romances and flirty glances. Freud and Jung expanded its repertoire to include all creative, life-producing drives.[10]

Design can be a medium for expressing libido, and sometimes, it is quite apparent. For example, sensual images in advertising (e.g., Calvin Klein Underwear ads) can be quite overt to create a desire for the products. Even though those ads often evoke controversy over ethical issues, they still exist.

---

[9] Kli (2018).
[10] Jung (2015).

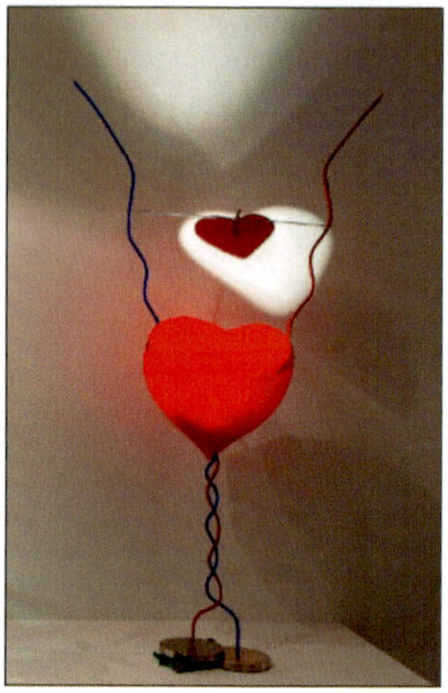

Fig. 14.7 One from the Heart, Ingo Maurer, 1989 (imageBROKER.com GmbH & Co. KG/Alamy Stock Photo)

But there's a subtler side to it as well. Libido in design can be a silent whisper rather than a loud shout, being at play in a more symbolic form. Consider how curves in design echo the natural contours of the human body, hinting at femininity and sensuality. Color, too, plays its part. Red, for instance, can be used to express passion and desire. Then, there are heart shapes and intertwined forms. These can be symbols of intimacy, of connection. A case in point is Ingo Maurer's clever design in Fig. 14.7. This design features a heart-shaped mirror with a movable spotlight attached to it. When you turn on the light, it makes the reflection of a heart onto the wall, bringing a sense of romance and playfulness into the room.

Destructive Beauty: Thanatos' Artistry

As the opposite drive of the libido, Freud provided the concept of the *thanatos* (also called the *death drive*).[11] It was a concept that Freud introduced later in his career and was somewhat controversial. It represents an instinctual drive toward death, destruction, and, ultimately, a return to the inorganic state of being. It is often manifested through behaviors that seem to counter the life instinct, such as aggression or risky behavior.

Similarly, a design that exhibits power, aggression, or a break from the norm can embody the death drive. Take the emblem of the Harley Owners Group, for instance (Fig. 14.8). The skull is a universal symbol of death, a nod to the death drive. Therefore, this emblem speaks to a shared boldness among members—a willingness to confront the danger and excitement inherent in motorcycling. It can also suggest the historical association of motorcycle groups with counterculture and rebellion.

[11] Mills (2006).

Fig. 14.8 Emblem of Harley Owners Group (Vladimir Zhupanenko/Shutterstock)

Let's turn our gaze to the "Porca Miseria!" chandelier in Fig. 14.9. Traditional chandeliers are all about order, elegance, and luxury, but Ingo Maurer shatters this concept, literally—broken plates, chaos in suspension. It's a visual protest against our standard notions of beauty, confronting us with the aesthetics of destruction and ruin, thus engaging deeply with the themes of the death drive.

Fig. 14.9 Porca Miseria!, Ingo Maurer, 2004 (Kay Ringwood/Alamy Stock Photo)

In these examples, the thanatos can be seen front and center, inviting us to embrace the thrill, the risk, and maybe even the taboo and the aggression. So, as Freud suggested, humans might have this thanatos as a basic human drive. We might be able to catch that even with the following remarks that people often say without much thought. We might politely say, "The last thing I want to do is hurt you." However, it unconsciously means "It's still on the list," doesn't it?[12]

Mind's Crafty Escape: Defense Mechanisms

Psychoanalytic theory also gives us the concept of *defense mechanisms*. They are mental strategies, primarily used by the Ego, to cope with unacceptable urges, not-so-pleasant feelings, frustration, or distress, sometimes caused by the conflict between the Id and the Superego.[13] Think of them as the mind's crafty tools to dodge discomfort or anxiety. Let's take a walk through ten of these ingenious mental tactics, as highlighted by Anna Freud, who added more to her father's theory.[14]

Displacement: It's rerouting our negative emotions from their true source to a safer target. This is like getting mad at your coffee maker when you're actually frustrated with your boss. Or, it's like squishing a stress ball—a harmless outlet for your inner Hulk, shifting the focus from the actual stressor.

Denial: It's refusing to accept reality. Ignoring a health issue, hoping it will just go away, is a good example. Or conversely, someone might say, "Hypochondria is the only illness that I don't have."[15] Also, consider how you think in a casino. You probably ask a security guard which machine people get the most money from, denying the fact that it is actually an ATM machine.[16] Likewise, if you plan to build a sea-level mansion, ignoring those pesky climate change reports, that's denial in a nutshell.

Repression: It's burying unsettling thoughts or desires deep within the unconscious. It's the mind's way of saying, "If I can't see it, it's not there." It's like not remembering a traumatic childhood event. Designers, too, might unknowingly shy away from certain colors or themes linked to personal traumas, like giving the cold shoulder to forest motifs after a creepy camping trip, without fully understanding why.

Suppression: It's consciously sidelining thoughts that we find uncomfortable at the moment. Thus, suppression is basically our "I will think about it tomorrow" approach.

---

[12] On December 31, 2023, extracted and revised from https://parade.com/1040121/marynliles/one-liners/.

[13] Cramer (2015).

[14] Cherry (2022).

[15] On December 31, 2023, extracted and revised from https://www.juliantrubin.com/psychologyjokes.html.

[16] On December 31, 2023, extracted and revised from https://upjoke.com/guard-jokes.

Avoiding looking at bank statements is a classic. It is like hitting snooze on an emotional alarm clock. If the designer knows deep in his mind that the client will decline his design because it costs too much but still continues his project without necessary corrections, that's also suppression. On the other hand, design can also stimulate these suppressed desires of the consumers when necessary. For instance, eco-friendly products nudge our suppressed guilt for the environment, offering an easy way to contribute positively.

Sublimation: It's redirecting unacceptable impulses into socially acceptable or even productive activities. It's like an aggressive person becoming a competitive athlete or turning your inner drama into a Broadway hit. Similarly, artists and designers often turn their emotional turmoil into masterpieces, making it a win–win for mental health and creativity.

Projection: It's casting or blaming our own feelings or flaws onto others—that is, the art of seeing your own quirks in others. This is the mechanism that we encounter every day. Real-life examples? What's most coworkers' favorite keyboard shortcut? It's "Shift + Blame," isn't it?[17] Also, we know that he who smiles in a crisis has found someone to blame. His ego is in peace because the path to inner peace begins with just three words—"Not my problem."[18] That's the projection in a nutshell. Similarly, designers might project their dislike for the color yellow onto their clients, conveniently leaving it out of their color palette.

Intellectualization: It's using excessive logic to sidestep emotional distress. It's like obsessing over the details of funeral arrangements to avoid confronting grief. Similarly, designers might drown themselves in the technicalities to avoid dealing with the real emotional undertones of a project when that project is personally and emotionally charged. Some people use it more often than others. If you have ever wondered why pizza is made round, packed in a square box, and eaten as a triangle, then you have a high probability of using intellectualization under stress.[19]

Rationalization: It's crafting excuses to make our actions seem reasonable. Ever called a shopping spree "retail therapy"? That's rationalization. Likewise, in the design world, it's making a product less durable and calling it "lightweight and portable."

Regression: It's reverting to behaviors of an earlier developmental stage. So, sometimes stress can turn us into toddlers. For example, stressed adults might throw childlike tantrums or suck their thumbs. Likewise, a designer might incorporate more whimsical, nostalgic elements in their work, echoing the comfort and security of childhood.

---

[17] On December 31, 2023, extracted and revised from https://upjoke.com/shortcut-jokes.

[18] On December 31, 2023, extracted and revised from HUMORTHATWORKS.COM and https://upjoke.com/inner-peace-jokes.

[19] On December 31, 2023, extracted and revised from https://upjoke.com/logic-jokes.

Reaction formation: It's acting the opposite of our true feelings. A person who deeply dislikes someone may display excessively friendly behavior toward that person to hide true feelings (the opposite can happen, too). In like manner, architects might suddenly dive into a completely different style when they hit a creative block.

Each of these defense mechanisms serves as a tool to manage internal turmoil. Handy? Absolutely. But, if overused or misapplied, they might lead to psychological issues or unhealthy behaviors. Therefore, understanding these mind tricks provides insight into human behaviors. Furthermore, as illustrated above, it's also true for designers, as these mechanisms can subtly influence their creative process and outputs.

Case in point—the creations of Tim Burton, a maestro of dark and gothic film, might be an example of "sublimation." In his works like "The Nightmare Before Christmas" (Fig. 14.10), "Edward Scissorhands," and "Beetlejuice," the loneliness takes center stage, the darkness gets the spotlight, and the bizarre becomes the norm. His characters are often outcasts or misunderstood, set in his whimsically eerie settings. They are Burton's way of turning his dark imagination into a parade of peculiarities that is not only socially acceptable but also celebrated for its originality. In Burton's world, even our inner oddities can have a positive role to play on the world stage.

Now, let's talk about the defense mechanism of customers reflected in the design they choose. Take the example of a fierce-looking car design (e.g., Fig. 14.11). This car can be a rolling piece of "displacement" for the driver. That is, the drivers might channel their anger received from the other into the road by letting this car run with the attitude of devouring the road.

Fig. 14.10 The Nightmare Before Christmas, produced and written by Tim Burton and directed by Henry Selick, 1993 (ScreenProd/Photononstop/Alamy Stock Photo)

Fig. 14.11 Car design with aggressive look (created by DALL.E, 2023, Author's Collection)

Next, consider the fountain design in Fig. 14.12, which could be interpreted as a metaphor for "repression." This fountain, with its water flowing somehow restrained, feels like it's holding back a secret. It also seems to represent the boundary between the conscious and the unconscious, where unacceptable emotions or thoughts from the unconscious are constantly trying to surface. Here, they are ever-present but not overtly acknowledged.

The "Cartoon Chair" in Fig. 14.13, made of stuffed animals, is also rich with psychoanalytic interpretation. This can be a ticket back to childhood against the harsh realities of the adult world—a "regression" armchair. The use of childhood toys, typically symbols of comfort and security, could suggest a yearning to reclaim those simpler, more secure times.

Fig. 14.12 Hyatt Hotel lobby, Tokyo, Japan (photographed by Jeongmin Lee, 2004, Author's Collection)

Fig. 14.13 Cartoon Chair, Fernando and Humberto Campana, 2007 (Nathaniel Noir/Alamy Stock Photo)

Each of these design examples reveals how defense mechanisms can be deeply intertwined with creativity, influencing both the creation process and output. They're reminders that in the world of design, sometimes the most compelling narratives are the ones we write in our subconscious.

Freudian Dream Scenarios: Dream Work

Freud's exploration of dreams is one of the mainstays of psychoanalytic theory. He believed that dreams are a gateway to our subconscious mind. He also suggested that dreams are a form of wish fulfillment. They might show the unconscious desires that we suppress while we are awake, hiding beneath layers of everyday politeness.[20] Imagine your most private wishes taking center stage in the safe nightly theater of your dreams, including those related to your suppressed sexual and aggressive impulses.

But there's a plot twist. Our dreams are the ultimate costume designers. They dress up our uncensored desires in more socially acceptable garb. That is, our dreams often disguise these raw wishes because they might be disturbing to our waking selves. Thus, the dream's surface story (the *manifest content of a dream*) is a more acceptable version of our hidden, true desires (the *latent content of a dream*). This magical transformation of the latent content into less shocking scenarios is what Freud called the *dream work*.[21]

---

[20] Jenkins (2017).

[21] Freud (1921).

Fig. 14.14 Show-window design of TSUM Department Store, 2015, Moscow, Russia (Sergey Bezgodov/Shutterstock)

Take Fig. 14.14, for instance. It's a show-window display design that utilizes dream imagery. It features knitting, spaghetti, and shoe sauce—a trio you'd never expect to see hanging out together. This illogical juxtaposition mirrors the nature of dreams, where logic often takes a back seat, and anything can happen. The surreal blending of spaghetti turning into knitting yarn also illustrates the dreamlike fantasy.

Then there's Hermès, the haute couture of dream weaving. See the whimsical, surreal themes of the show-window designs in Fig. 14.15. These are like a splash of dreamland—floating objects and whimsical creatures, much like the unpredictable and illogical nature of dreams. These displays captivate passersby, inviting them into a world where fantasy and luxury blend seamlessly.

Fig. 14.15 Show-window designs of MAISON HERMÈS Dosan Park, Seoul, South Korea (photographed by Jeongmin Lee, 2017, Author's Collection)

Freud's theory has been both influential and controversial. Nonetheless, Freud's emphasis on dreams as a window into the unconscious mind remains a significant contribution to our understanding of the human psyche.

More Design Insights Added to the Scene

Earlier in the episode section, *surrealism* has been touched upon briefly. Here, let me explain more about it because its legacy has left an enduring influence on the art and design world.[22]

Surrealism began in the early twentieth century as an artistic and literary movement and was greatly influenced by Freud and other psychoanalytic thinkers. It was all about tapping into the unconscious mind to unleash creativity. Surrealists believed that freeing the mind from the shackles of rational thought and societal norms could lead to revolutionary ideas. For a glimpse into this world, take a look at the paintings of Joan Miro, one of the leading Surrealists, in Fig. 14.16.

Therefore, Surrealists employed various artistic methods that aimed to bypass rational thought and to access the unconscious directly. For example, they used intriguing techniques like automatism, collage, displacement, exquisite corpse, and more. *Automatism* is a process of creating art without conscious thought, almost like doodling without a plan. It's like letting your hand do the thinking. *Collage* is another technique that combines disparate elements, often in surprising ways, to create a new, jarring image. *Displacement* is a method of placing familiar objects in

Fig. 14.16 Studio of Joan Miro at the Miro Foundation Museum, Palma de Mallorca, Spain (Mark Green/Shutterstock)

[22] Barnes (1999).

Fig. 14.17 Mae West Room in Dali Theatre-Museum, Salvador Dali and Òscar Tusquets, 1976 (Kozlenko Viktor/Shutterstock)

unfamiliar settings, making the familiar fantastically unfamiliar. *Exquisite Corpse* is a collaborative approach where each participant adds to a composition in sequence, often leading to unpredictable and whimsical results.

Some of these surrealist techniques echoed psychoanalytic practices like free association and dream analysis that aimed to reveal the unconscious. How do we know psychoanalytic techniques usher us into the subconscious mind? Think about the case of those brainstorming meetings at work, which utilize a method of free association or other surrealistic methods, allowing any wild thoughts. The meeting starts with the Ego's lead regarding sales and marketing but always ends with the Id's desire to have everyone's favorite pizza.

The grand finale of our exploration into psychoanalysis is Salvador Dali's Mae West Room (Fig. 14.17). In the mid-1930s, Dali, the renowned surrealist, envisioned the famous Hollywood star Mae West as a stylish apartment. Her hair turned into lavish curtains, her facial features into furniture and decorations, creating a surrealist depiction of a room. Later, with the collaboration of architect and designer Òscar Tusquets, this vision was realized into the Mae West Room in Fig. 14.17.[23] In this work, we can see that Dali blurred the lines between art, utility, and the subconscious.

In a nutshell, the surrealists were revolutionaries who harnessed the power of psychoanalysis to disrupt the mundane and to challenge our usual perceptions. They created a world where odd is the new normal, and beauty holds hands with the bizarre. It's their way of saying that beneath every creative endeavor, there can be a labyrinth of psychological intrigue waiting to be deciphered.

[23] Mugrabi (2018).

Now, let's wrap up our journey into the psychoanalytic world of art and design. We've uncovered how psychoanalysis reveals the intricate connections between the human psyche and the objects we create. Whether through the sensual curves of a Dali sofa or the aggressive stance of a sports car, the design might speak to our most fundamental drives. Therefore, let's give a nod to Freud and friends for their mind-bending contributions. However, it's also crucial to remember that psychoanalytic interpretations are just one lens through which to find meaning in human creations. Let us not forget that other elements, like personal experiences, cultural backgrounds, social contexts, economic factors, etc., also play a significant role in how the work is understood. In the end, the magic of true creativity lies in its open-door policy to diverse interpretations. This openness is the backbone of a creative world, a world of endless possibilities.

References

Barnes, R. (1999). *The 20th century art book*. Phaidon Press Limited.

Cherry, K. (Updated on 2022, November 1). *20 common defense mechanisms and how they work*. Accessed December 31, 2023. https://www.verywellmind.com/defense-mechanisms-2795960#toc-10-key-defense-mechanisms

Cramer, P. (2015). Understanding defense mechanisms. *Psychodynamic Psychiatry, 43*(4), 523–552.

Ferrari, S. (2011). Gombrich, art and psychoanalysis. *Journal of Art Historiography, 5*, 1–10.

Freud, S. (1921). *Dream psychology*. The James A. McCann Company.

Jenkins, W. J. (2017). *The interpretation of dreams*. CRC Press.

Jung, C. G. (2015). The concept of libido. In *Freud and Psychoanalysis* (Vol.4, pp.111–128). Routledge.

Kli, M. (2018). Eros and thanatos: A nondualistic interpretation: The dynamic of drives in personal and civilizational development from Freud to Marcuse. *Psychoanalytic Review, 105*(1), 67–89.

Lapsley, D. K., & Stey, P. C. (2011). Id, ego, and superego. Encyclopedia of Human Behavior, 2.

Mills, J. (2006). Reflections on the death drive. *Psychoanalytic Psychology, 23*(2), 373–382.

Mugrabi, C. (2018, June 13). Mae West Room. In *Minniemuse*. Accessed December 31, 2023. https://www.minniemuse.com/articles/musings/mae-west-room

Storr, A. (2001). *Freud: A very short introduction*. Oxford University Press.

Index

© The Editor(s) (if applicable) and The Author(s), under exclusive license to Springer Nature Singapore Pte Ltd. 2024

J. Lee et al., *The Psychology Behind Design*, https://doi.org/10.1007/978-981-97-3426-9

R

S

T

GPSR Compliance

The European Union's (EU) General Product Safety Regulation (GPSR) is a set of rules that requires consumer products to be safe and our obligations to ensure this.

If you have any concerns about our products, you can contact us on ProductSafety@springernature.com

In case Publisher is established outside the EU, the EU authorized representative is:

Springer Nature Customer Service Center GmbH
Europaplatz 3
69115 Heidelberg, Germany

Batch number: 10756376

Printed by Printforce, the Netherlands